Commentary on
1&2
Thessalonians

Commentary on
1&2
Thessalonians

Ronald A. Ward

WORD BOOKS, Publisher
Waco, Texas

First Printing—December 1973
Second Printing—March 1975
Third Printing—October 1976
Fourth Printing—May 1977
Fifth Printing—December 1980
Sixth Printing—November 1981

COMMENTARY ON 1 AND 2 THESSALONIANS

ISBN 0-87680-333-8

Library of Congress catalog card number: 73-87125
Printed in the United States of America

CONTENTS

1 Thessalonians

INTRODUCTION

1 Thessalonians

THE CITY

The east Macedonian city of Thessalonica—the Salonica of World War I—stood at the head of the Thermaic Gulf and to the northwest of the three-pronged promontory of Chalcidice. Its situation gave it certain natural advantages, which were augmented by the art of men. On the landward side lay a rich plain; toward the sea was a good harbor. When the Romans in 146 B.C. turned the conquered territory of Macedonia into a province, Thessalonica became the center of Roman administration and to all intents and purposes the capital. For the purposes of defense a highroad was constructed, the famous Via Egnatia, which joined Dyrrhachium (Durazzo) to Thessalonica by crossing the Balkans. It is said to have been the only good road in Albania until the Italians occupied it in 1916. Thessalonica was thus in the midst of a stream of traffic between Rome and the East; in addition roads from the North converged on the city.

Thessalonica obviously had political and commercial importance, and was a strategic center of missionary activity. It was prosperous and populous. Traveling salesmen and their associates would have appealed to a discerning missionary of the first century no less than to one of the twentieth. Just as Jeannie Lawson and Gladys Aylward were impressed by the many mule-trains traveling hundreds of miles in China and in consequence set up the Inn of Eight Happinesses, so Paul was struck by the possibilities for evangelism if converted businessmen "gossiped the gospel" in their travels. The two women missionaries to China told the stories of the gospel to the mule drivers in the inn. Paul preached Christ and started in the Jewish synagogue. The principle is the same.

At the end of the civil war which led to the establishment of the Roman Empire under Augustus, Thessalonica was rewarded for its support of the victors by being declared a free city. This ensured that it remained essentially Greek, not Roman like the neighboring city of Philippi. Philippi was a Roman colony, almost a miniature Rome, using Roman law and a constitution to match that of Rome. Free Thessalonica could summon its own assembly of citizens ("the people" of Acts 17:5) for legislative and juridical duties, and its magistrates bore the Greek name of "politarchs" or "city-rulers" (Acts 17:8). But the Philippian colonists with a touch of superiority prided themselves on "being Romans" (Acts 16:21, KJV).

There was a synagogue at Thessalonica, attended not only by Jews but by a large number of devout Greeks also, together with quite a few socially prominent women. These Gentiles, who were often called "the God-fearing," were attracted to the lofty ethical monotheism of the Jews and attended the imageless worship of the synagogue with profit without becoming full proselytes. It was from this congregation that Paul won his first converts to Christ in Thessalonica, mainly Gentile (Acts 17:4; 1 Thess. 1:9).

It is not easy to establish how long Paul and his companions spent in Thessalonica. On the face of it Luke seems to suggest three weeks (Acts 17:2). But is this long enough to accomplish all that is implied in the records? The great influence and wide reputation of the young church could hardly have grown out of a short mission. On the other hand the influence and reputation could have arisen out of the devoted evangelism of the members after the apostles had left the city. Paul may have planted a grain of mustard seed which grew into a large tree after his departure. Again, it may be argued that the Philippians could not repeatedly have sent aid to Paul in Thessalonica within a period of three weeks: one journey on foot would have taken five or six days (Phil. 4:16). But the Greek of the last mentioned text may mean that they sent help to him both in Thessalonica and repeatedly elsewhere—once when he was in Thessalonica and several times when he was in other places.

The problem, if it is a problem, will disappear with the exercise of a little imagination. We must not suppose that the preachers limited themselves to their sermons "in church" on the three sabbath days. There must have been intense and energetic religious activity on the ordinary days of the week. It is not necessary to save the three-week period by assuming the smallness of the new Christian community. The larger the group, the bigger the impact; and the resultant evangelistic outthrust and the attendant influence and reputation would be to some extent in proportion to the numbers of the church membership. Many evangelists have known what happens when their work "snowballs." Crowds beget crowds, and when the tides of the Spirit are running high, converts beget converts. A man with the untiring energy of Paul could find time to preach Christ to non-Christians and to teach the converted. And the fact that there were aspects of Christian truth about which he had to write later confirms the shortness of his stay in Thessalonica.

THE EPISTLE

For write to the church he did. From the First Epistle to the Thessalonians it is possible to discover his motives. Deep in his heart was a love of his new friends and fellow-believers and a great yearning to see them again (2:17–20). It was because the separation was unendurable that Timothy was sent back on a visit (3:1 f.). The good news which he brought increased rather than diminished the apostle's desire to return to the city (3:6–11), and in face of its immediate impossibility a letter was the next best thing. For he not only loved the Thessalonian Christians, he was concerned for them. Their conversion had involved them in affliction (1:6), for the attack on Paul and the uproar in the city had made them objects of suspicion and violence (Acts 17:5–7). The persecution had not ended and the question of their stability weighed on Paul's mind (2:14; 3:3–5).

There was also the question of slander. The enemies of Paul and of the gospel were getting at the church through attacks on the apostle's personal integrity. It was not his apostolic authority which was now challenged, as it was in Galatia. What was denied was his sheer, down-to-earth honesty. In that age traveling "preachers" swarmed everywhere: professors, doctors, men with quack remedies, sophists, artists, musicians, actors, and athletes. And they sought to pick up a living by imposing on the credulous. It would have been disastrous if Paul had become identified with parasites for, humanly speaking, the faith of the Thessalonians was bound up with the integrity of the man who had first brought them the good news of the gospel. Paul was therefore at pains to deny the rumors assiduously circulated by Jews and pagans. He was no flattering trickster, out for cash and glory (2:3–12). On the contrary he preached the gospel and pleased God—and earned his own living.

While with them he had given the believers a good outline of the Christian faith, a summary which today might be called an "intensive course" or a "crash program." But there were gaps to be filled in (3:10), problems to be answered (4:13–18) and moral guidance and challenge to be asserted (4:11–12; 5:14–15), spiritual exhortation to be given (5:16–22) and holiness to be upheld (4:3–8). All these desires and concerns mingled in the warm heart of the apostle and made him write his First Epistle to the Thessalonians.

Authorship

There can be no doubt that Paul wrote the epistle. The tone and character is distinctively Pauline if we regard it as a whole. The epistle rings true. Vocabulary, style, and thought accord with Paul's four major epistles. A forger would hardly have written 4:15, 17 after the death of Paul. To the charge that the epistle is lacking in originality and significant doctrinal ideas it is sufficient to reply that it expresses precisely what the situation demands. The Thessalonians had warmly received the gospel and were enthusiastic for it; but they were young in the faith. They had indeed stood up to persecution, but even so they lacked a certain religious solidity and experience. They needed to grow in the faith rather than to be corrected in their doctrine. They failed in maturity, not in orthodoxy. Accordingly Paul drew on his vast store of Christian truth in order to build them up, in the context of their existing situation. They did not need, for example, an Epistle to the Romans, though the doctrine of Romans is reflected in 1 Thessalonians. We have before us a letter, not a doctrinal treatise. It would be the same today if a theologian wrote a letter of pastoral guidance: it would reecho his theological writings but would not necessarily express everything which he elsewhere wrote more formally and systematically as doctrine. For the same reason it must not be said that the epistle gives us an early stage in Paul's theological thought. He had been a Christian for about twenty years and was to write Romans about five years later. He did not stand still for two decades and then jump forward to doctrinal maturity in a few years.

The epistle is mentioned in the Muratorian Canon and in Marcion's *apostolicon*. The former was discovered by L. A. Muratori in an eighth-century manuscript and published by him at Milan in 1740. It is the oldest extant list of New Testament writings, generally assigned to the second half of the second century. Marcion, who died in A.D. 160 or about that time, was an influential heretic of excessively Paulinist views. ("He was the only man who really understood St. Paul, and he mis-understood him.") Anti-Jewish to the fingertips, he excluded the Law and rejected the Old Testament completely. In about A.D. 140 he con-structed his own canon of scripture at Rome, consisting of an edited re-cension of Luke and ten of the epistles of Paul, the Pastoral Epistles being omitted. The ten were arranged and expurgated, and equipped with brief prologues which are found in most of the best manuscripts of the Vulgate. James Moffatt infers that 1 Thessalonians was in circu-lation by the first quarter of the second century.

Date

The date of the epistle is relatively easy to establish. It was written after the return of Timothy from Thessalonica to Paul (3:6) and by this time Paul was in Corinth (Acts 18:1, 5). As he was longing and praying to see the Thessalonians again (3:10 f.), it is unlikely that he delayed long before writing. Now Paul's stay in Corinth is one of the fixed points of New Testament chronology, as it overlapped that of the proconsul of Achaia, Gallio (Acts 18:11 f.). Gallio is mentioned in an inscription found at Delphi in 1905. From these remains of a re-script of the Emperor Claudius, which is dated, it is possible to infer that Gallio took office in the summer of A.D. 51. It is not known how long he had been proconsul when Paul was brought before him. If he had recently arrived, Paul may have already been in Corinth for eighteen months. It is thus safe to say that 1 Thessalonians was written at some time in the years A.D. 50 or 51. This makes it the first of Paul's epistles which have come down to us, with the possible exception of the Epistle to the Galatians.

THEOLOGY

Reference has already been made to the theology of the epistle and it must now be considered in some detail, though fuller discussion is reserved for the commentary. Our present purpose is to gather together the theological data and present them in some sort of logical order. This casts no reflection on the apostle: he drew on this or that element of his doctrine as and when he needed it; our business is to assemble the material coherently.

(1) Sin

We begin with the fact of sin. It is a black picture which Paul has painted. The Jews killed the Lord Jesus and oppose the salvation of the Gentiles and displease God. It is plain that the Gentiles are sinners also, as they need salvation; and in any case Paul saw a parallel between Gentile and Jewish persecution (2:14–16). Paul also spoke of evil (5:22) and of Satan (2:18), who hindered an eager pastoral visit and by temptation sought to detach the believers from their allegiance to Christ and so to nullify the apostolic work (3:5). A specifically religious sin, as opposed to a moral sin like murder, is idolatry, which is retrogression (cf. Rom. 1:23). In their conversion the Thessalonians had turned from idols to God (1:9).

The fact that Jewish sins displeased God shows that God has an attitude. He is not an impartial observer and it is not enough to say that he is a compassionate sympathizer. His attitude to human sin is summed up in the word "wrath," which is used three times in the epistle (1:10; 2:16; 5:9). The attitude is expressed in action. Transgression and wrong are punished: this is the meaning of the statement that "the Lord is an avenger" (4:6).

There was a time when such wrath was directed toward the Thessalonians. If this were not so, Paul would not have spoken of being delivered from it (1:10). But now a new factor must be mentioned —the love of God. Paul called his readers "brethren beloved by God" (1:4). He also spoke of grace (1:1), though in this greeting he did not say whose grace he had in mind. Even so we have already reached the heart of the problem: there is in God that which we call wrath and that which we call love; and both were directed toward the same object, in this case the Thessalonians. At the conclusion of the letter Paul spoke of the grace of our Lord Jesus Christ (5:28), and this is the heart of the answer.

(2) The gospel

The great historic facts of the gospel are clearly stated. The Lord Jesus was killed by the Jews (2:15); he did not merely die but was killed. This can only refer to the crucifixion. He must have been buried because God raised him from the dead (1:10). Jesus died and rose again (4:14). This was no mere exhibition; it was not an event unrelated to men. He died for us (5:10).

This is taken further in the statement that God appointed us to obtain salvation through our Lord Jesus Christ (5:9), a salvation which is simply summed up in the phrase "live with him" (v. 10). Salvation is contrasted with wrath. How could God vent his wrath on those who are living with his Son? We are not left with no more than an inference. We are specifically told that Jesus is the Deliverer from wrath (1:10). We have here a keyhole through which we can see Paul's whole doctrine of propitiation. And as salvation is through Jesus, the principle of mediation is apparent. Our Lord is the Mediator between God and men, not only the Thessalonians: salvation is also for the Gentiles (2:16).

Jesus died for us, and in him salvation is available. But men are not saved until they receive salvation. That is to say, they have to be told. They are not born saved because Jesus has already died for them; but they are born "savable," and they will be saved if and when they hear the good news and accept it by the exercise of faith. That is why Paul could speak of himself and his colleagues as apostles of Christ (2:6): they had been commissioned to make known the offer of salvation in Christ. They had been entrusted with the gospel and it was their task to make it known at any cost (2:4).

Their message is variously described as the word (1:6), the word of the Lord (1:8), the word of God (2:13), the gospel (2:4), the gospel of God (2:2, 8 f.), and the gospel of Christ (3:2). The Thessalonians had received the word (1:6); they had been converted and had turned to God (1:9). This must imply their salvation (2:16). The prominence given to the characteristic words meaning "belief" and "faith" is striking. Christians are called "believers" (1:7) and their faith was the subject of much talk (1:8). It is faith which has to be maintained (3:2 f., 5–7), and it is the deficiencies of faith which have to be made up (3:10).

The importance of faith becomes clear when we dwell on the situation. The apostles had preached and the Thessalonians had been converted and had received salvation. It is a fair inference that they had begun to believe when they heard the gospel. How otherwise could the apostles' labor prove to be in vain (3:5)? The hearers had put on the breastplate of faith (see discussion on 5:8). When, if not when they heard the gospel? The logical order is thus preaching, hearing, receiving, believing, and being saved. Christ crucified is preached; the hearer believes; he is saved. The link between the work of Christ and the salvation of men is constituted by faith. The Lord died for us men and our salvation, but we are not saved until we believe in him. This is very close in fact, if not in language, to Paul's doctrine of justification by faith.

Justification is not an experience which takes place at conversion and then is left behind. It is agreed that when a man puts his faith in Christ he is at once forgiven all his sins; and it is agreed that after thirty or forty years of living the Christian life he can look back with thankfulness to the day when he was justified. But justification is more than the first great red-letter day in the Christian life; it marks more than the "birthday" of the believer. Granted that it happens once, and once for all, but it sets up a relationship between God and the believer which is forever different from the relationship of his pre-Christian days. All through his Christian life he is a justified man, a child of God with a program and a destiny. This is reflected in Paul's teaching about God's call. God called us (4:7) at the time of our conversion, and he calls us still (2:12; 5:24), not indeed to be justified or converted but to follow more closely in discipleship.

It used to be the fashion to preach to the sinners at the Sunday evening service and to the saints in the morning. An old preacher once told me that when he started to preach in the first flush of his conversion, his evening message was "Come to Jesus" and his morning message was "Come closer to Jesus." The saints heard through him the call of God to come closer; they had already come. This is really what Paul meant. The double aspect of his doctrine of justification is thus present in the epistle even if he did not use the word "justify." The new status of believers established in justification looks back to their election (1:4) and forward through the present to the future, throughout which period they are delivered and kept (1:10; 3:13; 5:10). From the Parousia onwards they will be with the Lord (4:17); until then—kept (5:23 f.).

Conversion is the end or goal of the work of the evangelist, but it is the beginning of the Christian life for the man who has accepted the word. It goes on working in the believer. Justified as he is, he has new duties and privileges, and the word which continues to work in him (2:13; cf. 1:2 f.) both imposes duties and equips with power. Religious duties include the life of prayer (5:17); thanksgiving (5:18) and petition and intercession (5:25); personal holiness (4:3–7; cf. 5:23); and the work of evangelism (1:8). Evangelism is indeed spontaneous and joyous, but it is also a duty which the Thessalonians fulfilled and so became an example (1:7). In fact the will of God should be discovered and carried out (4:3; 5:18). Paul was himself an example of a life of prayer (1:2 f.; 2:13; 3:9–12; 5:23). Moral duties should be carried out in the sight of God and are thus not secular. Mutual love should grow (4:9–10), evil should not be repaid in its own coin but the good of all should be sought, life should be quiet and not meddlesome, and Christian men should be industrious and not parasites (4:6, 11 f.; 5:15). Religious and moral duties intermingle in the one life of Christian discipleship (5:12–22).

All this is, and should be, in the context of the church. Paul's readers were not, and were not meant to be, spiritual hermits. Each was to be found as a member of the Christian community (1:1; 2:14), which was "in Christ" (1:1)—a single signpost to a vast territory in Paul's thought and experience. They had been blessed by a past act, the work of Christ; they were kept by his power; and they enjoyed a hope which stretched out into the far distance of eternity, for it looked to the Parousia (1:3; 2:19; 3:13; 4:13–18; 5:23) and to God's own kingdom and glory (2:12). In their spiritual pilgrimage the believers were cared for by a simple and undeveloped form of ministry (5:12 f.), pastors who were over them "in the Lord" (cf. 1:1 above).

This relatively simple plan of salvation which we have disentangled from the First Epistle to the Thessalonians corresponds in broad outline to the Epistle to the Romans with its scheme of universal sin, the way of salvation, and the duties of the Christian. Points which Paul elaborated in some detail in Romans may be only touched on or implied in Thessalonians. But his essential gospel is the same in both epistles.

(3) God

So far our emphasis has been on soteriology but we ought now to consider Paul's doctrine of God as it appears in Thessalonians. In general all that is taught of God in the Old Testament may be regarded as Paul's belief. In particular God the Father is the eternal fount of deity (1:1, 3; 3:11, 13). He is real and true (1:9) in contrast to the many gods of paganism. He is the living God (1:9). This is also implied whenever the apostle calls on God as witness (2:5, 10): only the living can testify. (A corpse might be evidence but could not give evidence.) It was the living God in whose presence the preachers rejoiced (3:9).

God is not only living; he is loving (1:4). And he is all-controlling. This is suggested by the prayer concerning the journey to Thessalonica (3:11) and by the thanksgiving rendered to God (1:2 f.; 2:13). God is sovereign in nature, history, redemption and conversion. He is the God of peace (5:23). "Peace" is a rich concept (see on 1:1) and reveals God as the author of the atonement. The references to wrath are pertinent here (1:10; 5:9). In consequence of the work of Christ, God has a message for men, the active word of God (2:13) or the gospel of God (2:2, 8 f.), which he has entrusted to his servants to make known (2:4). In the gospel men are not merely informed of facts but they encounter a person, the living God. He is thus knowable and his believing people know him, in contrast to the heathen who do not know God (4:5).

God calls men in the preaching of the gospel, and he continues to call them when they have yielded to him (4:7; 5:24). He is to be trusted (1:8) and should be pleased (2:15; 4:1) throughout life, and he can and does recognize right conduct (2:10). He hears prayer and is responsive, or why should his people pray constantly (5:17)? He keeps and hallows his people (5:23). The Spirit whom he gives is the Holy Spirit (4:8) for the ministry of sanctification (cf. 4:3, 7).

The unity between Father and Son is suggested rather than asserted. For example, the church is "in God the Father and the Lord Jesus Christ," not "in God the Father and in the Lord Jesus Christ" (see discussion on 1:1). The preachers had been approved by God to be entrusted with the gospel, and it was the gospel of Christ as well as of God (2:8 f.; 3:2), and they were apostles of Christ (2:6). The churches of God were in Christ Jesus (2:14). The Jews who killed the Lord Jesus and oppose the preaching of salvation displease God (2:15 f.). God the Father and the Lord Jesus are together the subjects of the same prayer, and the verb is in the singular number (3:11). The will of God is in Christ Jesus (5:18). God appointed us to obtain salvation through our Lord Jesus Christ (5:9). (Compare also 3:13; 4:14.) The teaching is implicit rather than explicit, but for all that it is highly significant. It is not the teaching of an uninstructed enthusiast or of an amateur theologian. It does not spring from the formative years of Paul's thought. It is the natural language of a theologian who is a master of his craft and who, though not dealing specifically with the doctrine of God, yet finds his knowledge of it relevant to the situation.

(4) Christ

The Christology of the epistle is high. Paul could speak of Jesus (4:14), the historic man of Nazareth who was killed by the Jews, but he found it hard to restrict himself to this name. Even the Jesus who was killed was and is the Lord (2:15). This great Old Testament word, "the Lord" (see on 1:1), expresses the sovereignty of God, personally and legitimately exercised over the whole universe, animate and inanimate. God is sovereign of heaven and earth, ruler over creation and nature, over history and the affairs of men, over humans and demons alike; he is sovereign likewise in redemption and conversion. And such an exalted name is applied to Jesus. No more need be added at this point to our Lord's place in salvation. But attention should be recalled to the prayer concerning the journey to Thessalonica (3:11). If "our Lord Jesus" can "direct our way" he obviously is a master of providence and history is plastic in his hands. Although he is not actually called judge, it is implied that he will not be absent from the judgment (3:13; 4:17; 5:2). Note in 5:2 that an expression used by a Hebrew prophet in reference to God is quietly transferred to Christ. The full title, the (or our) Lord Jesus Christ (5:28) has an august solemnity, a certain atmosphere not unlike the hushed reverence of kneeling worshipers.

The Lord Jesus Christ (1:1) is also the Son of God who is in heaven (1:10). If anything further were needed to establish the close relationship between our Lord and God the Father, the term "Son" would do it. Jesus is a human name; Christ refers to the Messianic office; Lord expresses sovereignty. Whatever relationship exists or is possible or conceivable between one so named and God the Father, "Son" is the keystone to the whole. The relationship is personal. The exegete must always beware of reading in ideas which are foreign to his text. For example, he should not lightly and thoughtlessly, and certainly not at the first stage of his exegesis, read Pauline ideas into the Gospel of John. But in the light of the theology of the First Epistle to the Thessalonians, who could blame the exegete, still less the preacher, who saw in 1:10 a tap or faucet through which could be drawn the comparable water of life from the Fourth Gospel?

(5) The Holy Spirit

The references to the Holy Spirit are scanty, but his presence pervades the epistle. He is the gift of God and his ministry is that of sanctification (4:7 f.). It is not an independent or detached ministry but is in the closest association with the preaching of the gospel (1:5 f.). The bare words of the preacher, taken in the isolation of a tape-recorder, may be dull or interesting, plausible or implausible; they may tickle the ears or rivet the attention; but their essentially spiritual impact will depend on whether the man is an authentic preacher or whether he is merely a man who happens to occupy the pulpit. That is to say, the words as words may be everything or nothing. They may be of impeccable orthodoxy or have little or no theology. Even if they contain everything that is humanly possible of the truth of God, they make no spiritual impact and leave no spiritual mark without the ministry of the Holy Spirit. He is the source of spiritual power and conviction. It is through his silent influence in the mind and heart of the hearer that the words are driven home, conviction established, faith inspired and conversion achieved. In his hands the words are powerful tools in the creation of certainty. It is through his effective presence alone that men become holy.

It must not be thought that we are here erecting a large building on a narrow foundation (two verses) like an inverted pyramid. When Paul preached in Thessalonica he had his earlier ministry behind him, and when he preached in the power of the Spirit it was no new experience. The two verses, small as they may seem, really represent all his missionary activity up to that moment (cf. 2:1 f.).

Now the preaching of the gospel is the preaching of Christ. The Holy Spirit is thus closely linked with Christ. But he is, as we have seen, the gift of God. There is thus a harmony between Father, Son, and Holy Spirit, to say the least. This is not yet the specific doctrine of the Holy Trinity, but it accords with it and forms part of the material of it.

The ministry of the Holy Spirit may be resisted, in particular when he manifests himself in prophetic utterance (5:19 f.). The joy inspired by the Holy Spirit (1:6) was experienced by imitators—the plural term is significant. It was a group which rejoiced, not a solitary individual. This must not obscure the fact that joy is an individual experience, even in company with others. We all know what is meant by the fellowship of food, the eating of a common meal, but even here each man eats his own dinner. So the joy may be common but each member of the group has his own, inevitably private, psychological experience of joy. Apart from the view of common sense, the "privacy" of joy is proved by the fact that in a crowd a solitary man may be the exception: all may rejoice but one; all may be sad but one—and he might be filled with joy.

All this suggests that the Holy Spirit is the minister of personal experience. If there is any truth at all in "experiential religion," in what used to be called experimental religion—and there is—it is due to the presence of the Holy Spirit. And though Paul does not explicitly say so, his association of joy with the reception of the word suggests that those theologians are right who say that the Spirit is never to be separated from the Word; for he is the Spirit of Jesus (Acts 16:7).

In both the Introduction and the Commentary we have spoken almost indiscriminately of Paul, the apostles, the preachers, the missionaries or the writers, unless there has been some overriding reason for writing otherwise. This has been in the interests of variation and to avoid tediousness. It is justified by the fact that Paul was the dominant character, and that Silvanus and Timothy were associated closely with him. See on 1:1.

OUTLINE

1 Thessalonians

I. GREETING (1:1)
II. MATTERS PERSONAL AND FACTUAL (1:2–3:13)
   1. The Thessalonians: Their Conversion a Cause for Thanksgiving
      (1:2–10)
      (1) The gospel received (1:2–3)
      (2) Election demonstrated (1:4–5)
      (3) Affliction overcome (1:6)
      (4) Evangelism widespread (1:7–8)
      (5) Idols replaced (1:9–10)
   2. The Preachers: Their Blameless Conduct a Matter of Memory
      (2:1–12)
      (1) The preachers' effectiveness (2:1)
      (2) Persistence (2:2)
      (3) Motive (2:3–4)
      (4) Language (2:5)
      (5) Disinterestedness (2:6)
      (6) Tenderness (2:7)
      (7) Devotion (2:8)
      (8) Toil (2:9)
      (9) Standards (2:10–12)
   3. The Thessalonians: Their Persecution a Proof of the Reality
      of Their Conversion (2:13–16)
      (1) The Word of God received and active (2:13)
      (2) The experience of the churches repeated (2:14)
      (3) The character of the archetypal persecutors summarized
          (2:15–16)
   4. The Preachers: Their Inquiry an Occasion of Relief (2:17–
      3:10)
      (1) A visit prevented (2:17–20)
      (2) A mission inaugurated (3:1–5)
      (3) Good news reported (3:6–10)
   5. The Preachers and the Thessalonians: Both Parties as Subjects
      of Prayer (3:11–13)
      (1) Prayer for the preachers' journey (3:11)
      (2) Prayer for the church's growth (3:12–13)

COMMENTARY

1 Thessalonians

I. GREETING (1:1)

The introduction gives the names of the authors and readers, and a salutation. The form is conventional but it has been Christianized. A secular example appears in Acts 23:26. The same form is used in Romans, but there it has been richly "clothed" with doctrine (Rom. 1:1-7). Even so the very short form in the Thessalonian letter contains all the essentials: authors, readers, the divine names, and the characteristically Pauline *grace . . . and peace.*

Paul, Silvanus, and Timothy: Only the names are given, in the barest simplicity. The order of seniority is followed. The word "apostle" is not employed, mainly because Paul was on such terms of intimate friendship with the readers that it was natural to omit it. When a man is sure of his place in the hearts of his people he does not keep on saying, "I am the minister." In any case his apostleship was not disputed in the Thessalonian community. In a pleasing way Paul associates his helpers with himself. His spirit is that of the man who says "my colleague" rather than "my curate" or "my assistant." We should not think of three people writing a letter by each contributing a third of it. Paul is the dominant personality, though not domineering. The frequency of "we" should be noted. It is not quite true to say that "apostle" was omitted because only Paul was an apostle in the strict sense. He can use the term in a wider sense and include his colleagues (2:6). His aim was not to exclude. At times he had to emphasize himself (2:18), but "we" shows him as conscious of a background.[1] The three men had planted the church in Thessalonica (Acts 17:1-10) and were together in Corinth (2 Cor. 1:19) at the time of writing. They clearly formed a team (Acts 17:14-15; 18:5).

Paul stands first as the leader. The same order of the three is maintained elsewhere (2 Cor. 1:19), in spite of the rendering of the RSV. The proud Pharisee who had persecuted the church (Phil. 3:4-6), who was also a Roman citizen (Acts 22:27-28), encountered the living

---

1. See W. F. Lofthouse, " 'I' and 'We' in the Pauline Letters," *The Expository Times* 64 (May 1953), 241-45.

Christ on the road to Damascus and was transformed from Saul the persecutor into Paul the apostle to the Gentiles (Acts 9:15; 22:21). He
did not need to defend his apostleship when writing to the Thessalonians, but when necessary he could do it passionately (1 Cor. 9:1–5).
As "one untimely born" (1 Cor. 15:8), that is, born too early, he had
seen the Parousia-glory; the risen Christ was seen in his glory, not in
Jerusalem or Galilee.[1] As an apostle, then, Paul takes the lead, in
fulfillment of his commission.

Silvanus, called Silas in the Acts, is the Latin form of the name [2]
and accords with its owner's Roman citizenship (Acts 16:37). Silas is
not a contraction of Silvanus. Most likely it is a Greek form of an original
Jewish name akin to Saul.[3] The man in question was influential in the
church of Jerusalem (Acts 15:22), and was a prophet (Acts 15:32).
He was chosen by Paul (Acts 15:40) to accompany him on what is
traditionally called Paul's second missionary journey. The fact that he
was chosen by Paul gives him a subordinate position from the beginning.

Timothy is the junior, and somewhat of a minor character, though
not without importance. Years later he could still be regarded as young
(1 Tim. 4:12; 5:1–2). The product of a mixed marriage, he had a
religious background and some reputation in his "home church." He
joined Paul early in his second missionary journey (Acts 16:1–3) and
was constantly with him. He appears in the initial greeting in a number
of letters: 1 and 2 Thessalonians, 2 Corinthians, Philippians, Colossians
and Philemon. At times he represented the apostle (1 Thess 3:2). He
had an innate timidity (1 Cor. 16:10–11) and was affectionate and
emotional (2 Tim. 1:4–8). The fact that he was Paul's spiritual child
(1 Cor. 4:17) bound them together and fostered the dynamic leader-
ship of the older man.

The three men together point to the universal nature or catholicity
of the church. Paul and Silvanus are Jews, each possessing Roman citizenship; the name of Timothy is Greek and his father was a Greek.
Rome united the world of their day; Greek facilitated universal communication; the Jew stood for the Old Testament with its promise of
the coming Messiah. We may see an analogy in the title on the cross
(John 19:20).

The church: There was but one in the city and every Christian belonged to it. It was the church "consisting of" Thessalonians, not owned

---

1. Stephen Neill, *The Interpretation of the New Testament 1861–1961* (Lon-
don: Oxford University Press, 1964), p. 287, note 2.
2. Albrecht Oepke, *Das Neue Testament Deutsch: Die kleineren Briefe des
Apostels Paulus* (Göttingen: Vandenhoeck and Ruprecht, 1965), p. 160.
3. James Hope Moulton and Wilbert Francis Howard, *A Grammar of New
Testament Greek* (Edinburgh: T. & T. Clark, 1960), 2:109, 146. F. Blass, A.
Debrunner, and Robert W. Funk, *A Greek Grammar of the New Testament*
(Chicago: University of Chicago Press, 1961), paragraph 125.

by them. In relation to other groups of Christians in other cities or provinces Paul can speak of "churches" in the plural, the so-called local church (2:14). He also recognizes the one (universal) church (Col. 1: 18, 24). It is helpful to employ the Aristotelian concepts of form and matter and thereby to see that the "churchness" or form of the church is present in its totality in the local church even if its numbers (the "matter") are very few. This is what is meant when it is said that the whole church is present in the local church—it does not mean an innumerable company which no man can number.[1] In one and the same letter Paul can speak of the universal and the local church as "church" (Col. 1:18, 24; 4:16). The movement from the smaller (local) to the wider (universal) circle is analogous to Paul's similar transition from "I" to "we."

In God the Father and the Lord Jesus Christ: The association could hardly be closer. Even the preposition *in* is not repeated before *the Lord Jesus Christ*. The almost incidental linking of Jesus with God, without explanation and still less without apology, is highly significant. At this comparatively early date it would have been intellectually dangerous (if they were not right) for monotheistic Jews to speak thus of Jesus; as dangerous as if men today proclaimed the deity of, say, the late President Roosevelt. For there were still people alive to correct them. But there were nearly five hundred alive to support them (1 Cor. 15:6); and the resurrection of Jesus was crucial (Rom. 1:4). It signalized his sonship and lordship.

The Father expresses not only divine identity but spiritual experience. Men may know God (Rom. 1:21) in some measure, but it is only in Christ that God has given himself to men as Father, and only through the Spirit of Christ that they know him as such (Gal. 4:6; Rom. 8:14–17).

Lord Jesus Christ is the full title. *Jesus* is the name of the historic person who was seen in Nazareth, Jerusalem, and elsewhere in Palestine. It is the Greek for a late form of the common name Joshua (compare the KJV and RSV of Heb. 4:8). We are so familiar with the sacred name that we miss its impact. But if we imagine the Savior's name to have been John instead of Joshua we can savor the feelings of unbelieving Jews at hearing the sound of *Lord* John. The divine is linked with the common—quite rightly, because "God sent forth his Son, born of woman" (Gal. 4:4), and he was "the man Christ Jesus" (1 Tim. 2:5). The name *Jesus* is appropriate (Matt. 1:21).

Lord (Greek *Kurios*) is the word used in the Septuagint (Greek) version of the Old Testament for the divine name traditionally ren-

---

1. Compare Moule's instructive note. C. F. D. Moule, *The Cambridge Greek Testament Commentary: Colossians and Philemon* (Cambridge: University Press, 1957), p. 154.

dered Jehovah, now Yahweh. It is of the deepest significance that the word used to translate the ineffable name of God should be applied to *Jesus* (Exod. 3:14–15; Phil. 2:11). The name of *Jesus* is *Lord*.

Christ is Greek for the Hebrew Messiah, the Anointed One. It is instructive to look at Psalm 2:2 and Acts 4:26 in both KJV and RSV. The king who was the subject of prophecy has actually come (Mark 8:29; 14:61–62). Popular expectation had thought of a deliverer from the Romans, but for Jesus, Messiahship was a task involving the cross— the supreme service. He linked the Messiah with the Servant (Mark 1: 11; Ps. 2:7; Isa. 42:1).

In what sense is the church *in God the Father?* Neither writer nor readers can have been thinking of it as a terrifying prospect or experience (Heb. 10:31). The absence of fear is due to being in Christ also. The famous Pauline formula, "in Christ," has been thoroughly investigated, and some regard it as a social concept. So it must be, if the church is in Christ. But it is also individual and personal. At the heart of a highly individualistic passage Paul can state his purpose to "be found in him" (Phil 3:9). The believing church is in Christ because its individual members are, and each of them becomes so when he first believes. And being in Christ they are safely and peacefully *in God the Father.* This Pauline language corresponds to that of John: " . . . no one shall snatch them out of my hand . . . out of the Father's hand" (John 10:28–29). Both Paul and John are far removed here from the experience of the natural man: " 'In him we live and move and have our being' " (Acts 17:28).

Grace to you and peace: The source and the result. *Grace* [1] is one of the great New Testament words. The original is Greek (*charis*); it is flavored with the *hen* of the Septuagint and has been born again, like the apostle himself, on the road to Damascus. It moves from the superior to the inferior, from the greater in character and power to the lesser. It is from God to man and not from man to God. It is entirely undeserved. God is not in any sense obligated to be gracious, a fact which is illustrated in the doctrine of election (1 Thess. 1:4; 2 Thess. 2:13) and in Paul's rejection of the picture of an employer paying wages. Wages must be paid for work done—a debt. Grace is free—*gratis* (cf. Rom. 4:4).

The term itself is abstract though convenient for use. It means that we are concerned with a gracious God who acts personally in dealing with men. We must not make *grace* a thing-in-itself, working impersonally. Grace means God himself working for and in men; and he thus works in Christ. In fact grace is alive in Christ, who embodies it. When we speak of it we should think of Christ-crucified-and-risen.

---

1. For a profound study of the meaning of grace, see T. F. Torrance, *The Doctrine of Grace in the Apostolic Fathers* (Grand Rapids: Wm. B. Eerdmans, 1959), pp. 1–35.

Thus we should never isolate grace from Christ and should never isolate Christ from his cross and resurrection; and never isolate Christ from God. Grace is thus a particular case of love. It is love loving the unlovable and pardoning the unpardonable. It is utter purity cleansing the defiled. It is the perfectly clean touching the leper. It is the exalted coming down to lift up the fallen. There is love between Father and Son but never grace. How could there be?

Salvation is due to grace (Eph. 2:5, 8; 2 Tim. 1:9). It is through grace that we receive the call to accept salvation (Gal. 1:15). Christian service is the gift of grace (Eph. 3:8). Equipment for the varying tasks is a grace-gift (Rom. 12:6; Eph. 4:7; 1 Pet. 4:10), diverse though the tasks may be. Justified men stand in the new territory of grace (Rom. 5:2), in which soil the Christian can grow to maturity (2 Pet. 3:18). It is grace which makes the Christian what he is and grace which gives him any success he may have in evangelistic and pastoral toil (1 Cor. 15:10). In grievous personal situations which need to be interpreted in order to be endured, grace is enough (2 Cor. 12:9). Grace means—the Christ of the cross (Rom. 3:24–25; 2 Cor. 8:9).

Peace is an apparently simple word but one with deep undertones. In the normal Greek sense it is the opposite to war (Luke 14:32) or danger (Luke 11:21). But it was used in the Septuagint to represent the Hebrew *shalom*. (Many will be reminded of the salutation *salaam* from their reading of oriental stories.) The Hebrew contains the idea of completeness, wholeness or welfare. (It is easy to see the connection with the absence of war. In war there are obviously *two* parties, fighting each other. When they are at peace there is *one* circle of friendship—obviously a "whole.") In particular the prophets saw such peace as a mark of the Messianic kingdom, and the Christian concept of peace was correspondingly filled out. It is almost the same as salvation (Isa. 52:7; Acts 10:36). In other words the Greek word (through the Septuagint) has taken on a Hebrew meaning. Three elements may be distinguished. The believer has peace *with* God (Rom. 5:1): the divine opposition has ended and in Christ God is "for us" (Rom. 8:31–32). By the combination of petition and thanksgiving he may dispense with anxiety in the knowledge that he is protected by the peace *of* God (Phil. 4:6–7). This is no mere subjective feeling, which as feeling might be a fool's paradise, but is grounded in God's work in Christ. There is no turmoil in the inner citadel of his heart, whatever happens outside (Matt. 10:34–36). It is the fruit of the Spirit (Gal. 5:22). The believer should also work for peace *among* men (Rom. 12:18; 14:19; Eph. 4:3). This goes back to Jesus (Mark 9:50). Paul prays that the "peace of God" may not have even the slightest crack (Rom. 15:13—"all . . . peace").

Thus the believer has peace with God; he may have the peace of God; and he ought to work for peace among men.

This salutation is thought by some to combine Greek and Hebrew greetings: *grace* (*charis*) from the normal *chairein,* and the Hebrew *peace*. But the Jews tended to identify them, even translating *shalom* on occasion by *chairein* (Isa. 48:22; 57:21, LXX; cf. Luke 1:28 [1]). The decision on this question does not greatly matter in comparison with the doctrinal message. The greeting is no mere form of words. The world gives a mere salutation; Jesus gives his peace (John 14:27). For how many does "goodbye" mean "God be with you"?

There is no verb in the Greek. We may understand the thought as a statement, a hope, or a prayer. "Grace and peace are actually yours." This is true in fact. But the hope and prayer are appropriate, for grace and peace may be multiplied in men's experience (1 Pet. 1:2). To all comments should be added the extensive use of the concordance.[2]

---

1. Theodor Zahn, *Introduction to the New Testament,* 2nd ed., rev. (New York: Charles Scribner's Sons, 1917), 1:119, note 7.

2. A convenient study will be found in Leon Morris, *The Apostolic Preaching of the Cross* (London: Tyndale Press, 1955), pp. 210–17.

II. MATTERS PERSONAL AND FACTUAL (1:2–3:13)

Paul and his companions recalled with thanksgiving their earlier visit and the sound conversion of the Thessalonians. They were sure that the readers would remember the evangelistic zeal and pastoral care of the writers and their own warm response to the preachers and to their message, in spite of persecution. They had been warned of persecution in advance and had survived it. All the more were the authors longing to see their beloved readers. The epistle gives the impression here that Paul was on the defensive against slander.

1. The Thessalonians: Their Conversion a Cause for Thanksgiving (1:2–10)

Thanksgiving was inspired by the remembrance of the Thessalonians. They had received the gospel, the power of which had demonstrated their election, sustained them joyously in affliction and made them widely known as evangelistic believers. Negatively, they had abandoned their dead idols; positively, they were serving the living God and awaiting the Advent of his Son.

(1) The gospel received (1:2–3)

Unceasing thanksgiving was being offered to God for all the Thessalonian Christians: the faith had taken deep root and was being shown in strenuous lives.

Verse 2: We . . . give thanks always for you all—no break and no exception. The three authors must be regarded as speaking together, whoever actually used the pen. This should be kept in mind throughout the epistle. The thought anticipates that of verse 7, in which the church is an example. It is not stated whether the prayer of thanksgiving is individual or corporate: probably both. It is quite likely, in view of the writers' vivid memories, that Thessalonians were mentioned by name. Paul frequently began his letters with thanksgiving. Galatians is a striking exception, not unnatural in the circumstances. Paul strongly emphasized the duty as well as the privilege of thanksgiving, sometimes

[27]

explicitly saying so (2 Thess. 1:3; 2:13 "we are bound to") and sometimes just implying it (Rom. 1:8 "First, I thank . . ."). He bluntly
told his readers to give thanks (1 Thess. 5:18). It is thus an act of
obedience, a recognition of all God's mercies generally, and a mark of
spiritual alertness in that it recognizes answers to prayer when they
come. Prayer is not a vague broadcast sent out into the open and forgotten. It is directed to God in Christ, and it should look for the answer,
recognize it, and immediately give thanks for it. The movement is
circular: spiritual vitality recognizes the answer and the answer fosters
and even renews the vitality.

Always . . . constantly: The attitude of thanksgiving is continuous
and the *mentioning* is regular. The *always* may be represented by an
unbroken line thus ——————— and the *constantly* by a series of dots
. . . . *Constantly* means that no "dot" is ever missing. The
two words reflect the true life of prayer. We cannot always be mentioning, though we should be regular, but the attitude can be permanent.
The essence of prayer is not the utterance of words, however regular,
but the lifting up the heart to God and keeping it "up." The outer expression of thanksgiving lies in the mentioning.

Verse 3: Remembering is the cause of the thanksgiving. It is not a
secular remembrance but is consciously in God's presence. Some scholars transfer the adverb from verse 2 to verse 3, translating it "constantly remembering." It is a small point. The main fact is that they
gave thanks *always,* which must mean that they were always *remembering.* The actual *mentioning* in words is secondary, though obviously
desirable.

Work of faith—an arresting juxtaposition in the writings of Paul. It
is as striking as such an expression as "a democratic Republican" or
"a republican democrat," which could be quite nonpartisan. Paul is the
great antagonist of works—but only as a means of justification (Rom.
3:28). The latter is the celebrated verse into which Martin Luther introduced the word "alone"—by faith alone—for which he has been
severely criticized. But Origen used the word here long before him,
and even technically, from the point of view of language, Luther was
correct.[1] "A cup of water" (Mark 9:41) must mean "only a cup."
Works do not count for justification—but they count. Paul can speak of
"faith working through love" (Gal. 5:6) and even of "keeping the
commandments of God" (1 Cor. 7:19). He means in the verse under
discussion that the Thessalonians had put their trust in Christ, had believed in him and still did so, and that therefore they had worked. More
simply, faith works.

Labor of love: Faith works, but *love* goes the extra mile (Matt. 5:

---

1. Joachim Jeremias, *The Central Message of the New Testament* (London:
SCM Press, 1965), p. 55.

41). The order is first faith, then love (1 John 4:19), though love does not replace faith but expresses it. *Labor* means work that is energetic and wearisome, toil. It is a paradox of the Christian faith that our Savior calls to him "all who labor" (Matt. 11:28), who toil to the point of weariness, and then inspires them to further toil—though perhaps of a different sort. James would understand this (Jas. 2:14–20).

Steadfastness of hope: That is, endurance. The Christian hope is the motive power by which faith continues to work and love to toil, even though we encounter stern opposition and feel that we have come to the end of our tether. The object of hope is Christ (Col. 1:27). It is not quite impossible but linguistically unwieldy to take *Lord Jesus Christ* in relation to each member of the triad: *work of faith* in *Christ, labor of love* toward him, endurance of *hope* in him, though of course it is true in fact that we trust him, love him, and hope in him.

The triad *faith, love, hope* can be used as a summary of Christianity. Faith looks back to the cross, with all its wealth of meaning; Christians love the brethren in the present; and hope has its eye on the future, sure and certain. The association is not uncommon (5:8; 1 Cor. 13:13; Col. 1:4–5; Heb. 10:22–24; cf. 1 Pet. 1:21–22). The phrase *work of faith* appears again in the second letter (2 Thess. 1:11).

The words *before our God and Father* are placed by the RSV toward the beginning of the verse, naturally enough, to be taken with *remembering*. In the Greek they come at the end of the verse, after *hope in our Lord Jesus Christ*. This position, together with identical language in a text concerned with the Second Advent (3:13; cf. 2 Cor. 5:10), gives to the remembrance a certain solemnity. The Christian hope, the Lord's coming, and the judgment seat of Christ combine to remove any shallow lightheartedness from the remembrance which occasioned the prayers of the writers and their thanksgiving for the Thessalonians.

(2) Election demonstrated (1:4–5)

The preaching of the gospel with spiritual conviction and converting power had shown, by its effect on the listeners, that they were among the elect.

Verse 4: For we know states the ultimate reason for the thanksgiving. Undoubtedly they gave thanks for the work as evidence of faith, for the drudgery as evidence of love, for the endurance as evidence of a hope really felt; but all this was itself evidence of what was prior, their election. The short clause is a single word in the Greek (*eidotes*, literally "knowing"), a participle which is a regular formula with Paul. Its frequent use is not without significance (Rom. 5:3; 6:9; 13:11; 1 Cor. 15:58; 2 Cor. 4:14; 5:6, 11; Eph. 6:8). We live indeed by faith and not by sight, but even so we have much which is worthy of the term "knowledge." And from knowledge, inferences may be drawn. Take one of the examples: "We rejoice in our sufferings, knowing that suffering produces endurance" (Rom. 5:3). We can turn this around to show the development of the thought, the drawing of the inference, thus:

What produces endurance is a matter for rejoicing.
Suffering is what produces endurance.
Therefore: Suffering is a matter for rejoicing.

It is plain that the Christian should be a man of faith, knowledge, and reason. A detailed study of the "inferential" words of the New Testament ("therefore," etc.) could be illuminating, especially to Christians suspicious of reason.

Brethren beloved by God: The warm affection expressed in the vocative "brothers" is deepened by the reference to the love of God. The word *beloved,* a perfect participle, expresses the abiding result of a past act. (As a popular instance, "he has scored" means that "we are now winning" or "we *are* now doing better." It might even mean "we *are* on top." The point is that the bare statement "he scored" would leave the door open for a swift addition "but they equalized at once" whereas "he has scored" leaves us cheering!)

Now this perfect participle combines two lines of thought. It is not always realized how often the New Testament uses a past tense (an aorist) for the love of God. God so *loved* the world (John 3:16); we are more than conquerors through him who *loved* us (Rom. 8:37); and likewise elsewhere (Eph. 2:4; 2 Thess. 2:16; 1 John 4:10, 11, 19; cf. Gal. 2:20; Eph. 5:2, 25). Why the past tense? Does not God still love us? Assuredly he does; but the past (aorist) tense draws our attention to the point of impact of his love—the cross of Christ. There in that historic place the love of God was most eloquent. There it is concentrated. There the words of prophets before him and preachers after him are gathered up into one great utterance of the Son of God. There all the hidden deeds of a loving providence and all the scattered acts of divine mercy in Galilee and Jerusalem are brought together in one utterance and one act of almighty and eternal love.

This is one line of thought. And the New Testament safeguards itself against any suggestion that God did indeed love us but has since ceased to do so, by the occasional use of the present tense (2 Cor. 9:7; Heb. 12:6), and by the great affirmation that *God is love* (1 John 4:8, 16). This is the second line of thought. God loved; God loves. These two are brought together in the perfect tense: "you have been loved by God" means that "God loved you" and "you are now in the circle of his love." The impact of the cross has eternal results—in God and in you.

It must not be thought that for Paul the love of God was a theological commonplace. He gazed in wonder at it all his days. It may be that many

today are innoculated by the movies against understanding the nature
of God's love. So much goes by the name of love that we may miss the
essential in the love of God. His love is not impulsive but is derived
from his will. He willed to love us. It was not induced in him by anything
lovable in us; it is spontaneous, its cause being in God himself and
not in us. Hence it is not limited to a few choice spirits but is universal.
"God so loved *the world* . . . ." It is act rather than emotion or feeling.
It has been customary to emphasize God's love as an activity and the
stress is wholesome. But the attitude behind the act must not be
forgotten. Paul could speak severely about apparently beneficent
actions which were devoid of love, because the subject did not really
care (1 Cor. 13:3).

There are three "moments" in which the love of God is discerned,
and they are cumulative; that is, the later adds to the earlier by drawing
our attention to it and impressing it on us. The first may be stated thus:
Christ has been crucified. The tense is again perfect (cf. 1 Cor. 1:23;
Gal. 3:1). The historic fact with its inner meaning is the objective evidence for the love of God (Rom. 5:8), and the evidence lasts for ever.
Secondly, God has called (1 Cor. 7:15, 17; cf. v. 18). There was a time
when the man who is now a believer heard God speaking to him and
calling him to faith in his Son. The invitation was self-authenticating
though it is beyond rationalization. The call was decisive. We have
been called—and we still have a vocation. In our experience the love
of God in Christ crucified shines before us, and we need no further proof.
Thirdly, in our experience of conversion or later, the love of God has
been poured out in our hearts through the Holy Spirit given to us. It has
been poured out like a refreshing shower of rain and therefore, in the
spirit of the metaphor, "we *are now* wet through." The Holy Spirit has
made us aware of the love of God and the individual knows it in the
depths of his heart (Rom. 5:5).

The message of the cross is heard in the call. The call continues all
our lives (1 Thess. 2:12; cf. Phil. 3:14, where the call says "up-
ward!"),[1] and through the Holy Spirit in his heart a man knows the
love of God in Christ for him (Rom. 8:35 compared with v. 39). This
Paul and his readers understood.

It is plain that we must also not say that we know what love is and that
"God is like that." Rather we must look at Christ crucified and then say
that "the love of God has now been brought out into the open for us to
see it" (cf. 1 John 4:9). We must not say that we have been deeply
loved in our family and that our experience of God is like that. Rather
must we say that we have never known a love like that in which as
sinful men we have been accepted in Christ by a God of utter holiness,

1. L. H. Marshall, *The Challenge of New Testament Ethics* (London: Macmillan and Co., Ltd., 1946), p. 308.

and that family love must look up to this as its highest pattern and example. We must not say that we love our family and indeed our fellow-men and that this is what we are supposed to do. Rather we must say that we reach the highest point in our love for others when it is inspired by God in Christ: "we love, because he first loved us" (1 John 4:19; cf. 1 Thess. 4:9–10).

That he has chosen you: Literally, "your election." The doctrine of election goes back to ancient Israel. It is seen in patriarchal history (Rom. 9:11–13). On a broader field all Israel was elected in the fathers (Rom. 11:28); on a narrower scale part of Israel was elected (Rom. 11:5).[1] The supreme example is our Lord himself (Luke 23:35; cf. John 1:34 where a variant of great antiquity reads "elect" for "Son"). But he was not only the elect; he himself elected: "You did not choose me, but I chose you" (John 15:16–19; cf. 6:70; 13:18). God's choice is God's chooser.[2] There is thus unity between Father and Son. Judas was chosen to fulfill the Scripture, God's Word. It is thus not because of election that men are holy but because of the atonement.[3] And Father and Son unite to keep them (John 17:11–15).

Paul reverts to this subject in the second letter (2 Thess. 2:13), but for our present purpose we find more detail further afield. Election means that God "chose us in him before the foundation of the world, that we should be holy and blameless before him" (Eph. 1:4). The phrase "in love" in the following verse (Eph. 1:5) is the subject of dispute. Some scholars take it with "chose" and some with "be holy" and some with "destined." However the question is finally settled, it can hardly be denied that God chose us in love. And he did so in Christ. It was not an arbitrary act and certainly not an act of naked will. But does it refer to the church in general or to the sum total of believing individuals?

It is hard to see how the church can be holy unless its members are. "Holy" is a cultic word; he who is holy can approach the holy God— which the believer does in Christ. "Blameless" is moral as well as religious and occurs in the parallel passage to the verse in Ephesians: "to present you holy and blameless and irreproachable before him" (Col. 1:22). The word *irreproachable* savors of the forensic. In its verbal form it is used by Paul in his great question: "Who shall bring any charge against God's elect? It is God who justifies" (Rom. 8:33). All

---

1. G. Schrenk in *Theological Dictionary of the New Testament,* ed. Gerhard Kittel, trans. Geoffrey W. Bromiley (Grand Rapids: Wm. B. Eerdmans, 1967), 4:179–80. Cf. also the "election within election" in H. L. Ellison, *The Mystery of Israel: An Exposition of Romans 9–11* (Grand Rapids: Wm. B. Eerdmans, 1966). The whole book is suggestive.

2. L. Coenen in *Theologisches Begriffslexikon zum Neuen Testament* (Wuppertal: R. Brockhaus Verlag, 1967), 3:289.

3. Otto Procksch, in *Theological Dictionary,* ed. G. Kittel, 1:106, note 59.

these high privileges belong to the believer because he is in Christ, and he is in him by faith—which is individually exercised. A man must be holy to approach God; he is holy in Christ. He must be blameless; he is blameless in Christ. He must be immune to accusations; he is so immune in Christ. The ultimate purpose may indeed be that believers may attain to character and holiness in themselves. But in the meanwhile— and it will be a long time—they bear the imputed righteousness of Christ. (The verb "present" in Col. 1:22 may be eschatological—cf. v. 23, "continue"; 1 Cor. 1:8). The purpose extends to the church (Eph. 5:27) which is to be holy and blameless; the church which is constituted by individual believers in their relation to Christ and to one another.

Election then is of individuals, in love, and in Christ. The process is surveyed by Paul in Romans 8:29–30. It is God's purpose and he is completely free, uninfluenced by anything outside himself, and sovereign, having all things and all men at his disposal.

This is not just a doctrine. It is that by which believing men have lived and died, sometimes in stress and tragedy. Even so it is a doctrine—a doctrine for believers, and believers only. It must not be interpreted mechanically, for in spite of all the laws discovered by the psychologists, man has reserves of mental energy in his central self, certainly enough to make him a morally responsible person. In one sense he is bound in his sins; in another he is free enough to accept or refuse the gospel responsibly. In his dealings with men God does not turn them into machines but works through their will and choice. To take a simple example: if a man for some reason of his own wants his son to marry a French-speaking girl he does not choose the girl and present her to his son. He sends him to France—where he falls in love with the girl of his own choice! He fulfills his father's purpose by exercising his own choice.

The question of the nonelect must be treated with great reserve. We have no proof positive that this or that man belongs to their number. Any objection that election is not "fair" is quite out of place. God is not a democrat. All humanity deserves to die for its sins—and in infinite mercy God has chosen to save a great number which no man can number, by his own self-sacrifice, summed up in the expression "the precious blood of Christ." Who knows what this cost to God? The initiative was with God and it has been effective.

Far from leading believers to complacency, a true grasp of the doctrine will impress on men that it is all of grace and not of merit. And to find oneself among the elect is to discover moral obligations, a life of strenuous moral effort (Col. 3:12–14). The obligation includes evangelism. Election does not imply the need for restrictive practices. The converted man is not afraid to make known the saving name on the score that the nonelect may be offered a blessing to which they are not entitled. His first characteristic act is an exultant shout of invitation in the words of Jesus, "Come to me, all who . . . " (Matt. 11:28). He rejoices in the word "whoever" (John 3:16).

But how may the elect be recognized?

Verse 5: For our gospel: The preached gospel was divinely owned and effectively applied. The authentic Christian is evidence that the God who elected and destined him for salvation has called him out of the world into Christ. *Our gospel* means primarily "the gospel which we preached." But the preachers were not mercenaries in an ecclesiastical army, merely doing what they were told but without any personal interest in their message. They had themselves tasted its power (Paul of Tarsus!) and had made it their own. They preached the Word of God as it came through their own experience of it. There is an analogy here between evangelistic and pastoral work. Comfort is given through comfort received (2 Cor. 1:3–7). The *for* gives the reason for the knowledge of verse 4.

The gospel did not come to them only in word, but it did come in word. Without speech there would have been no preaching. We cannot explain the operation of the Holy Spirit which charged a bare verbal cable with high-voltage spiritual power. But we can ask what are the constituents of a good "cable." How should the preacher speak? At the least he should deliver Christian truth; he should speak with personal conviction; he should use the form of direct address ("you"); his thought and expression should be clear; boldness and "the wooing note" should intermingle; personal testimony should be given but not obtrude; and the trumpet should give no uncertain sound: he has been sent as an ambassador. Without hypocrisy there should be an atmosphere of personal holiness. The epistle points in this direction (2:1–12).

All this is on the human level. The gospel so preached came to the Thessalonians *in power.* Now power means the ability to do something. The preached gospel was able to arrest the attention, convince the mind, convict the heart, convert and save the man, and inspire to evangelism and good works. The secret of this lies with *the Holy Spirit,* who applies the spoken word to the listeners. They recognize that God is speaking to them and calling them (4:7–8). This applies in all evangelism. "Power" and "Holy Spirit" represent one fact—the Spirit at work. It should not be forgotten that the *gospel came* to the Thessalonians. It had to—or they would never have known it. It does not arise from within the heart of man. It is not human nature and it is not human discovery. God sent his Son; that is, he came from outside history into history and he still has to be proclaimed (Rom. 10:14).

Full conviction: Christian certainty. Notice the advance in the thought. An atheistic politician can deliver a powerful and persuasive speech, but here we have the converting power of the Holy Spirit. The *full conviction* is possessed by the preachers for they already know the *power* of the gospel. Conviction is that attitude of mind in which we persist in a belief or a course of action in spite of evidence to the contrary or practical opposition. We know that the "evidence" is not the whole story and are sure that the opposition can be overcome (cf. Rom. 4:21; 1 Thess. 2:2). Conviction of this kind is based partly on the belief of God's Word, partly on prior experience of its power, and partly on a theological knowledge and attitude. There may be opposition to the gospel, and it may be rejected. But the doctrine of election suggests that "I have many people in this city" (Acts 18:10). When Jesus spoke, the audience was split in two (John 7:40–43; cf. 9:16; 10:19). There are those who are deaf to the most persuasive of appeals; but there are those who will respond. It is this prior theological knowledge which encourages the true evangelist to expect conversions, to make arrangements in advance for them to be received and counseled, and to preach *with full conviction*. The one sun melts wax and hardens clay—but it is one sun and it is God's (Rom. 9:18). The evangelist has behind him the sovereignty of God, and he knows it.

You know: The writers confidently appealed to their readers for confirmation of what had just been said. They had come to the city as strangers (Acts 17:1). What kind of men were they? They *proved to be,* turned out to be, men through whom God worked mightily to transform lives—just as the good Samaritan turned out to be a good neighbor (Luke 10:36–37). The preachers were already powerful evangelists before they arrived, but their prior character had been manifested in their ministry. The impact on the city must have been tremendous: uproar, attack, charges of sedition. Turning the world upside down had indeed "upset" the community (Acts 17:6). The gentle appeal anticipates the second chapter.

For your sake: This is the ultimate purpose of God, but there may be an underlying feeling of apostolic motive. They did not come and preach for their own gain, as they make plain in the following chapter (2:5–6). The same phrase is used to the church at Corinth: "though he was rich, yet *for your sake* he became poor" (2 Cor. 8:9). The preachers were indeed imitators of their Master (1 Cor. 11:1).

(3) Affliction overcome (1:6)

The pressure which had been put upon the Thessalonians by their persecutors had been neutralized by the joy inspired by the Holy Spirit.

And you became imitators: Further proof of the election of the Thessalonians. The word *and* links on to the *for* at the beginning of verse 5. Their election had been shown by the fact of their reception of the gospel and by the manner of receiving it. The imitation cannot have been deliberate. The writers observed the similarity of which the readers were at first unconscious. Paul could speak of the duty of imitation (2 Thess. 3:7, 9), when, of course, it would have to be deliberate. The modern preacher is diffident about asking his people to copy him, and it may be due to the fact that he may stand closer to them than Paul did to his converts. They had come out of heathenism (v. 9), whereas congregations today have at least nominally been heir to the Christian tradition of generations. But the missionary may tell his people to "do as I do," and even in the settled city church a preacher may challenge his congregation to join him in a Christian practice or rule of life. But he must be sure that his own conduct reflects the life of Jesus.

"Imitation" has value as a practical illustration of what has been the subject of exhortation in words. The call to imitate directs the attention from moral and spiritual theory to concrete fact. It is a salutory reminder to the preacher that he lives in the public eye. He must not preach a Lord whom he may possibly know but does not obey.

The motive of imitation is important. The imitation of Christ is not the way to salvation; it is a significant signpost to the way in which those men should live who have already received salvation.

In much affliction, with joy—the heart of the unconscious imitation. It cannot rightly be said that they were like the Lord in receiving the Word. They received it. He gave it. He was the Word. The point of comparison is the union of affliction and joy. The word *affliction* is not used of our Lord in the four Gospels, though the English verb is in one of the Servant Songs (Isa. 53:4). But it is plain for all the world to see that Jesus suffered. Perhaps the best comment is the statement that he "for the joy that was set before him endured the cross" (Heb. 12:2). *Affliction* and *joy* are found together in the churches of Macedonia (2 Cor. 8:1–2) and in the life of Paul himself (2 Cor. 7:4). Affliction is part of the Christian life and supplements the mystical (but not the atoning) afflictions of Christ in his church (Col. 1:24). It does not overwhelm "boasting" (Rom. 5:3) because it has a ministry of spiritual education. It is one of the experiences which cannot separate us from the love of God in Christ and in which we are "super-conquerors." (In Rom. 8:35 "tribulation" is affliction.)

Paul returns to the subject later (1 Thess. 2:14). The joy which the Holy Spirit inspired has an organic connection with the Spirit's presence in the heart. "The fruit of the Spirit is . . . joy" (Gal. 5:22).

(4) Evangelism widespread (1:7–8)

Because of joy of the Holy Spirit, the Thessalonians had spontaneously shared their faith far beyond their own city, as everybody knew. Such a fulfillment of Christian duty had made them a pattern church.

Verse 7: So that you became an example: This is a further stage,

for they were not always so. (This must be true of all who ever *became*
anything.) Paul was here giving yet another proof of their election:
they had received the gospel, their joy in it had not been outweighed by
affliction, and now they went further still in spreading the good
news. Without denying the actual result, *so that* places some emphasis
on the natural consequence of their welcome of the gospel. Their joyful
though afflicted conversion was the cause of their becoming *an example.*
The singular should be noted. (The plural "examples" is found in quite
a number of manuscripts and is probably due to the plural *you.* But the
singular is the preferable reading and it has the support of Pauline
usage elsewhere: Phil. 3:17; 2 Thess. 3:9.)

It is widely held that it is the church, the Christian community col-
lectively at Thessalonica, which constitutes the *example.* This may well
be right. A church may be exemplary, even though some members are
open to criticism (5:14), and encouragement of the church as a whole
may have some effect on individuals. But Nigel Turner [1] has recently
produced evidence to suggest that Semitic practice is being followed
for a singular noun being used distributively, which would imply that
each member is an *example.* This is not impossible, as the idleness of
5:14 may have been due to the love of spiritual work rather than of
earning a living. There is the additional fact that they were *an example
to all the believers* and not to "all the churches." It is not easy to over-
throw Turner's evidence, and it has the effect of making the Thessalonian church even better than we had thought it!

The word *example* is the Greek word *tupos,* our "type." Its verbal
form means to "strike." The noun means a "mark left by a stroke," as
in the mark or print of the nails (John 20:25).[2] From this it comes to
mean a "copy" and then an "image," the "figures" of Acts 7:43. It is
not a big step from this to "pattern," as in the pattern or "standard of
teaching" in Romans 6:17 (cf. Acts 7:44—same word as "figures").
Thus the Thessalonians became a "prototype." A somewhat similar
word occurs in Hebrews 1:3, where Christ bears the very "stamp" of
God's nature. He is, as it were, the replica or facsimile of God, whereas
the Thessalonians are themselves the model of which others are to be
the replica. Allowing for the fact that other believers should imitate
them, we may say that a *striking* example leaves an *impress.*

Of what were they an example? Obviously evangelistic zeal, "for
. . . the word . . . sounded forth" (v. 8), but this must have a base
and the authors have given it. Their *faith* is the talk of everybody.

---

1. Nigel Turner, *A Grammar of New Testament Greek* (Edinburgh: T. & T.
Clark, 1963), 3:25.

2. In this verse the word *tupos* is used twice in the text of the five Bible
Societies, as in Souter's text. Others adopt the readings *tupos* and *topos* (place)
respectively. See Kurt Aland et al., eds., *The Greek New Testament* (New York:
American Bible Society, 1966), p. 409.

They are hence typical examples of sound conversion, persistent faith, and zealous proclamation. They were typical because unconsciously they were imitating the case of Paul himself, the most normal of all instances (1 Tim. 1:16).[1]

To whom were they an example? *To all the believers* who were in Christ before them, i.e., in Philippi in Macedonia; and to those who were converted subsequently to the Thessalonians, i.e., in Beroea in Macedonia and in Athens and Corinth in Achaia up to the time of the writing of the letter—which came from Corinth (Acts 16:9–12; 17:1, 10, 15–16; 18:1). The flames of piety were fanned by reports of the Thessalonians (cf. 4:10).

In Macedonia and in Achaia: These were the two Roman provinces which comprised Greece—Macedonia to the north, and Achaia to the south. Albrecht Oepke[2] remarks on the fondness for "thinking in provinces" manifested by Paul. Free of the empire, this Roman citizen let his eye sweep over whole provinces which he would fain win for Christ: the converts of Philippi, Thessalonica and elsewhere were but the firstfruits. He saw in Epaenetus the firstfruit of Asia (Rom. 16:5) and in the household of Stephanas the firstfruit of Achaia (1 Cor 16:15), with the implication that more were to follow. Paul's range indeed was wider than the provincial: "I must also see Rome" (Acts 19:21). But even the imperial vision would not finally satisfy him. In a remarkable passage (Rom. 10:18) Paul quotes from the Septuagint version of Psalm 19:4 to compare nature's universal glorification of God with the universal proclamation of the gospel. Without speech or word, nature proclaims her Creator "to all the earth . . . to the ends of the world." But the gospel transcends nature both in message and in range. Paul was feeling here for language to describe his cosmic thinking—the world was vaster than even the Roman Empire. And Jesus would be worshiped and confessed as Lord "in heaven and on earth and under the earth" (Phil. 2:10–11). That would be the climax of his "thinking in provinces." Nothing less than the whole universe is to be brought to the feet of Christ. (This has nothing to do with the so-called doctrine of universalism. Every knee will bow to Jesus Savior and Lord. Even the enemies who reject his salvation will acknowledge his authority.)

It should be noticed that even if it is the church as a whole that is the example, it is an example to all the individual believers in the two provinces. All advocacy of the "social gospel" should maintain the perspective and proportion of this model church.

---

1. The normality of Paul's conversion has been worked out in R. A. Ward, *Mind and Heart: Studies in Christian Truth and Experience* (Grand Rapids: Baker Book House, 1966), pp. 78–96.

2. Oepke, *Das Neue Testament Deutsch,* p. 161.

Verse 8: . . . has . . . sounded forth from you in . . . : The words in the verse should be carefully grouped. It is not "from-you-in-Macedonia-and-Achaia" but "sounded-forth-in-Macedonia-and-Achaia." In the Greek the words *from you* are emphatically at the head of the sentence.

Has . . . sounded forth: The language is vivid. As a violent clap of thunder may be followed by reverberations rumbling round the enclosing hills to remind us that the storm is still with us; as the blare of the trumpet with its call to arms leaves the unresponsive sluggard disquieted in conscience and still hearing the tuneful note; as a sensational tale starts its course and is blown through all the streets like autumn leaves before the wind: so, starting *from you, has the word of the Lord sounded forth.*

We need not suppose that all the Thessalonians were preachers in the ordinary sense of the word. Some of them no doubt were. But the Acts of the Apostles gives us glimpses of the life of the early church and what was done in one place by aroused and determined men may well have been done in another. A vibrant and living faith could not be silent. The story of Philip and the Ethiopian eunuch (Acts 8:26-40) is but one example. More striking still is the dispersal of what today would be called laymen after the "affliction" or pressure that arose over Stephen (Acts 11:19-21). The fellowship was scattered—not like dust but like seed (cf. Matt. 13:38).

Not that the Thessalonians were scattered as a whole. Most of the church stayed in their city. But Thessalonica was a great metropolis and junction, situated on the main route from Italy to the East, a seaport and a busy center of trade. We cannot suppose that no Thessalonian Christian ever went anywhere. And with all the coming and going of such a city is it not likely that men came to Thessalonica as pagans and left as Christians—to spread the good news themselves?

The word of the Lord is the gospel. It had come to them in power (v. 5), and in it they "had received the word" (v. 6). This is the plain meaning, but the expression must be examined in greater detail. The phrase *the word of the Lord* comes from the Septuagint, and it is instructive to observe some of its uses. In the prophecy of Jeremiah, for example, there are some significant variations. The word came "from" the Lord to Jeremiah. We read of the word of the "mouth of the Lord"; false prophets do not speak from the mouth of the Lord. The word of the Lord "came" to Jeremiah. It was the word which the Lord commanded to Jeremiah, the word which the Lord showed to him. It was the word which the prophet spoke to the people in the name of the Lord. In startling contrast stand the two expressions: hear the word of the Lord *which I speak;* and *thus saith the Lord.*

It is clear that there are two speakers: God speaks and the prophet speaks; and the prophet speaks what has been given to him by God. The word is thus authoritative.

So far we have been thinking of the God of the Old Testament, Jehovah or Yahweh, and his prophet. But now we must notice a change. In Old Testament times God spoke fragmentarily, piecemeal, in various ways; he has now spoken decisively and finally (Heb. 1:1–2) —and what he said was Christ. The Word of God is Jesus Christ. Just as Jeremiah spoke what God had said, so the Christian witness speaks what God has said—Christ. Only this time the speakers are not prophets in the sense that Jeremiah was a prophet. To judge by Paul's language they were the ordinary members of the Thessalonian church. This does not mean that any and every Christian in a sort of religious private enterprise can decide that next Sunday he is going to be the minister and address the church! Paul would hardly countenance such a procedure (1 Thess. 5:12–13). It does, however, imply the prophetic nature of the church and what has been termed the apostolate of the laity. Not all members have "gifts" (1 Cor. 12:4–11) which obviously fit them for the pulpit or for public speech in the name of the Lord. But even the humblest member with no apparent "gift" at all can say Amen to the prayers audibly (1 Cor. 14:16 and RSV footnote), and thus identify himself with the believing church. Even he can stand with the preacher and "support" him by the silent testimony of his presence. Thus we can imagine the church member speaking: *the word of the Lord* means Christ; it means Christ made known by me; it means Christ made known by me at God's command.

It would seem that the word *Lord* here has blurred edges. It is not entirely precise. With the rich background of Old Testament usage and New Testament gospel it cannot help suggesting two meanings: the Lord God Almighty, and his Son our Lord Jesus Christ. The gospel is of both and from both, for God was in Christ (2 Cor. 5:19).

(The above does not invalidate the statement that the Scripture is the Word of God. Christ is the living Word and the Scripture is the written Word; yet there are not two Words but one. The generic Word is specifically present in two modes, each testifying to the other.)

In Macedonia and Achaia: Note the significant omission of "in" before Achaia. In the previous verse the two provinces are thought of separately; here they are regarded as a single expanse of territory in contrast to *everywhere*.

It ought to be said that the RSV has given us as balanced a translation as possible, but that Paul's Greek bears the mark of an earnestness of spirit which cannot stop; hence some features are grammatically irregular. Literally he said: "For from you has sounded forth the word of the Lord not only in Macedonia and Achaia but in every place." Here he ought logically to have stopped. But he sped on to tell the story of common talk everywhere. Not only were Christians spreading the good news. Men were talking, Christians and non-Christians alike, about what had happened in Thessalonica. Apart from the differences of number of converts, size of audiences, and the presence or absence of already existing churches, we might compare the events in Thessalonica, their local impact and the spread of "talk" about it, with the effect of a Graham crusade in a major city. The story spreads far and wide. Discouraged Christians speak to one another in hushed and awed tones of the conversions they had never expected to see again. The man in the street (in the earlier days at least) is curious to know what has been going on, and talks and listens. Paul did not trace the various places in which the "talk" took place. He was content to say that (in every place) "your faith toward God has gone forth" and (perfect tense) is still there, being discussed. The natural consequence was that he and his partners had no need to say more. All was too well known!

Faith in God: The God who is revealed in his Word (v. 6). Strictly we should translate it "faith *toward* God" (Greek *pros*), which suggests the direction of their faith in contrast to their previous "faith" toward idols (v. 9). Their faith was expressed in their "turning toward God" (v. 9). Other prepositions used elsewhere in connection with faith convey delicate shades of meaning. Faith is directed "into" and sent right "into" Christ and the believer is consequently in Christ and continues to believe "in" him. Now in Christ he rests his faith "on" him. If we feel that the spacial metaphors are in conflict with one another, we might find it helpful to visualize the believer's commitment to Christ as a movement *into* a room—or a fortress—*in* which he stays *on* the floor, the foundation of which is rock.

In all true faith, credence and trust mingle. Credence means that there are certain statements which are regarded as true, however simple (e.g., "Jesus is Lord"). This is implied by the fact of preaching: the preachers must say something *about* the Savior. If this element is lacking, the sermon has little content and the believer's trust is hazy. On the other hand, trust means that the believer confidently hands himself over to Christ, puts himself into his hands. If this is absent, we have no more than "signing on the dotted line," a mere intellectual assent.

The phrase *the word of the Lord* is quite common in the Acts of the Apostles but is used only once more by Paul (2 Thess. 3:1). It is thought by some scholars that the use of the word *everywhere* is an exaggeration—understandable and pardonable but still an exaggeration. It is wiser to see in the expression an understanding of the significance of what is taking place. There is undoubtedly much talk. And with all the movement in a city like Corinth, where Paul was, information would constantly be coming in to him. What gossip takes place in seaports! How many men from out of town would encounter the apostle with the remark that he was the man who had started that business up in Thessalonica which everybody was talking about? What news did Timothy pick up on his journey (1 Thess. 3:1–6)? Did Aquila and Priscilla hear some rumors in Rome (Acts 18:1–2)? Treason (Acts 17:7) is an ugly word, and Rome must have heard of it. Was the report secret, confined to the diplomatic bag? Or did officials let out the information, to provide fuel for the gossips? These questions cannot be answered with certainty but shrewd guesses are not out of place. And Paul saw in the whole situation the beginning of winning the world for Christ. It would be pedestrian and dull if we were to see in his attitude no more than exaggeration.

(5) Idols replaced (1:9–10)

This could have only one explanation—their conversion. On hearing the gospel they had turned from idols to God. They were now serving him, animated by the expectation of his Son's return from heaven.

Verse 9: For they themselves report: The explanation of the need for no further comment (v. 8). *They* refers to the people, implied but not explicitly mentioned, who live *everywhere*. Their report must not be thought of as the result of journalists covering some special event. Newspaper men are sent with the specific task of finding out what has happened and then writing a report for their paper. Here on the other hand the report is humanly unpurposed. It is human talk resulting from sensational events. The same word is translated elsewhere simply by "told" (Luke 8:34, 36). The constant wagging of tongues can be brought out by translating "they are spreading reports about us and telling what a welcome . . . . "

What a welcome we had: Literally "what kind of entrance." In itself the Greek word is neutral. The entrance might have been "in vain" (as in 1 Thess. 2:1), but in reality it was highly successful. Paul was mentally walking along the road into the city and rethinking his thoughts as he first approached it: What would be the attitude of the inhabitants? Some of them believed and became the church of the Thessalonians. In consequence Paul let his preoccupation with the thought of their possible attitude determine his choice of language. They did believe; any uncertainty was at an end. He therefore used the word "entrance" to cover the whole visit. This justifies the use of *welcome*. The simple *had* is very graphic. We see Paul going over the scene as he wrote, entering the city and preaching the Word. The *had* takes us (with Paul) up to the moment of the first conversions, when the question was decided. What would be their attitude? Look! Conversions! The Greek aorist could be brought out by rendering "what kind of entrance we got." The "got" is not elegant but it takes us to, and expresses, the moment when the matter was settled.

How you turned to God: The expression of their faith. The life of faith is both negative and positive. It abandons idols and abstains from certain activities (1 Thess. 4:3). It positively turns to God and stays in fellowship with him in Christ. The evidence suggests that the converts were a number of Jews of the synagogue and many devout Greeks (Acts 17:4). In other words, the church was mainly Gentile. The epistle reflects this. It is more appropriate to speak of Gentiles turning away from idols than of Jews doing so. And it is appropriate also to speak of Gentiles turning to God. When Jews are converted they turn specifically to the Lord—Jesus Christ. (The Jews of Thessalonica were persecutors: 1 Thess. 2:14–16; Acts 17:5–7.) Similar language is used of Gentiles in Acts 15:19, "those of the Gentiles who turn to God." The Thessalonians had faith toward God and they turned toward God. Repentance, "turning" and faith are related (Acts 3:19; 11:21; 26:20). The Thessalonians had moved from darkness and the power of Satan to light and to God; such a movement of faith had brought them forgiveness and a place among the sanctified (cf. Acts 26:18; also Acts 15:3, the "conversion," literally "turning," of the Gentiles).

From idols: That is, heathen gods. The idol is, as popularly supposed, a material image, generally made by man. (But cf. Acts 19:35.) Its very existence is forbidden in the Second Commandment (Exod. 20:4). For it is by definition an image of the divine, and God is spirit (John 4:24). As an image of a god, it is an object of worship. But though materially solid it is spiritually emptier than the air. The prophetic denunciation of idolatry is scathing. A man cuts down a tree and burns some of the wood: some is firewood for cooking and some for human warmth; and with the rest he makes a god which he worships (Isa. 44: 9–20). At times the message is conveyed with grim humor. In a picture of the evacuation of a city before its conqueror arrives we see gods themselves being rescued. A god should carry his people. But Bel and Nebo have to be carted away on beasts of burden (Isa. 46:1–7)! Men pay cash to have an idol made—and then bow down before it. It can neither move nor speak. (Cf. Jer. 10:1–10.)

This attitude is inherited by the New Testament and emphasized anew. For example, the idol is still dumb (1 Cor. 12:2). It is still no more than a thing, a nothing (1 Cor. 8:4–6), even though there may be many of them. But a "nothing" can be a serious spiritual danger. It establishes a link with a transcendent realm which is not God's realm (1 Cor. 10:19–22, 28–29). Idolatry and the Christian faith are incompatible: "What agreement has the temple of God with idols?" (2 Cor. 6:16). Idolaters will not inherit the kingdom of God. But they may be cleansed and justified in the gospel. The Corinthians were evidence that the idolater can be saved—but he must be like the Thessalonians and "turn to God." "And such were some of you" (1 Cor. 6:9–11). The opposition of the New Testament to idolatry could hardly be put more strongly.

The idol is a substitute god and therefore a false god. It is dead—and has never lived. Its deadness is like that of a stone rather than that of a corpse. It cannot think or speak, and it cannot answer prayer. It is a liability and not an asset. He who worships it performs no religious duty but sins. The highest concept of a heathen god cannot be compared with the revelation of God in Christ. Was Zeus crucified for you? Does any god combine righteousness and mercy as the God and Father of our Lord Jesus Christ?

It may be asked how a "nothing" can involve so much spiritual danger. Is it not all rather harmless? The answer is plain. If a military commander in a spirit of irresponsibility commits his troops to an impossible engagement, wildly confident that strong reinforcements are on the way, and if he has no reason to believe even in the existence of the reinforcements, then the reinforcements, though they do not exist, constitute a positive danger. The more frequently he is guilty of such folly the greater is his blameworthiness. If it be argued that the fault lies in the man and not in the supposed forces, the answer is again at hand. It is the man who will be punished, not the "reinforcements." And it is the idolater, not the idol, who will not inherit the kingdom of God. (Cf. Gal. 5:19–21.)

So far idolatry has been considered in relation to the cultus, the practice of worship. But a man can be an idolater who never thinks of worship, pagan or Christian. For an idol is anything which takes the place of God in the life of man. Thus covetousness is idolatry (Eph. 5:5; Col. 3:5). The idolater does not know God, is still in his sins, is in a state of slavery, and has an object of worship or service which can never satisfy the deepest longings of the human heart. Idolatry is bankrupt from the start. It cannot enrich or inspire. If it be said that some forms of non-Christian worship give peace and harmony to some people, it is the peace of the cemetery. They may represent the ideal of an atheistic psychiatrist, but they are unreconciled to God, unforgiven, and have no hope of heaven. For idolatry has no cross, certainly no cross of Jesus. To become an idolater is to turn backward (Rom. 1:18–32), and has fearful moral consequences (cf. Gal. 4:8–9). It is no stage on the gradual ascent to the true faith, a harmless or even a valuable stepping stone. The New Testament writers, who lived close to idolatry and saw it in action, and who at the same time walked with God, were antagonistic both to the characters of its gods and the practices of its devotees. The missionary, therefore, while mindful of the duties of courtesy, must be extremely cautious in all modern "dialogue" and must certainly not join with non-Christians in the search for spiritual truth. "We have found the Messiah" (John 1:41). To err here is to deny the prophetic office of the church and her commission from the Lord.[1]

It may be asserted that the human heart craves for some image of the divine. We already have such an image in Christ, for "he is the image of the invisible God" (Col. 1:15) and "we ought not" to require any other: to do so is ignorance and sin (Acts 17:29–31). Some ancient statues may make us catch our breath at the perfection of the sculptor's art, but the many-breasted Artemis (cf. Acts 19:24, 27–28, 34–35) reveals the inner shame which no aesthetic value could finally hide. (Cf. 1 John 5:21.)

To serve a living and true God: One God only, with the emphasis on the attributes *living and true.* To speak of *a God* in the present context does not mean that he is one God among many. For example, a man might say: "I married her in order to get a loving wife." He does not imply by the use of "a" that he has more than one wife. He is merely emphasizing the "loving." So it is here with reference to God. (Cf. Heb. 1:2, "a Son," with its heavy emphasis on the category of revelation, divine personality.)

To serve is often taken as purposive. But whose purpose is expressed? A close parallel is seen by some in the statement "I turned to see . . ." (Rev. 1:12). This would suggest the purpose of the Thessalonians. The thought is perhaps not impossible, but it does involve difficulties. It is conceivable that the thought of these converts in their turning to God was: "our purpose in abandoning our idols . . . is to serve the true God." But coordinate with *to serve* is *to wait for.* Are we to suppose that at the time of their conversion their purpose in turning to God was explicitly to wait for his Son? They had still a great deal to learn (1 Thess. 4:13). We can evade the difficulty by saying that ultimately we are concerned with the purpose of God. After all, he was the author of their call (1 Thess. 2:12; 4:7; 5:24; 2 Thess. 2:14), and this was why he had called them. There is truth in this explanation, but it is an over-simplification. It is better to take the two infinitives as an example of the mingling of the purposive with the epexegetic. The latter is explanatory of what is involved when men turn to God. If they have had a glimpse of this, then to some extent they share God's purpose for themselves.

Living is in pointed contrast to the dead idols. It means more than the truth that "God is alive." He acts (Josh. 3:10; Acts 14:15–17), and he gives life (John 5:26, 40).

True, genuine, again is in contrast to idols. The thought is that God

---

1. An important article which is relevant here was published in the student magazine of Wycliffe College, University of Toronto. J. Jocz, "Syncretism or Faith?" *Cap and Gown* (1967), pp. 22–28.

is real. We sometimes say that "this man is *really* an American," and we mean that you can investigate every detail of his life and you will find nothing to disprove his claim: he can prove his citizenship. He is a citizen *in fact*. Advertisers tell us to avoid substitutes and to buy the real thing, the genuine article. Such is the meaning here, as well as in the reference in the Nicene Creed to "very God"—no substitute, no false claim, no mere appearance. The God to whom the Thessalonians had turned was in fact—God. The New Testament witness is to a God who is not an illusion.

Verse 10: And to wait for a compact body of divinity. *His Son* clearly refers to God the Father and the Lord Jesus Christ, already mentioned in this chapter (vv. 1, 3). The gospel (v. 5), the word (v. 6) of the Lord (v. 8), had come to the Thessalonians in the power of the Holy Spirit. Father, Son, and Holy Spirit are thus implicit in verse 10. *Jesus,* the historical character, is the Son and is to come *from heaven*. How did a man from Nazareth get to heaven? Obviously the ascension of our Lord is implied. His resurrection is specifically mentioned. The fact that he *delivers us from the wrath* suggests the atonement.

Now this is not the rich doctrinal elaboration of the Epistle to the Romans, and it is not intended to be. And it is not presented as a coherent system. It is rather what should have been expected in a warm letter to people who had welcomed the gospel when preached to them as it always should be preached—warmly, with vitality and animation and in terms of doctrine. (This does not imply heavy theological dogmatics. If does mean that however many the illustrations, however much the gospel is preached in popular language, there is an inner core of Christian truth. Without this it is not the gospel and it is not preaching.)

The standpoint of the apostle is worth observing. He was speaking at what for him was "the present moment" from which he was looking back through the ascension and through the resurrection to the cross. It was from the same standpoint that he affirmed that "we preach Christ crucified" (1 Cor. 1:23). If he had taken up his position at Bethlehem and from there had looked forward, there might have been some grounds for the criticism that we preach a dead Christ. But it is not so. We know what is meant by the crucifixion, which was a historical event. But "the word of the cross" (1 Cor. 1:18) is more than the story of the crucifixion, though it includes it. The cross, for Paul and for us, is the crucifixion with its inner meaning and the event which followed it, the resurrection. It may be doubted if Paul ever thought of the cross in any other way.

Wait for combines a joyous expectation (cf. 1 Pet. 1:8), a sure hope (1 Thess. 1:3) and a certain solemnity. This prepares the way for later treatment of the theme (4:13–18). The emphasis in *heaven* is not location in space but divine authority. In heaven the Son is at

the right hand of God, interceding for us (Rom. 8:34), and is the head
of the realms of nature, history and grace (cf. 1 Cor. 15:24–28). The
Christology is high. Although the term *Son* is of moderate frequency in
Paul's writings, it is sufficiently established. (Cf. Rom. 1:3–4; 2 Cor. 1:
19; Gal. 2:20; Eph. 4:13.) Paul's doctrine of the divine sonship of
Jesus is one of the links between him and John. Notice how John 3:
16–17 and Galatians 4:4–5 overlap. (Cf. similarly the first chapter of
Hebrews with Col. 1:13–20.) The framework of Paul's doctrine of the
Person of Christ and of salvation is present in the Epistles to the Thes-
salonians and it coheres with that of the New Testament generally.

Whom he raised: Proof of the deity of Jesus (Rom. 1:4).

Who delivers us: The present tense does not exactly imply "he is
doing it now" but rather "he is permanently our Deliverer." (Cf. 1 Thess.
5:9.) He will prove to be still our Deliverer when the coming wrath
actually arrives, the certainty of which is grounded in the resurrection
of Jesus (Acts 17:31). The speech from which the last named text is
taken was given in Athens not long before our epistle was written
from Corinth. (For "assurance" in the RSV read "grounds for belief,"
"evidence.")

Wrath to come refers to the eschatological wrath on the Day of Judgment. It is now clear why Paul could use the present tense *delivers.*
Believers have already been delivered from that which is still to come.

The reason for this is, in technical terms, that justification is eschatological. When a man puts his faith in Christ he is justified, pardoned,
forgiven. In terms of a court of law he is acquitted; a judgment has
been given. But judgment belongs to the Day of Judgment. In other
words when a man is justified he receives a verdict, and for him the
Day of Judgment has been brought forward. The eschatological or final
verdict of the last day has already been given. This decides the question of whether a man goes to heaven or hell. Believers have, however,
the judgment of awards when the character of our work will be tested.
Even if the work does not pass the test the believer himself will be
saved (1 Cor. 3:12–15; cf. 2 Cor. 5:10).

The concept of the wrath of God has come under heavy fire within
the last generation; it has been interpreted merely as objective events
inevitably resulting from sin. It looks very much as if the moral universe
has been mechanized. But it is no more valid to make this the last word
in a moral universe than in the universe of nature. The mechanistic
concept has been applied fruitfully to nature, but it must not be assumed
that God is no more than a machine-minder. He operates the machine;
indeed he is present and active in every part of it. We speak of the
"laws of nature." They are not self-existent, and in themselves they
do not "cause" anything. They rather express the uniform way in which
God works. For in Christ he creatively upholds the universe. In him all

things cohere in the system which they are (Col. 1:17). The rising of the sun each day may be described in terms of natural law, quite rightly within a limited field, but ultimately "he makes his sun rise on the evil and on the good" (Matt. 5:45), and he does it regularly. So it is in the moral realm. Sin certainly has consequences. But God is more than a moral machine-minder. He operates the moral universe and is present in every part. His providence is ever at work and "in him we live and move and have our being" (Acts 17:28).[1]

At this point it is appropriate to ask certain questions. Does God know what goes on in the world? Is he interested? Has he an attitude? Does he approve of certain acts and disapprove of others? May we speak of "degrees of intensity"? That is to say, does he approve of some activities more than of others; and does he disapprove of some more than of others? (For example, for him is murder worse than a slap on the face?) If he disapproves does he "do anything about it"? Or does he contemplate any action? Does he uphold the right and does he refuse to let men permanently do evil and "get away with it"?

If the answers to these questions are in the affirmative—and it is difficult to see how they can be other than this, at any rate for a Christian and a student of the Bible—then we can sum up by saying that God has an attitude which is (or will be) expressed in action. Attitude and action: this is what is meant by the *wrath* of God. It is not emotion, temper, irascibility, spite, malice, or malignity. It is the reaction of a holy God to all evil. Miracle, it might be said on some interpretations of miracle, is an invasion of the natural order. It implies that the established order is "not good enough" and is invalid. This interpretation perhaps might not matter so much, and in any case it is God himself who is the author of miracle. But evil is an invasion of God himself. It says to him in effect, "You are not valid." It is thus an affront to utter goodness, and God will not finally tolerate it. In the end goodness is left on the throne. This is what is meant by *the wrath to come*. In the mercy and long-suffering of God it is dammed up in order to give men the opportunity to repent and believe and receive salvation. But in a sense it is "on its way" and is anticipated (Rom. 1:18).

Wrath was manifested by Jesus against men who combined strictness in religion with moral blindness (Mark 3:5). He also spoke of it explicitly (Luke 21:23) and implied it in his parables (Matt. 18:34; 22:7; Luke 14:21). John can use the significant word "abide" ("abide in me" John 15:4) of the wrath of God which abides on the man who is disobedient to the Son (John 3:36, "rests" in RSV). Wrath is prominent in Pauline thought (Rom. 1:18; 2:5, 8; 3:5; 4:15; 9:22; 12:

---

1. The reader would profit by consulting Frank H. T. Rhodes in *Christianity in a Mechanistic Universe*, ed. Donald M. MacKay (London: Inter-Varsity Fellowship, 1966), pp. 11–48.

19; Eph. 2:3; 5:6; Col. 3:6; 1 Thess. 1:10; 2:16; 5:9). In one passage (Rom. 5:8–9) love and wrath are closely associated. Either both
are real or both are to be rejected. It is from the love in the cross of
Christ that we derive salvation from wrath.[1]

2. The Preachers: Their Blameless Conduct a Matter of Memory (2:1–12)

The readers were aware of the impact of the preachers. They were
fresh from ill-treatment and insult but nevertheless overcame opposition
to their bold proclamation, sincerely carrying out the task divinely laid
upon them. They did not deceive or flatter, nor did they seek their
own advantage, glory or convenience. Tenderly they gave of themselves
in their ministry of evangelism and edification. They earned their own
living and their lives would bear the closest examination.

(1) The preachers' effectiveness (2:1)

The readers were reminded, not informed, of the tremendous events
which took place when the preachers came. What kind of men could
they be? All that follows (vv. 2–12) gives the answer.

For you yourselves know is a confident appeal to known facts. *For,*
as a conjunction, introduces a clause giving a reason for something,
but its function here is not self-evident. The writer is following a rather
common Greek idiom in which a reason is given for a statement understood but not expressed. Reference has already been made (1:9)
to the widespread talk about the preachers' "entrance" (the "welcome"
of the RSV) and its effect, and it is continued in thought though not
openly stated. In consequence we must read the beginning of the chapter
thus: "(This rumor is true.) *For* . . . . "

It must not be thought that this is illegitimately reading into the text
what is not there. It is there, implied by the word "for," and it is a test
of our skill in exegesis and interpretation. Sometimes our translators help
us by actually translating the Greek word *(gar)* by "for" and sometimes
they do not. Consider as an example the following (Jas. 4:14): "What
is your life? (Precious little!) *For* you are a mist . . . . " The "For"-
clause explains the words in parenthesis. Or take a similar instance
(2 Cor. 2:16–17): "Who is sufficient for these things? (We are.) *For*
we are not, like so many, peddlers of God's word . . . . " This is con-
firmed by the apostle's words a few verses later (2 Cor. 3:5), *"our
sufficiency is from God . . . . "* On the other hand, the "for" is sometimes omitted though the *gar* is present in the text. Thus we might have

---

1. For a study of the wrath of God in the teaching of Jesus, see R. A. Ward,
Royal Theology: Our Lord's Teaching About God (London and Edinburgh:
Marshall, Morgan & Scott, 1964), pp. 88–100.

expected the following: " 'Do you understand what you are reading?'
And he said, '(No.) *For* how can I, unless some one guides me?' "
(Acts 8:30–31). Evidence is to be found again in the passage in Romans which reads: " . . . provided we suffer with him in order that
we may also be glorified with him. I consider that the sufferings of this
present time are not worth comparing with the glory that is to be revealed to us" (Rom. 8:17–18, RSV). Professor C. K. Barrett, who
bases his commentary on his own translation, boldly and rightly
begins verse 18 with "The glory is as sure as the suffering, *for* I consider . . . . " [1] He has done full justice to the *gar*.

With warm affection *(brethren)* the earlier situation was recalled.
It was an important point, in the interests of the gospel, to scotch any
false rumors. The ancient world abounded with itinerant "preachers"
of philosophies and quack remedies who sought by these means to pick
up a living. Paul could not let himself be regarded at any time as a
parasite. As he wrote the present verse he still had in mind the picture
of his "entrance" into the city (see on 1:9). The "welcome" of 1:9 and
the "visit" of 2:1 both represent an original "entrance." When the
preachers entered Thessalonica they did not come as parasites, seeking
to get what they could from a gullible population. They came rather
with their hands loaded with the gifts of the gospel. Hence their *visit*
was not *in vain*. The latter expression literally means "empty." Thus
"our entrance was not empty" means "we did not enter the city
empty-handed." (Cf. Mark 12:3.) The effectiveness of this (or any)
mission depends on whether the missioner has something to give. Has
he a gospel? Paul and his companions had.

Was not: The original is in the perfect tense, "our entrance has not
proved to be, or turned out to be, empty-handed." The thought might
be paraphrased thus: "As you look back now on events then, you know
that you have received men bearing gifts and not demanding them." The
emphasis at this stage is on what they brought rather than on the "success" of the mission, though obviously the success was in the background. The preachers were not mere talkers (cf. 1:5) and certainly
not windbags or "puffed up" (cf. 1 Cor. 4:19, KJV).

The confidence of the writers is impressive. They were sure of their
facts and sure of their readers: the Thessalonians would not be prejudiced against them.

(2) Persistence (2:2)

In spite of their previous experience they were not deterred from
taking the risks of preaching still.

Suffered . . . shamefully treated at Philippi: Insult added to injury.

---

1. C. K. Barrett, *A Commentary on the Epistle to the Romans* (London:
Adam & Charles Black, 1957), p. 165.

The events in question have been recorded by Luke (Acts 16:19–24), and they left their mark on Paul (Phil. 1:30). A few years later he gave to the church in Corinth a summary of his sufferings (2 Cor. 11:23–27) and a fearful list it is. Even so the apostle gives the impression that indignity affected him as much as, if not more than, pain. He was a sensitive soul, not pompous, but with a lively sense of the respect due to him. He was embarrassed at having to be lowered in a basket through a slit in the city wall at Damascus (2 Cor. 11:30–33; Acts 9:23–25). His nature and background would prevent him from regarding the episode as merely an enjoyable schoolboy prank. At Philippi he had felt keenly the insult to his Roman citizenship and the degrading punishment of being beaten with rods. When the time came for him to leave, he made the officials change their tune and give him an escort to conduct him out of the city (Acts 16:35–39). It was bad enough to receive punishment without being condemned in a proper legal process. To be beaten in full view of the populace ("publicly") was the last straw.

Then Paul and his companions Silvanus and Timothy had come to Thessalonica. It is not hard to imagine their emotions as they made their "entrance" into the city. Would it be *Philippi* all over again? We may see here an anticipation of Paul's thought and experience. In every city it was being brought home to him the painful cost of preaching the gospel (Acts 20:23). Many a lesser man would have faltered and even given up the work. But Paul took a strong line with a deserter and did not spare himself any more than he did John Mark (Acts 12:25; 13:13; 15:38).

To be *shamefully treated* is an example of the famous Greek concept of *hubris*. Aristotle has defined it as bringing disgrace on a person by injury or annoyance with the sole motive of the pleasure of doing so, the pleasure of showing one's superiority. (A characteristic of the young and the wealthy, according to Aristotle.) In Athens it was the subject of criminal prosecution and the penalties were severe. It is significant that it could not be done to slaves. Treat them as spitefully as you like, it could not be *hubris*.[1] Men guilty of such wanton injury and outrageous maltreatment were included by Paul in his list of men "given up" by God (Rom. 1:30, "insolent," RSV). He himself once was guilty of this sin (1 Tim. 1:13, "insulted him," RSV). Now at Philippi he had been the victim of it. He had borne it in good heart. He was in a good tradition, following in the steps of the prophets and of the Lord (cf. Luke 20:11—the dishonoring was a form of *hubris;* Luke 18:32). But he did not merely "bear" it. He harnessed it to the power of Christ. It was the Philippian church to which he confided his great ambition to know

---

1. Aristotle *Rhetoric* 2. 2. 3–6 (1378*b*); 2. 24. 9 (1402*a*).

Christ and the power of his resurrection and the fellowship of his sufferings (Phil. 3:10). In spite of all the pain and insult suffered in Philippi, *as you know,* he pressed on with the work in the city of Thessalonica.

We had courage—the original New Testament "boldness." The noun suggests an outspokenness which hides nothing and omits nothing (cf. Acts 4:29). "To speak boldly" is easily derived from "to say everything" and it is only one step further to the meaning "to be bold, courageous." It should be noticed that we should not think here of an even flow of courage, but rather of a fountain suddenly bursting forth. The idea is that "we took courage," or "we became bold." The expression conceals the emotional life of the apostle, with fightings without and fears within (cf. 2 Cor. 7:5). We may see an analogy in the life of our Lord and find our best comment in Luke 9:51: "he set his face to go to Jerusalem." Paul and his companions set their faces to preach in Thessalonica—a decisive act of courage. But it was not merely human dash. They were not alone.

In our God: A blessed intimacy for those who can see it. The church is always *in God* (1:1), the preachers included. But at the critical moment there was an influx of divine power (cf. Phil. 4:13). "Our God" appears again (3:9) in the present epistle, twice in the second letter (2 Thess. 1:11–12) and once more (1 Cor. 6:11). The expression is appropriate to *the gospel of God* later in the verse and suggests: the God who is revealed in Christ; the God who is known in experience by the preachers; the God who is "common" to all the members of the Christian "community," here particularly the Thessalonian church; the God who is preached; and the one true God who is distinguished from the false gods (1 Thess. 1:9); the God, it must be added, whom his people are pledged to serve. The phrase does not rule out the other term, "my God" (Rom. 1:8; 2 Cor. 12:21; Phil. 1:3; 4:19; Philem. 4). The latter implies the intimacy of personal religion and the closed door of individual prayer (Matt. 6:6). When, however, we say "our God" we know that others of the faith understand from their own experience the language of the individual Christian. It is the characteristic of the Christian religion that it combines without imbalance the individual and the social or collective. The individual believer is not an unrelated atom, settled forever in an ecclesiastical pigeonhole; nor is he lost in the crowd. He believes—in the company of his fellow-believers. He has ample scope for his own spiritual development and growth in grace, and he gives and receives support and encouragement from his fellows. The true Saint (with a capital S) is far in advance of his fellows; but he recognizes them as brethren. There is one way to heaven for both parties.

To declare to you the gospel of God: This gives the lie to certain half-truths. It is sometimes said that Christianity is caught, not taught. It is a brilliant epigram but dangerous. It suggests, quite rightly, the evidential power of a living Christian community, but it forgets that if the gospel is to be known, if the faith is to be "caught," it must be made known. A man who has really "caught" something will become an inquirer first. He needs to be told, either by word of mouth of preacher or teacher or in conversation, or by the printed page. There is indeed "the infection of a good courage," but Christianity is not a disease to be caught but a gospel to be proclaimed.

The gospel of God is capable of the widest interpretation. It means the good news which originates in God. It is not man's discovery or invention. It is not even true to say that it originated in Christ, for he was sent by the Father to make it possible for a gospel to be preached. It is the good news about God: it tells not only what he is like but what he has done; and not only what he has done but what he offers. It is the good news which God brings, for the human preacher on his own is powerless. After all the strenuous activities of Paul's first missionary journey and all the preaching involved, the preachers reported all that God had done in their company (Acts 14:27; 15:4). The Lord gave his testimony when his grace was preached (Acts 14:3), and thus added his witness to that of the preachers (cf. Acts 13:31), for he is still the faithful and true witness (Rev. 3:14; cf. Acts 11:21).

In the face of great opposition is a metaphor from sports. We can illustrate today from the Olympic Games. Competitors assemble to engage in various contests—running, boxing and so on. In Paul's day each race or bout was an "event," a sporting event, to which the name *agōn* was given, the word used in this verse. Obviously there were competitors against whom Paul was striving. There were men "preaching" their philosophies and others crying their wares and panaceas. Paul had to divert the attention of their listeners. In addition he had to contend with those who positively set out to silence him: jealous Jews; men who used political arguments to cover economic interests; loafers who were always ready to make trouble about anything for the sake of its entertainment value; rabble-rousers and the rabble generally. All were the preachers' "competitors," and the "event" or "conflict" (Phil. 1:30) made strenuous demands on them. In the end the preachers won. They gained a hearing—and converts. (The metaphor is much more prominent in 1 Cor. 9:24–27, and Heb. 12:1.) The "arena" in Thessalonica was external. Elsewhere the "contest" was within (Col. 2:1, cf. 4:12, literally, "always contending for you"). We still speak of "wrestling in prayer."

(3) Motive (2:3–4)

Far from being deluded or giving way to the sensuality of heathen religions or tricking their listeners, the apostles were obeying the divine commission at any cost.

Verse 3: For our appeal does not spring from . . . states the reason for the bold proclamation of the gospel of God. The *for* is similar to that in 2:1 (see explanation). The thought is: "(It really was the gospel of God.) For our appeal . . . . " Notice the use of the present tense. It is not said that the appeal *did* not spring, although this would have been quite appropriate. But a general principle is being applied to a particular case. "It is always like this." *Appeal (paraklēsis)* is a word which in different contexts is translated "exhortation" (Acts 13:15), and "comfort" (2 Cor. 1:3–7); sometimes "encouragement" (Rom. 15:4; Phil. 2:1) and, as here, "appeal." In its broadest sense it means something like "persuasion with authority." It is less than a bare command and more than a mere request. The apostle did say that "we persuade men" (2 Cor. 5:11, but a different Greek word), and as a preacher he certainly had authority. A poignant example of the corresponding verb *(parakaleō)* appears when the father of the prodigal son went out to the elder brother and "began to appeal to him" (Luke 15:28, literal). It is similar in "God making his appeal through us" (2 Cor. 5:20).

Error or uncleanness, nor . . . with guile: These are three possible explanations of preachers with no real message (2:1), however great their impact. They may be themselves deceived and in *error;* they may be sensualists; or they may be deceivers of any who will listen to them *(with guile),* deliberately tricking them with a message which they know contains no truth.

When men are in *error* they are astray and they do not know it. They may be perfectly sincere, but in fact they are wrong. How could Paul and his companions be wandering now (to err is to wander)? Their wandering was a fact of the past and they had been sought and found (Matt. 18:12; Paul employed the metaphor of pursuing and overtaking in Phil. 3:12; cf. Rom. 9:30; Christ had overtaken him). How could they be wrong when they knew the Scriptures and had experienced the power of God (Matt. 22:29; cf. 1 Cor. 15:3–4)? How could they be now astray from the truth, when they had been brought back to the truth (Jas. 5:19)—in Jesus (Eph. 4:21)?

Uncleanness is taken by some scholars in the sense of covetousness, a defilement of the spirit (2 Cor. 7:1). This would imply that the preachers were spellbinders with their tongues in their cheeks, hoping to extract money from their deluded audiences. There is little or no evidence to support this interpretation, though the idea is familiar: sordid money, filthy lucre, filthy rich. The money would have been earned at great cost! The hazards were great and the converts poor (2 Cor. 8:1–2); the preachers had to earn their own living (2 Thess. 3:10–12).

It is more likely that the preachers were rejecting a charge of immorality. They lived in a day of sexual looseness, very much like our own. Gentiles who were converted had to be taught (1 Thess. 4:3; cf.

1 Cor. 6:13–7:2). And it was not only a question of a general looseness of living characteristic of heathenism. The laxity had entered the domain of religion. There were such people as temple prostitutes. Even Israel had had to be warned against allowing them (Deut. 23:17–18), and their Hebrew name is significant—the sacred ones. Herodotus [1] records a disgraceful custom of the Babylonians. Every woman, once in her lifetime, had to sit in the temple of Aphrodite for the sexual pleasure of some stranger, thereby making herself holy in the sight of the goddess. It is quite possible that enemies accused the preachers of practicing such temple craft. But would such men preach the gospel of God with its ethical demands on the converts? Would they have preached it with such power? That is ultimately to say, would God have blessed their work so signally? They had already been tested and proved by God (2:4).

Guile is sheer cunning. The preachers did not trick their audience for the sake of personal gain, nor did they distort the Word of God (cf. 2 Cor. 4:2). How could they, when they were responsible to God? They were neither deceived nor deceivers (cf. 2 Tim. 3:13). Error and immorality were not the source of their work, and trickery was not their method.

Verse 4: But just as we have been approved: They had passed the test. The verb in question *(dokimazō)* is an interesting one. It figures in the *Polity of the Athenians,* often referred to as the *Athenian Constitution,* only discovered in A.D. 1890 in an Egyptian papyrus. It is here used in the sense "to examine and admit . . . to the rights of manhood" and "to approve after scrutiny as fit (for an office)." [2] The verb thus means more than the bare test. It implies the hope that the test will be passed. One of the excuses made in the parable of the great supper is: "I have bought five yoke of oxen, and I go to give them a trial, to put them to the test" (Luke 14:19, author's translation). If, as a careful buyer, he has already done this, he knows what the result will be; but if he has not hitherto examined them, he certainly hopes that he will approve them after scrutiny. If men advance far enough to be considered as candidates for the diaconate, the officials who test them surely have the expectation and hope that they will prove blameless, not susceptible of any charge against them (1 Tim. 3:10).

It is one of the blasphemies of wicked men that they "examine" God and, when they ought to have had the expectation that he would pass, they award him a failure and dismiss him from their recognition, thereby incurring the judgment themselves of having a "disqualified mind" *(adokimon,* Rom. 1:28). Our Lord was "rejected after examination" (Mark 8:31, cf. 12:10).

---

1. Herodotus 1. 199.
2. Aristotle *Athenian Constitution* 42. 2; 45. 3.

In modern times when men are security-conscious, officials who are likely to have access to classified or secret documents are subjected to a strict security test. When it is all over, it is sometimes said that "these men have been screened." This is the thought in the Thessalonian passage, in which the perfect tense should be noted. "We have been screened—and therefore we possess credentials now."

By God: There are always men who want to "screen" the ministry, and sometimes it is merely the desire of malcontents. There is a place for the human test, as with the deacons. At times the wish may be conscientious ("however did that man get into the ministry?"), and at times no more than critical. Paul had to deal with men who wanted proof of the Christ who was speaking in him (2 Cor. 13:3); ultimately the authorization is from God and from his Son (2 Cor. 10:18).

We must not suppose that God, as it were, searched for men whom he could approve. The doctrine of election (1 Thess. 1:4) suggests that God prepared his men in advance. They were thus able to meet the test which he imposed.

To be entrusted with the gospel—because God had found them trustworthy (cf. 1 Tim. 1:12). In the case of Paul, God chose him in eternity, separated him, set him apart before he was born and called him through his grace. Paul could never forget the gracious call which had come home to him on the road to Damascus. It is the secret of his faithfulness and the method by which God had prepared him to meet the test.

He revealed this partly to the Galatians (Gal. 1:15) and partly to the Corinthians: "I give my opinion in the conviction that I have been pitied enough by the Lord to be trustworthy" (1 Cor. 7:25, author's translation).[1] The experience of mercy inspired the trustworthiness. For this reason he had been "passed" by the searching eye of the examiner with a high enough grade *to be entrusted with the gospel.*

It is sometimes said that God has faith in men. It is an unfortunate expression for God the omniscient, but it stands for something which should be stated differently. A clue may be found in Paul's statement that "I have been entrusted with a stewardship" (1 Cor. 9:17, author's translation, cf. 4:1–2 for the same imagery, and Luke 16:1–10 for the literal use). Now in any story of an unjust steward, it is conceivable that the owner might have deep suspicions of the man whom he proposed to employ; he might even have proof already that he was a rogue. Yet he might tell the man that he was entrusting his estate to him for management. It is thus possible to entrust something to a man whom you do not trust. This is paradox, oxymoron, or what you will, but it is

---

1. See the already cited *Grammar* of Blass-Debrunner-Funk, paragraph 425(3). Cf. also C. F. D. Moule, *An Idiom Book of New Testament Greek* (Cambridge: University Press, 1959), p. 127.

possible. It would obviously be absurd to say that an owner in such circumstances "had faith" in his steward: it was the last thing that he had. But he still entrusted his estate to him. Still less must we say that God has faith in men, even though he entrusted his oracles to the Jews and his gospel to Paul. (Cf. Rom. 3:2; Gal. 2:7; 1 Tim. 1:11; Titus 1:3.) When God entrusts he does not have an emotional "faith." It is a deliberate act of his will, as the passage from the Epistle to Titus shows ("entrusted by command of God"). And he knows the end from the beginning.

So we speak: A statement of general principle. It is not said, "so we spoke," though it would have been true. But the thought is of the preachers' regular habit—"so we always speak"—in a way which tallies with the divine approbation and commission. To *speak* covers everything from a whisper (Luke 12:3) to a proclamation (Mark 2:2); from an audience of one (John 4:27) to a vast crowd (Luke 9:11, 14).

Not to please men, but to please God: Not a spasmodic purpose but an abiding consciousness. The preacher must not set out to antagonize. Paul himself could begin a speech with remarkable tact and grace and could pay a compliment on occasion (cf. Acts 24:10; 26:2–3). The offense of the cross may be inevitable but the preacher should avoid being offensive in himself if he is to "persuade men" (2 Cor. 5:11). Paul was here considering his ultimate motive. In matters of courtesy and in nonessentials generally, he did not set out to displease everyone but to win them. But whatever conflicted with his gospel, impeded its progress, or sought to divert his attention from it, had to be opposed.

In interpreting the apostle and in coming to a final decision about how far the Christian should please men, we must give due weight to his other statements. It is a serious matter to please men if we keep God out of our thoughts and live in the power of the old self (cf. Rom. 8:8), because then we shall not please God. On the other hand, we have the example of our Lord, who did not please himself. "We who are strong" should without exception ("each") please his neighbor so that he may have the blessing of being built up (Rom. 15:1–3). Paul's own practice was first and foremost to please God. Provided that was done, he could say that "I try to please all men in everything I do, not seeking my own advantage, but that of many, that they may be saved" (1 Cor. 10:33).

Paul was well aware of the dangers in merely "pleasing men" (cf. Gal. 1:10; Eph. 6:6; Col. 1:10; 3:22). It is to be noticed that, apostle though he was, Paul put himself on the same level as his readers. It is not only apostles who must please God: he called the Thessalonians to do so likewise (1 Thess. 4:1). There is no double standard of Christian ethics. The apostle is as the ordinary layman, and the layman as the apostle; both should please God.

Who tests our hearts: The certificate of divine approval is constantly being brought up to date. A university graduate is always a B.A., but he can spend his life breaking the academic "rules" of his discipline. Not so with the preachers, who maintained a constant and living relationship with their teacher. It does not imply a cat-and-mouse procedure, but that God's searching eye is always on his ministers, and they in turn should always be conscious of his gaze, as Paul and his colleagues were. They were constantly being "screened" and they knew it. And in the confidence in their trustworthiness which was inspired by their gratitude for the grace of God in Christ they preached the gospel and challenged any traducers. We must regard this as more than a mere emotional certainty.

Hearts—the whole inner life. The use of the term "heart" in the New Testament is a study in itself. As in our modern usage it is the seat of the emotions, both good and bad (Rom. 1:24; 10:1). But it is far more. It is the seat of the intellect, from which come thought and reflection (Mark 11:23; Acts 7:23; Rom. 1:21, where the RSV's "minds" represents the Greek "heart"). It is the seat of the moral consciousness and of the will (Acts 11:23, "with purpose of heart," KJV; 1 Cor. 4:5; 2 Cor. 9:7, KJV), and even the scene of the imagination (Eph. 1:18). It stands for the ego, the whole personality. God has put the "earnest," the first installment, of the Spirit "in our hearts" (2 Cor. 1:22), that is, he has given it (the earnest) to *us* (2 Cor. 5:5). The heart is the seat of religious experience from which springs moral conduct. The "hidden person of the heart" (1 Pet. 3:4) is that to which God looks for the truth about men (Luke 16:15; cf. 1 Sam. 16:7).[1]

It should be observed that any charges against the preachers in verse 3 are answered. They are not deceived, because the gospel is of divine origin. They do not act from uncleanness because they have been tested and approved by God and are constantly being so tested. They are not guilty of guile and trickery because they are responsible to God and are pleasing him.

(4) Language (2:5)

They did not flatter, as the readers knew. They did not cover their avarice with specious talk.

For we never used either words of flattery: The general truth (vv. 3–4) is supported by the particular case. The readers could not know directly the general principles which governed the preachers' labors, but they could, and did, know how they had been applied at Thessa-

---

1. See Johannes Behm in *Theological Dictionary of the New Testament,* ed. G. Kittel, 3:612. Cf. also W. David Stacey, *The Pauline View of Man in Relation to its Judaic and Hellenistic Background* (London: Macmillan & Co., 1956), pp. 194–97; and H. Wheeler Robinson, *The Christian Doctrine of Man* (Edinburgh: T. & T. Clark, 1913), pp. 104–107.

lonica. Hence, in this verse (but not in vv. 3–4) the confident assertion *as you know* is in place. Flattery is the insincere use of conversation to tell the listener that he is better than he actually is. Its object is not merely social acceptance, the comparatively harmless "saying nice things." The ulterior motive is the advantage of the speaker. The flatterer thus gives more than he gets: he expresses the esteem in which the listener is held and therefore gives him pleasure. But the flatterer also gets more than he gives. If he is successful, he hopes for gifts of money, or social or political support, and so on. The point is the deliberate purpose of the flatterer. The merely "nice" man is just "nice." The "niceness" of the flatterer is a matter of policy: he is out for what he can get—and conversation is cheap.

This is a far cry from the apostle Paul and his companions. The man on whom lay the necessity to preach, with all the violence of a storm at sea (1 Cor. 9:16; cf. Acts 27:20), was hardly likely to seek the safety of the harbor of flattery.

Or a cloak for greed: A plausible story to cover an inner covetousness, An analogy is to be found in the conduct of "preachers" when Paul was in prison. Some were envious of him and inclined to quarrel with him; they wanted the glory of the popular preacher for themselves and their motives were mixed. In their hearts they wanted to show him that he was not the only pebble (or preacher!) on the beach, and thus to tighten his bonds. They preached Christ, with the ostensible motive of making him known; but it was a cover for their inner spirit of rivalry and even malice (Phil. 1:12–18; cf. Luke 20:47, and 1 Pet. 2:16, though the word here is "covering"). The *greed* is more than a mere love of money; it has no thought for others at all.

It is possible to translate the first part of verse 5 as "we did not resort to" the speech of flattery. This is of the same spirit as "we took courage" (v. 2) and perhaps reflects the pressure felt by the preachers. But they did not give way. The readers were not called to witness the excuse for greed. Reasons can always be given for a policy or practice. Only God really knows the heart. The invocation of God as witness reveals the necessity felt to establish the truth, and the certainty of the divine knowledge, interest, and aid. The God of truth would not repudiate truth. Later (v. 10) both God and the readers are witnesses. (Cf. Rom. 1:9; 2 Cor. 1:23; Phil. 1:8.)

(5) Disinterestedness (2:6)

They did not seek to gain a reputation. It was enough to be apostles of Christ.

Nor did we seek glory from men: "He must increase, but I must decrease" (John 3:30). They did not seek it but they found it (1 Thess.

1:9). This takes *glory* in the almost certainly correct sense of reputation, renown. But there may be an undertone of glory in the other sense, as when we speak of the glory of God. Paul was no idolater; God's glory belongs to him. But in his mercy, glory is for his people also, in which Paul delighted. But it could not come from men. (Cf. Rom. 8:30; 1 Cor. 2:7; 2 Cor. 4:17; 1 Thess. 2:12; 2 Tim. 2:10; Heb. 2:10.)

Whether from you or from others: This analyzes the *men*. There is ample room for "the encouragement of the preacher." But it is to the preacher's peril if he seeks to build a reputation for himself on the foundation of the saints' appreciation. It is even more dangerous if he seeks it from the world. "Woe to you, when all men speak well of you, for so their fathers did to the false prophets" (Luke 6:26). We have to have "church publicity," but it is fraught with spiritual danger to the ministry.

Though we might have made demands: Literally, to be in (a position of) weight. They could thus have exercised their rights. But is the weight the weight of influence or the burden of hospitality? A final answer is not possible. The immediate context speaks of seeking glory from men. It would be natural, therefore, for the writers to mean that they had no need to look for human regard; they had it already. They were apostles. On the other hand only a little later (v. 9; cf. 2 Thess. 3:8) we read that they toiled and labored with the purpose of not imposing a burden on anyone. Paul was very sensitive about these matters. He insisted on the apostolic right to hospitality, and he used his own discretion about whether he exercised it or not (1 Cor. 9:4–18). On the whole it seems wisest to combine the two interpretations. The preachers had no need to seek human glory; they already had the authority of apostles, both to preach and to be given food and lodging. The reflection is suggested that in our modern world the business executive who is given a credit card to cover hotel expenses is not entirely without his "glory." In the light of this we can see how questions of hospitality can be associated with matters of reputation.

As apostles of Christ: As those who were sent as missionaries. Notice how Silvanus and Timothy were linked with Paul. The word "apostle" has a narrower and a broader sense. The apostle *par excellence* was a witness of the ministry of Jesus and of his death, resurrection and ascension, and of the continuity of these events (Acts 1:21–22, 25–26; cf. Mark 3:13–15; 6:30). These were members of a sort of College of Witnesses and bore the title of "the Twelve" (1 Cor. 15:5—even in the absence of Judas). (A note to illustrate: in soccer the team is often called "the eleven." An excited schoolboy could easily shout "our eleven is winning," blissfully ignoring the fact that one member of the team is off the field, injured. "The eleven" in fact is a title—like "the Twelve.")

Paul himself is a special case (see discussion on 1 Thess. 1:1). In the wider sense apostles were preachers and missionaries, sent by the Lord to preach the gospel. Barnabas was an apostle in this sense (Acts 14:4, 14), and Andronicus and Junias were conspicuous among the apostles (Rom. 16:7). Paul seems to distinguish between the Twelve and the apostles generally (1 Cor. 15:5, 7). Silvanus and Timothy would be members of the latter. (Timothy cannot be excluded, on the grounds of 2 Cor. 1:1; Col. 1:1; Phil. 1:1.)

The apostolate is of divine appointment (1 Cor. 12:28–31) and is God's gift to the church (Eph. 4:11). Its characteristic is spiritual power (2 Cor. 12:12). The "ordinary" apostle can witness to the resurrection of Jesus Christ (cf. 2 Tim. 2:8) like any modern preacher; but he cannot testify to it in the same way as apostles in the strict sense (Acts 1:21–26). In the nature of the case such men can have no successors. Their apostolic testimony is preserved for all time in the New Testament. Apart from this distinction in the manner of their witness, the work of both kinds is itinerant preaching. The apostolic testimony in the New Testament is thus the standard for faith, doctrine and practice. We hear much today about "ascertaining the mind of the church" and it is understandable and laudable (cf. Acts 6:5). But the church can appeal, if necessary, against itself; against its preachers and leaders and bishops, to the first apostles; and that means to the New Testament. And from this there is no appeal.

(6) Tenderness (2:7)

The preached Word was a manifestation of power, but the preachers were as gentle as a nurse with children.

But we were gentle among you: There was no apostolic high-handedness. The translator cannot sit on the fence, though here he might well prefer it. Behind *gentle* stand two readings in the Greek, differing only in one letter (*nēpioi* and *ēpioi*). To complicate the matter the immediately preceding Greek word ends in the letter "n"; if a scribe thought he had written it twice when he had only written it once, he would reduce *nēpioi* to *ēpioi*. On the other hand if he absent-mindedly repeated the letter he would increase *ēpioi* to *nēpioi*. *Nēpioi* is better attested; but recent textual critics tend to adopt *ēpioi* in their editions (Souter, Kilpatrick, Nestle, Aland). The former means "babes" and the latter *gentle*. "Babes" involves a violent change of metaphor and simile, from "babes" to "nurse," which is not impossible, especially to a Hebrew, though it puts rather a strain on the reader. It tallies with the description of members of the kingdom of heaven (Matt. 19:14), though the word for "children" is not the same. (Cf. Matt. 11:25.) But other uses do not lend encouragement to this interpretation (Matt. 21:16; 1 Cor. 13:11; Gal. 4:1). On the other hand *gentle* is regarded by some as tame. If we insist on following the better reading we must explain it by reference to Paul's tendency (like a preacher!) to extract every possible turn of thought from an initial metaphor. (Cf. Jesus' treatment of the sheepfold, shepherd metaphor in John 10:1–16.) The probabilities must be balanced: the better reading against the view of common sense.

We incline to the reading *gentle,* which need not be interpreted as tame. It is a fine foil to the "weight" of the previous verse. The apostles "did not throw their weight around." It is the opposite of quarrelsomeness (2 Tim. 2:24), a gentleness not so much of spirit, though it is that, as of external behavior like word and gesture.[1] "A soft answer turns away wrath" (Prov. 15:1).

The picture which follows is tender and beautiful. The *nurse* combines the skill of her profession with the outflow of mother-love. We see *taking care* in another context in Ephesians 5:29 (cherishes). The Greek word appears elsewhere for the mother bird "warming" her young (Deut. 22:6, LXX; cf. Job 39:14, LXX). The preachers' evangelistic and pastoral activity was not a cold-blooded, detached affair but a loving, heart-warming concern. There is room for "pulpit vigor" and fighting the fight of faith in the sermon; but sometimes the *gentle* preacher inspires his hearers to receive the Word with gentleness, not resistance (cf. Jas. 1:21). Some see an allusion to Numbers 11:12; but it is better, if there is an allusion at all, to refer to the birth of Moses, whose mother, in the providence of God, was both nurse and mother (Exod. 2:7–8). The *children,* in an unstudied way, preserves the thought of the permanence of the Christian fellowship. Children are always the children of their parents, however far away they may be. Forever the preachers and the Thessalonians would be united in the one family of God.

(7) Devotion (2:8)

They spoke the words of the gospel, but into it they put all their nervous energy, and in personal counseling they did not hold themselves back.

So, being affectionately desirous of you: The previous figure is continued. The rare Greek verb is possibly a nursery term to express endearment. The insight of a young mother is here needed for the best comment.

We were ready to share with you: With delight as well as by decision. The word *share* can be used of getting or giving a share. Here it means to give. There is a slight paradox in the thought of "desiring" you and giving to you. The idea in *share* must not be pressed too much. It does

---

1. Cf. C. Spicq (Études Bibliques), *Les Épîtres Pastorales* (Paris: Librairie Lecoffre, J. Gabalda et Cie, 1947), p. 360.

not mean "only a share and no more." The preachers were glad to give
the whole gospel to the Thessalonians and at the same time to keep it
themselves. The reason lies in the nature of Christian fellowship. At the
heart of fellowship or communion is that which is common. If things
like money are common (Acts 2:44; 4:32), they are shared and shared
out—the greater the number of people the smaller the share. But with
the "common salvation" (Jude 3; cf. Titus 1:4, "a common faith"),
it is shared and not shared out. Each believer is offered "full salvation."

Not only the gospel of God: See the discussion on verse 2. It is also
"our gospel" (1:5; see discussion). No conflict is involved.

But also our own selves: Nothing was held in reserve. The word behind *selves* has been given more than one interpretation. *Psuchē* can
mean barely "life," as when we hear of a man "risking his life" (Phil.
2:30); or it may mean "vitality," "energy"; or it may stand for no
more than the individual person (Rom. 2:9; 13:1; 2 Cor. 12:15).
Now the preachers did not give their lives for their listeners; if they
had, there would have been no letter. They might have given their
energy or even their vitality as they worked for their living to avoid
making impositions (v. 9). This rather restricts the scope of the passage. We are left with the thought of their giving their individual persons, of sharing themselves with the Thessalonians. *Our own selves* is
an admirable rendering and catches the spirit of the text.

It is not only a question of giving time and energy in the interests of
inquirers. Most of us know people of reserved character. Even in
intimate conversation there is a final barrier which we cannot pass. The
other man will not expose his soul completely, and we come away
realizing that we do not really know him. Hidden depths of personality
are unplumbed. The Thessalonians did not find Paul and his colleagues
men of this stamp. For example, it would be understandable if the
former persecutor wanted to soft-pedal his pre-Christian activities.
But he might have found, in the work of counseling the hesitant, that
his greatest power came in telling of his feelings as he looked back on
the days when he had harried the church. "I received mercy." The
whole context (1 Tim. 1:12–17) can be interpreted as an instance of
the apostle's "giving himself."

In the social life of the church the preachers also gave themselves.
There are people who "look in on" the church social as the king looked
in on the wedding guests (Matt. 22:11). Perhaps they belong to a high
social class and do not feel at home; perhaps their interests are severely
academic and they feel like fish out of water at innocent games and
festivities. Whatever the reason they are not "one with the people,"
still less "one of them." It was not like that with the missionaries. They
met the Thessalonians at their own level. They thus gave their *own
selves.* This illustration—and it is only an illustration—must not be

misunderstood. It is extremely doubtful if the Thessalonians had church socials in the modern sense, and it is certain that the apostle Paul would have wanted to use the time to better advantage! "Being one with them" and "being one of them" must mean that the preachers identified themselves with the people and sympathetically entered into their experiences and interests. They loved them as they were. It does not mean that at any time they laid aside their role or forgot who had sent them. They were always ministers of Jesus Christ. In fact, as true ministers, they were "one with the people" without being "one of them." Their authority as apostles and preachers was not lost. But it was not the bare and abstract authority of office. It was steeped in love, because the preachers both gave it and received it. The Thessalonians had become *very dear* to them.

(8) Toil (2:9)

They preached at their own expense, imposing no burden of a financial nature on their converts.

For you remember our labor and toil, brethren: This is no new information. *For* introduces the reason to support earlier statements: no greed (v. 5) but rather readiness to share and love for the Thessalonians (v. 8). For some reason the RSV later reverses the order of *labor and toil* (2 Thess. 3:8) though the Greek order is unchanged in a Pauline set phrase (2 Cor. 11:27). The preachers had worked in order that they might not be a burden; and in order to set an example (2 Thess. 3:8–9). It is striking that thanksgiving should be offered for the Thessalonians' *labor* of love. (See discussion on 1 Thess. 1:3.) Paul's work was tentmaking (Acts 18:3). It may well be that he used leather for other objects than tents, though still retaining the trade name of tentmaker. We have seen a similar practice in our own time. A man has been called a saddler but has been involved in leather goods other than saddles. In touching words the apostle told the Ephesian elders that "these hands ministered to my necessities" (Acts 20:34). These hands: who can doubt that he held them up as he spoke, the soiled hands of a manual worker? (Cf. 1 Cor. 4:12.) It has been conjectured that Paul the scholar was embarrassed and self-conscious. Do not manual workers use their hands almost without being aware of it? But the work was not new to him. It is a nice point whether Saul of Tarsus in Cilicia was trained to work in the celebrated *cilicium,* the coarse cloth of Cilician goat's hair.

Labor and toil together suggest drudgery, the irksome task, all that is uncongenial, wear and tear, hardship: everything in fact that is bothersome.

We worked night and day, that we might not burden any of you, while we preached to you: They used a strenuous earthly means to a heavenly end. The main activity (and interest) lies in *we preached*. It is not necessarily implied that they worked twenty-four hours every day. They did not keep "office hours." Paul's practice is reflected in the episode at Troas (Acts 20:7–11). Many of the members would be free only at night, and they seem to have met at the house of Jason (Acts 17:5–7). The preachers did not want to burden *any one* of the Thessalonians, a fact which shows a concern for individuals. It is not hard to visualize the scene: Paul with the company of young believers about him in the house, speaking incessantly about the kingdom of God and working with his hands while he did so. We have heard of preaching under strange conditions (barns, open air, theaters), but on few occasions as odd as here. But it gave a demonstration of his love of the congregation. Not a cent from them!

The gospel of God: See discussion on 2:2, 8. There is a remarkable parallelism between the preaching of Paul and that of Jesus. Jesus was "preaching the gospel of God, and saying, ' . . . repent, and believe in the gospel' " (Mark 1:14–15). Paul testified "of repentance to God and of faith in our Lord Jesus Christ." His ministry was to "testify to the gospel of the grace of God" (Acts 20:21, 24). In the fulfillment of such a ministry he would deny himself material support from his immediate listeners but accept it from a beloved church at a distance which he could trust (Phil. 4:16).

(9) Standards (2:10–12)

The readers themselves could give evidence—as could God—of the impeccable conduct of the preachers as they presented the moral and spiritual demands of discipleship.

Verse 10: You are witnesses, and God also: Everything has been observed. The thought involved in the word "witness" is twofold. The witness is one who has himself seen and heard, and can in consequence tell his story at first hand. An obvious example is the apostolate (Acts 1:8, 21–22; see discussion on 2:6). The Thessalonians were witnesses to all that they had seen and heard; to everything external at the very least, like the absence of words of flattery (v. 5); and to what was inner and spiritual so far as they were in spiritual fellowship or *en rapport* with the preachers. They experienced it and could speak if they wished. God likewise had seen and heard, and he knew perfectly not only the external but the secret man of the heart. Thus he knew, if the Thessalonians did not, whether the preachers were motivated by greed or not. In a sense the Thessalonians would testify, at least to themselves, whether they wanted to or not. *For you remember . . .* (v. 9). The writers were confident of the response. But was it God's will to testify?

According to the New Testament God does testify. He testifies to his

Son (1 John 5:9–11) and to men (Heb. 11:4; Acts 15:8; cf. Acts 14:3; Heb. 10:15). It would seem that Paul could have called on the readers to answer two questions. Was his life—and those of his coworkers—in accordance with the Scripture? Did God work through his servants to cleanse the hearts of men through the Word? If the preachers had been charlatans, how could the new life of the Thessalonians be explained? What had made them turn from idols to the living God? God, in fact, had already given his testimony to the preached Word. He had owned the preachers as his servants. The genuineness of the religious life of the Thessalonian church stood or fell on the genuineness of its founders. A bad tree cannot produce good fruit. (Cf. 1 Sam. 12:3–5.)

How holy and righteous and blameless was our behavior: An impossible claim to make unless it were true. The three adjectives are not mutually exclusive but have a cumulative effect. The preachers were *holy* not only in being separated (cf. Rom. 1:1) to fulfill a duty laid upon them but in their actual attitude toward God—even when they gave themselves completely to their friends.

Righteousness is a vast study in itself. It is well to remember that the noun interlocks with the adjective *righteous* and with the verb "to deem righteous," generally translated by "justify." Noun, adjective, and verb are used in Romans 3:25–26. In one sense to be *righteous* means to be in conformity to the standard laid down by God, both in relation to him and in relation to one's fellowmen. This is the meaning of the word, though nobody attains to the standard (Rom. 3:10–18). In another sense a man is deemed righteous by faith and is thus one who is acceptable to God. (Cf. Rom. 1:17; 10:3–6.) This "ranking" as *righteous* is through the obedience of the cross. Now the apostle Paul bases his Christian ethic on the work of Christ. The "therefore" of Romans 12:1 is highly significant. The believer is to put his body, "members," at God's disposal as instruments of righteousness (Rom. 6:13, 19). If he is an obedient believer he is not only righteous by faith but righteous by using his members as "tools" for carrying out the requirements of God's righteousness. When it is said that the missionaries behaved righteously, it cannot mean a secular righteousness. It was the behavior of men justified by faith who were obeying God in their dealings with him and with the Christians at Thessalonica.

Blameless is a negative term which rounds off the writers' claim. Though it hardly adds anything to the meaning of the other two adjectives it provides a climactic ending. It should be regarded as a statement of fact rather than a defiant challenge. It is a curious fact that Saul the Pharisee could claim to be blameless (Phil. 3:6). But that was a legal righteousness and "confidence in the flesh," rather like the Pharisee in the parable (Luke 18:9–12). The blamelessness of Paul the apostle was the outworking of divine grace in the heart of a man justified by faith. In fact Paul corresponds to the tax collector in the same parable.

You believers: Those with whom the preachers had the closest relationship. The description is not meant to exclude others. Note the basic word for Christians—"men who trust (God in Christ)."

Verse 11: For you know how, like a father with his children: The sex is changed from verse 7 but not the tenderness. The nurse has become the father. Once more an appeal was made to the Thessalonians' knowledge; once more we see apostolic confidence.

We exhorted each one of you: The sermon was followed by counseling. No member of the church could say afterwards that "in all his ministry the pastor never spoke to me." This may have some bearing on the length of the preachers' visit and the size of the church. The figure of father is here slightly more appropriate than that of nurse, especially if she appeared to have charge of babies. The noun corresponding to *exhorted* is used in verse 3 (see discussion); we "persuaded with authority." This was not flattery (v. 5) though it was aimed at individual need as well as the general good of the church.

And encouraged you and charged you: The words are addressed to the feelings and to the will respectively. The former is an address to the faint-hearted (1 Thess. 5:14) amid affliction (1:6) and suffering (2:14). It can be consolation to the bereaved (John 11:19, 31). *Charged* is more solemn. It virtually insists on a response and has an atmosphere of a divine requirement being made known by God's messenger.

Verse 12: To lead a life worthy of God: The whole life should exhibit Christian conduct. *To lead a life* is the RSV rendering of the familiar Hebrew idiom "to walk." It is a fruitful figure of speech. The Christian walk is *worthy of God,* negatively, if it is not: like the Gentiles (Eph. 4: 17–19); in darkness (John 8:12); according to the flesh (Rom. 8:4); in a secular manner (Eph. 2:2). It is *worthy of God,* positively, if it is: by faith (2 Cor. 5:7); with thoughtful care (Eph. 5:15); in newness of life (Rom. 6:4) (cf. Col. 2:6 "in him"); according to love (Rom. 14:15); to please him in everything (Col. 1:10); as he walked (1 John 2:6). The Christian must "keep on following him" (Matt. 8:22, literal) because he is then on the right Way (Acts 9:2; cf. John 14:6). (Cf. Eph. 4:1.)

Who calls you: The original call never stops. It leads to our conversion. In the order of experience (Rom. 8:30), Paul used the past tense: God called; God justified. But once converted we are not left on our own. God does not indeed call converted men to be converted, but he still calls them. There is a time when our Lord says, "Follow me," and we hear it for the first time and do follow. After that he still calls us onward, "in his steps" (1 Pet. 2:21). It is not possible to follow anyone unless he is moving. The picture is of the advancing Christ constantly reassuring his disciples: "Keep following me; keep moving; do not stop." The Christian maintains his discipleship, not because he is like a dog tied to the rear axle of a farm cart, but because he constantly hears the voice of God bidding him continue what he has begun. The translation *who calls you* is better than the static "God your caller."

Into his own kingdom: Not yours! "Thy kingdom come" (Matt. 6: 10). The subject of the kingdom of God has been the aim of much research and the literature is immense.[1] The following points should be kept in mind. *Kingdom* does not mean a place, a realm ruled by a king, but an activity; God's royal rule or sovereignty is meant. The kingdom of God existed in the Old Testament. "Thy kingdom is an everlasting kingdom, and thy dominion endures throughout all generations" (Ps. 145:13; cf. Ps. 103:19). When Jesus preached the kingdom of God he was not merely reiterating the Old Testament teaching. The *kingdom,* the royal rule, "has drawn near" and therefore "is at hand" (Mark 1:15). God is no longer ruling, as it were, at a distance. (This does not mean deism. It does mean that God was inaccessible to men who would oppose him. In Christ the metaphysically distant God who rules everything entered history.) "The kingdom of God is among (*entos*) you" (Luke 17:21, literal). There stood Christ in their midst, the embodiment of the kingdom, of God ruling. After the cross, resurrection and ascension, and the outpouring of the Holy Spirit, the kingdom was within believing men, for Christ dwells in their hearts through faith (cf. Eph 3:17). God is over all in his providential rule, he was among men in the days of the ministry of Jesus, and he is in believers. He is still "over" all, only we now know that it is in Christ (Col. 1:13–18); and he is "in" all believers in Christ through the Holy Spirit.

The kingdom is present (Matt. 12:28; Luke 11:20). It is "righteousness and peace and joy in the Holy Spirit" (Rom. 14:17). "Thine is the kingdom . . ." (Matt. 6:13, RSV footnote). The manuscript authority for this last portion of the Lord's Prayer is not good, and it is often regarded as an ecclesiastical addition. But recent Semitic scholarship has shown the unlikelihood of a prayer ending without a doxology.

---

1. For excellent surveys and bibliographies see George Eldon Ladd, *Jesus and the Kingdom: The Eschatology of Biblical Realism* (New York: Harper & Row, 1964; reprint ed., Waco, Tex.: Word Books; London: S.P.C.K., 1966); and Gösta Lundström, *The Kingdom of God in the Teaching of Jesus: A History of Interpretation From the Last Decades of the Nineteenth Century to the Present Day* (Edinburgh and London: Oliver and Boyd, 1963).

The manuscripts may just assume it. And if the church added it, why is there no normal Christian ending like "for Jesus Christ's sake"? [1]

The kingdom is also future. All attempts to limit it to the present (realized eschatology) break down in the face of one piece of evidence: "Thy kingdom come."

The New Testament speaks of entering the kingdom (Matt. 23:13; cf. 7:21; 18:3). It means consciously putting oneself under God's royal rule in Christ ("Jesus is Lord" cf. Rom. 10:9), and this involves conversion. It is a striking fact that we read of a man "discipled to the *kingdom*" (Matt 13:52, literal), and of one "discipled to Jesus" (Matt. 27:57, literal). In fact it amounts to the same thing whether we inherit eternal life, follow Jesus, enter the kingdom, or are saved (Mark 10:17–26), as it is all one experience. Paul's great aim of testifying to the gospel of the grace of God was fulfilled when he went about preaching the kingdom (Acts 20:24–25).

Providentially and invisibly God still in Christ rules nature and history. Invisibly in Christ he rules in the hearts of believers. In the final consummation of all things he will in Christ rule openly: all things, all people and especially his own believing people. Christ is already Lord of nature and history ("at the right hand of God"). He is King in the realms of nature, history, and of grace. At the end he will be known of all as Creator and Sustainer of the universe and Head of the Church. And his people will continue to rejoice to be under the rule of him who is Lord, and to say "that there is another king, Jesus" (Acts 17:7).

And glory—hitherto unattained (Rom. 3:23). God's *glory* means God as revealed, particularly in his being, character, majesty and might; and the "radiance" which is the sign of his presence. He has revealed himself in nature and history. "The heavens are telling the glory of God" (Ps. 19:1; cf. Rom. 1:19–20, 23); "I will get glory over Pharaoh" (Exod. 14:4; cf. vv. 17–18). There is enough in nature and in the affairs of men for humanity to know that God exists and that he is God; that he is righteous and holy; that he is worshipful and omnipotent. The "radiance" appeared in the wilderness (Exod. 16:7, 10); on Mount Sinai (Exod. 24:15–18) and in the tabernacle (Exod. 40:34–35); in the Temple (1 Kings 8:11); and in prophetic vision (Ezek. 1:28). It is referred to also in Luke 2:9.

These two meanings of *glory,* which we may call "revelation" and "radiance," are distinct, though in the New Testament they tend to merge. At the transfiguration the disciples "saw his glory" (Luke 9:32; cf. 1 Pet. 5:1). It was more than "radiance": "listen to him!" (Luke 9:35) they were commanded. God's creative illumination has shown us "the glory of God in the face of Christ" (2 Cor. 4:6). "The glory of his

---

1. W. D. Davies, *The Setting of the Sermon on the Mount* (Cambridge: The University Press, 1964), Appendix VIII, pp. 451–53.

grace" (Eph. 1:6, KJV) is more than surpassing brilliance, as the context shows. We read of "the might of his glory" (Col. 1:11, literal; cf. 2 Thess. 1:9, "the glory of his might"). There are grounds for saying that Jesus Christ is the glory (Jas. 2:1). All God's revelation is concentrated in him, radiant in light (Heb. 1:3).

To this glory—to Jesus Christ who is himself the glory—Christians have already been called (1 Pet. 5:10) and are still constantly being called (see discussion above). When they come to Christ, they are not moving away from God. On the contrary, they are going to where God is to be found in all his fullness. In that they have received Christ (Col. 2:6), they have already participated in the glory. But all that is implicit now will be explicit later, for there is glory yet to be revealed (Rom. 8:18): "we shall see him as he is," and "we shall be like him" (1 John 3:2), "similar in form to the body of his glory" (Phil. 3:21, literal). The scene will be one of surpassing grandeur. But all this is merely scenery compared with the essential glory, the presence of God in Christ, before which glory Christians will be presented. Thus they will be forever with the Lord (Jude 24; 1 Thess. 4:17).

The Greek text uses only one article in this phrase, which has the effect of closely linking both nouns. We might bring this out by translating it "his own kingdom-and-glory." The ideas overlap. God in Christ is present (glory); but what is he doing? Ruling! God in Christ is ruling (kingdom); but how? Manifestly! All will see that God is God, that he is holy, righteous, love, worshipful, and mighty. The light in his presence makes the sun a mere candle. "The Lord God will be their light," and believers will joyfully be under his rule and will recognize it with adoration. They will find that to serve and worship God in Christ is to share his throne. For his service is perfect freedom (Rev. 22:3–5).

3. The Thessalonians: Their Persecution a Proof of the Reality of Their Conversion (2:13–16)

The writers offered thanksgiving to God without intermission because the readers had received the authentic Word of God and it was still active in their lives. They had no need to be surprised by persecution, as their experience corresponded with that of churches elsewhere. The Thessalonians had suffered at the hands of their own compatriots, just as the churches in Judea had suffered from the Jews. The latter may be regarded as typical of all persecutors of the church.

(1) The Word of God received and active (2:13)

It was no mere human speech which the Thessalonians had heard. Speech it was indeed, but it conveyed the Word of God, and they had both heard it and received it so deeply that it was still at work in their hearts.

And we also thank God constantly for this, that: The thanksgiving is pushed further back, as it were. The apostles have already spoken of remembering the work and toil and endurance of the Thessalonians (1:3). At this point they revert to the beginning of it all. Faith comes before works, conversion before service. And there is a logical order in the experience of conversion. The Word is first heard (as by a tape-recorder), then received and welcomed. First the head and then the heart. In the act of reception we should notice a complex response. The truth of the statement given in the preached Word is believed. This involves an attitude: what the preacher is saying is not his word but the Word of God. In addition it is not only the truth which is received, as when, for example, a man says for the first time that "I accept the teaching of the church." The truth must indeed be believed, but this by itself is no more than intellectual assent. There is a further step. In genuine conversion a man receives Christ, the living Christ. Thus the Word is heard and understood. Its "content" is believed as being the Word of God and not of man, and its subject is received into the heart. The writers were conscious that they had preached the Word of God, and gave thanks that it had been received as such.

Received: a "tradition" word. (See discussion on 2 Thess. 2:15.)

Accepted: a "hospitality" word. The Greek verb has some suggestive uses. " . . . the Galileans welcomed him" (John 4:45). Note the context: it was a welcome of honor. The ingenious scheme of the unjust steward had as its aim that people might "receive me into their houses" (Luke 16:4). Paul asked the Colossians to receive Mark if he came to them (Col. 4:10); obviously he was not to be turned away. The Galatians received the apostle Paul himself "as an angel of God, as Christ Jesus" (Gal. 4:14), a statement which recalls words of Jesus (Matt. 10:40–41). The very people who had been treated as tenderly as children (v. 7) had clearly received the kingdom of God as a child receives it (Mark 10:15). In this they were unlike the "unspiritual man" (1 Cor. 2:14).

As . . . the word of God: This occasions the thankfulness for the attitude of the Thessalonians. The *as* is important in interpretation. It was not being suggested merely that Paul had preached the word of God. He had certainly done that; but his point was that his hearers had recognized it as such. However imaginatively and vividly the preachers had spoken, the essence of their message had been truth. The *word of God* is analogous to the *gospel of God* (see discussion on 2:2, 8–9). In the present context the latter gives the content of the former. It is conceivable that in some situations the message might be exclusively that of judgment. It would seem therefore that *word of God* is the wider term.

Which is at work in you believers: No dead letter! The thought is that the *word* has done its work and goes on working. The human side is to be observed in the parable of the sower, from which certain points may be extracted. The seed fructifies; it is the word of the kingdom and must be understood (Matt. 13:8, 19, 23). The hearers of the word accept it and bear fruit (Mark 4:20). The seed is the word of God and the hearers hold it fast in an honest and good heart and bring forth fruit with patience (Luke 8:11, 15). (The "patience" is the "steadfastness" of 1 Thess. 1:3.) The close association of word, gospel, and kingdom should be noticed.

The word goes on working because it is "living and active" (Heb. 4:12). The (literal) "word of hearing" (which means the "word heard") is almost identical in the Greek of verse 13 and Hebrews 4:2. The latter text shows that the message when heard benefits only when it is met with faith. This the Thessalonians continued to exercise.

Other forces are at work also. We read of "the power at work within us" (Eph. 3:20) and of "faith working through love" (Gal. 5:6). The word and the power are divine; the faith is human. The human and the divine interpenetrate within us and though we may distinguish them in thought we cannot look into our own minds and say that "this means me-believing" and "this means God powerfully working in me." In the one consciousness (and perhaps unconsciousness too?) divine and human intermingle. There is an analogous example in the ministry of the Holy Spirit. He comes into our hearts crying "Abba! Father!" (Gal. 4:6). He does the shouting. But so do we. We too cry "Abba! Father!" (Rom. 8:15–16). We do the shouting. The Spirit's witness is joined with our witness that we are children of God—just as the activity of the word and the power are joined to the activity of our faith. Great is the mystery of piety! (Cf. 1 Tim. 3:16.)

(2) The experience of the churches repeated (2:14)

The readers were not to regard themselves as an exceptional case, with a unique "problem of suffering" on their hands. They were in the true and noble succession.

For you, brethren, became imitators of the churches of God in Christ Jesus . . . in Judea: Proof that the word was still at work in them. Notice how *you* picks up the expression "you believers" in the previous verse. The imitation was hardly deliberate. The readers were here made to feel that they belonged to a wide fellowship. They were *imitators* of the apostles and of the Lord (1:6; see discussion); they were not a little coterie with no connection with anybody. The *churches . . . in Judea* were older, established churches. To continue their existence they must have shown steadfastness (cf. 1:3) and were thus apt examples. It would encourage the Thessalonians to know that Christian fellowship was holding out in the heart of Judaism, where many Christians would be Jews. The Jewish attack (Acts 17:5) was not new.

For *churches* see discussion on 1:1. They are both *in Christ Jesus* and *in Judea*. This is the distinction between spiritual and physical geography. *Judea* stands for a place on earth, for earning one's living, for all the hazards of the concrete situation: stress of climate, social and economic conditions, and the unrelenting struggle for existence, not excluding possible persecution. The words *in Christ Jesus* remind us of the higher, hidden life of the believer (Col. 3:3). The fight continues below but the direction, the supply, and the inspiration is from above. Cf. "the churches of Judea in Christ" (Gal. 1:22, literal).

For you suffered the same things: The pattern was reproduced. Christians in Judea were persecuted by Jews, those in Thessalonica by Macedonians. Persecution may have been instigated by Jews but the local population took it up (Acts 17:8). The *countrymen* were Gentiles, and the church at Thessalonica was largely Gentile also. A possible translation is "you were treated in the same way by your own countrymen . . . . " This leaves much to the imagination of the reader and can be very effective.

(3) The character of the archetypal persecutors summarized (2:15–16)

The writers were not anti-Semitic; but they saw in the rejection of the Messiah and the subsequent attitude of the Jews the essence of all persecution.

Verse 15: Who killed both the Lord Jesus and the prophets, and drove us out: Historic facts. It might be argued at first that the Romans killed the Lord, and in point of fact it was the soldiers who carried out the deed. But it is here a question of responsibility. The soldiers were obeying orders (Mark 15:15–16, 20, 24); and Pilate's authority to execute was derived from above. The greater responsibility and the greater sin was laid at the door of those who had delivered Jesus (John 19:10–15). Our Lord's words, "he who delivered me to you," point to Judas. Judas set the proceedings in motion, in consequence of which the Lord's "own nation and the chief priests" handed him over to Pilate (John 18:30–31, 35). The complicity of priests, scribes, rulers, and people may be traced in the Gospels (Mark 14:43, 55, 63–64; 15:1–3; Luke 23:10, 13–18; Mark 15:8–15, 29–32).

Thus we can say that the Roman soldiers killed Jesus and that the Jews killed him, and apportion the responsibility accordingly. An analogy is to be seen in the record that a soldier of the guard beheaded John the Baptist and that Herod beheaded him (Mark 6:16, 27).

Emphasis is laid on *the Lord* which may be brought out by rendering the phrase *who killed both the Lord—Jesus—and the prophets.* The word *Lord* heightens the enormity (see on 1:1) and anticipates 1 Corinthians 2:8; *Jesus* identifies the human person. (Cf. Luke 23:34).

The *prophets* are those of the Old Testament. The best comment is Matthew 23:29–39; Mark 12:1–12; Acts 7:51–52.

And drove us out: A "typical" action. The anticlimax is only apparent. It could be argued and, as far as it goes, rightly, that it was not *the Jews* who drove out the preachers but "some Jews." But that is just the point. It was an act characteristic of the nation as a whole, and it reproduced the same pattern as in the killing of the Lord and the prophets. The spirit of the utterance would be shown in the remark of, say, a Dutchman who said that "the Germans engaged in two World Wars and blew up our house and made us homeless." Strictly speaking it was "some Germans" who blew up the house; but it was characteristic of a nation at war. It was a hostile act. So it is here in the epistle. The Jews are represented as in opposition to their covenant God. His cause is not their cause. Hence their attitude to the Messiah, to the prophets who had looked for his coming (cf. Rom. 1:2; 10:11; 1 Pet. 1:10–12), and to the preachers who proclaimed him.

Deep feeling is manifested here, as well it might be. The calculated murder of the one who had loved him and delivered himself (Gal. 2: 20; same Greek word as Mark 15:1, 10) up for him could not and should not be contemplated by Paul unmoved. But it was not uncontrolled passion or rancor. Paul loved his Jewish kinsmen, prayed for their salvation, and would almost have sacrificed his own in order to gain theirs. Anguish and sorrow balanced his anger (Rom. 9:1–5; 10:1–4; cf. Acts 17:5, 13.)

And displease God: A verdict on the historic acts, but not only on the ones in the past. The thought is that "they go on habitually displeasing God."

And oppose all men—by their opposition to the gospel, which is for the benefit of all men. We need not see here a reference to heathen misunderstanding of Jewish exclusiveness. The explanation is given in the first part of the next verse. Jewish hindrance of evangelism both displeases God and harms men.

Verse 16: By hindering us from speaking to the Gentiles that they may be saved: The two ideas are to be taken together. We must not regard this as the expression of petty annoyance such as a speaker may feel when he is interrupted or "heckled." The Jews were attempting to thwart the salvation of men. They did not themselves look at it in this way. They did not believe that Jesus was the Messiah (Acts 3:13–14). They objected to Paul's doctrine of justification by faith in their zeal for the law (Acts 18:13; cf. 21:20–21). The spiritual needs of the Gentiles did not worry them (Acts 22:21–22). The former champion of Judaism was therefore the object of their implacable opposition (Acts 9:22–23) from the first. (Cf. Acts 13:45–46; 18:5–6; 28:19, 22.) From their own point of view, with which Paul agreed, they had a zeal for God; hence their opposition. But it was not enlightened zeal (Rom. 10:2). Therefore, in opposing the gospel and particularly in their opposing the preaching of it by Paul, they were hindering the salvation of the Gentiles. Thus they were "contrary to all men" (v. 15, literal). Paul has himself described the lengths to which they were prepared to go in their "hindrance" (2 Cor. 11:24; cf. Deut. 25:1–3). It should be observed that the *hindering* is conative: they were "trying to hinder," with only partial success. There is a parallel to this in the life of Saul the persecutor in Acts 26:9–11. Note the similar "opposing the name of Jesus of Nazareth"; the succession of hammer blows: "I did . . . I shut up . . . I cast my vote"; and then the check to his plans, "I tried to make them blaspheme." The persecutor in time past and the Jews still could only try, he to force the Christians to blaspheme and the Jews to prevent the apostle from preaching salvation to the Gentiles.

The place of language is worth reflection. If the Jews could have silenced Paul, their main object would have been achieved. Salvation is the great act of God, objectively in the work of Christ on the cross and subjectively in a man's heart when he believes. The first part is accomplished; it is "the finished work of Christ." The second part takes place with the act of faith, and faith is born when a man responds to the preaching of the gospel. Words are not to be despised.

There is a permanent element in the apostle's teaching here which should not be forgotten. Jewish scholars are still writing books to show that Jesus is not the Christ, the Son of God. The cross is still a stumbling-block.

So as always to fill up the measure of their sins: This is somewhat unexpected, as the context prepares us for the result of the Jewish opposition rather than the purpose or aim. It is quite true that the filling up is the consequence of the acts of the Jews. But the construction is one of purpose. Whose purpose? This is an example where the grammatical subject must give way to the theological. The result or consequence is not unforeseen by God, and it is taken up into his eternal purpose. Other examples of purpose, of which the "doers" are unconscious, may be seen in Romans 1:20 (KJV) and 4:11. Jewish blindness at last became absolute and ceased to be merely a spiritual phenomenon; it became a divine sentence. There is an analogy in Romans 1:24.

It is sometimes asked how it is possible for a holy God to use the deeds of sinful men for his purpose. The answer has been vigorously given that "we give him little else to use." If God is indeed the sovereign ruler of the world of men, he must either ignore their deeds, which is abdication, or use them even if they are sinful. Illustrations of this may be seen in the life of the Old Testament Joseph; in the betrayal by Judas; and in the cross itself. When Joseph privately made himself known to his brothers, he made two striking statements. "I am your brother, Joseph, whom you sold into Egypt. . . . So it was not you who sent me here, but God" (Gen. 45:4, 8). Again, it was Judas by whom the Lord was delivered up (John 19:11; see on 1 Thess. 2:15); but the fearful sin was taken up into God's purpose. God delivered up his Son (Rom. 8:32; the "giving up" here does not mean anything like "going without," as when a man says that "I have given up half my house for these people" or "I gave up my son for the sake of the school team, when I wanted him to work in the garden." It means "handing over" and has a somber hue: cf. Rom. 1:24, 26, 28). In addition Jesus delivered up himself (Gal. 2:20; Eph. 5:2). The synthesis of the deliverance of Jesus by Judas, by God, and by Jesus himself is stated in Acts 2:23. The brothers sent Joseph into Egypt—and God sent him there. The lawless men encompassed the death of Jesus—and it was God who spared not his Son (Rom. 8:32). Thus does God take up the deeds of sinners into his eternal purpose. "O the depth of the riches and wisdom and knowledge of God! How unsearchable are his judgments and how inscrutable his ways!" (Rom. 11:33). But God has revealed them to us through his Spirit (cf. 1 Cor. 2:6–13).

The metaphor of "filling up to the brim" goes back to Genesis 15:16 (LXX) and is used by our Lord in Matthew 23:32 (cf. v. 35), where once more purpose is to be seen. Two points deserve attention. First, is it fair that those who "top up" the cup should be guilty of the full contents of the cup? The answer is to be found in an illustration from momentum, which involves of course a quite different metaphor. Suppose that some freight cars are running loose on the railroad tracks in a marshaling yard. They are slowing down but still have some momentum, given to them by some pranksters who originally gave them a start. In their path is an automobile, stuck on the tracks because its driver has stalled his engine. It is likely that the freight cars, if left to themselves, will gently come to a stop before they reach the automobile. But more pranksters take advantage of the existing momentum and give the cars a further push so that they collide with the automobile and kill the driver. It could be argued that in giving the extra push *to what was already moving* they were morally responsible for the whole movement of the cars, from beginning to end. If the cars were not already in motion, the second group could not have mustered the strength to start them. They "took over" the momentum and added to it—with disastrous results. So did the Jews take over the moral momentum of the opposition to God.

Secondly, the *always* needs some explanation. It would fit in better if we could understand the meaning to be that the Jews were always engaged in the process of filling up. But the Greek aorist tense is against this interpretation. Paul's mind sums up the process, *so as . . . to fill up,* and he is best understood as seeing the level of the (liquid) contents rise swiftly to the top. Then at once a further reflection came into his mind. "I do not mean merely the Jewish opposition to us. I mean everything: the murder of the Lord and the prophets; our own expulsion; the failure to please God and the hostility to men." All this he summed up in one word, *always,* at the very end of the clause. We can do some justice to the completeness of the action and to the word *always* by rendering: "so as to bring their sins to the top of the vessel —always." The implication is that the vessel was already partly full; the Jews filled up the top half as it were. (Cf. the social expression, "May I fill up your cup?" when you have drunk only half of your coffee.)

But God's wrath has come upon them at last: Present fact and prophetic anticipation. Jewish obduracy was in itself a punishment (cf. Rom. 1:24). Former threatenings were not final (Jer. 4:27; 5:10, 18; 30:11; 46:28), but this was final. The Old Covenant was at an end and its blessings transferred to the church (Luke 20:16; cf. Acts 13: 46). The unbelieving nation was hurrying on to its destruction, marked by the fall of Jerusalem in A.D. 70. Yet still there is hope (Rom. 11:1, 25–32). (For the concept of wrath see discussion on 1 Thess. 1:10.)

This text appears in almost exactly the same form in the *Testament of Levi* (6:11), part of the *Testaments of the Twelve Patriarchs.*[1] This work is of Pharisaic origin and may be dated just before 100 B.C., though it has some later Jewish and even Christian additions. It was never canonical Scripture. Either the similarity is pure coincidence, or it is a Christian interpolation, or Paul was quoting from his *vade mecum* (as Charles calls it) or pocket companion. If it is a genuine quotation, Paul was turning the language of the Jews against themselves.

The words *has come* represent a single Greek verb which originally meant "to do something before someone else does" and so "to anticipate." A stock example would be "I anticipate you in reaching the city," which means that I arrived before you did. The verb is used in 1 Thessalonians 4:15 in the sense of "precede" or "forestall." It came to mean "to have just arrived" and "to arrive," and is used appropriately for the breaking in of the kingdom of God (Matt. 12:28; Luke 11:20). It brings out the sureness of the arrival. J. H. Moulton has a pleasing story of a tourist in the island of Cos (Acts 21:1) who called for a cup of coffee. The waiter, instead of responding with the possible "Coming, sir," cried out *ephthasa* (our verb). He implied that he was already at the table, presumably with the coffee! Perhaps we can retain the original meaning of the verb by putting some colloquial words on his lips: "I beat you to it!"[2]

---

1. See R. H. Charles, *The Apocrypha and Pseudepigrapha of the Old Testament* (Oxford: Clarendon Press, 1913), pp. 282–315.

2. J. H. Moulton, *A Grammar of New Testament Greek* (Edinburgh: T. & T. Clark, 1919), 1:135, 247.

Such is the Pauline certainty concerning the wrath of God. For the eye of faith, it is an observable phenomenon in its outworking, though the divine, personal attitude is not visible. It is a matter of desperate seriousness to reject the Messiah, and equally serious to spurn his messengers (Matt. 10:14–15, 40; John 13:20).

4. The Preachers: Their Inquiry an Occasion of Relief (2:17–3:10)

Separation from the beloved people was anguish and the apostles were eager to pay a return visit, but were prevented. Unable to endure the uncertainty, they sent Timothy to stiffen the morale of the church in its afflictions and to find out how the people were faring in their spiritual warfare. His return brought good news of the Thessalonians' steadfastness in faith and love and their constant regard for the preachers which the apostles thankfully received as if it were life itself. It sustained them in their affliction and in their longing to return once more to round off the faith of the Thessalonians. The whole section throbs with deep feeling.

(1) A visit prevented (2:17–20)

In their feeling of desolation the preachers resolved more than once to return to the Thessalonians, but Satan blocked the fulfillment of their plans. This was all the more frustrating as they had entertained such high hopes for the church: it would be their joy and glory at the Second Advent.

Verse 17: But since we were bereft of you: The picture of the nurse and the father (vv. 7, 11) has given way to that of the orphan. The word *bereft* occurs rarely in the Greek, and in its simple form of "orphan" it can be used of people deprived either of their children or of companions. Used literally in James 1:27, it has a wider reference in John 14:18 ("desolate"). It was appropriate to masterless disciples. Paul reversed the process. He and his colleagues were "discipleless apostles."

The Greek paragraph begins with a strong contrast—"But we, brethren." This is either a merely linguistic contrast with the "you" of verse 14, or is in contrast to the Jews who "oppose all men" (v. 15). How different were the apostles! Some evangelists today do not favor a return visit as they feel that the follow-up should be left to the local ministry. It is a reasonable point of view and emphasizes the itinerant nature of the evangelist's task. But Paul could not put aside his pastoral concern, any more than he could stifle his personal sense of loss. He was not content to say "separated," "torn away," "parted" or "deserted." He felt as desolate as the orphan who feels that the separation is forever. The intensity of his emotions may be judged by the fact that it was only *a short time* before thought was given to a return visit.

Perhaps as an implicit defense against possible slander ("he will not return; he has milked you dry"), the point was made that the separation was a physical one and no more than that. In a sense the preachers were still "with" the Thessalonians for the separation was *in person not in heart*. (See discussion on 2:4.) They felt the separation. They thought about the infant church. In imagination they saw its individual members as they had seen them a little while earlier. They willed to return to them. The whole personality of each preacher was directed to the Thessalonians. (The thought may be compared with Phil. 1:7.)

When the writers said *we endeavored,* they were saying more than that they had tried. The word implies speed, eagerness and seriousness. The preachers wanted no delay. They were not listless, and they did not treat the question as of little importance. (For speed cf. 2 Tim. 4:9, 21; for eagerness cf. Gal. 2:10; for seriousness cf. Eph. 4:3; 2 Tim. 2: 15. These distinctions are not watertight. Thus Titus 3:12 may combine speed and seriousness.) Intensity is expressed by *the more eagerly* and it is reinforced by *with great desire.* It is not an example of tautology. This is one of the few cases in the New Testament where *desire* has a good meaning (cf. Luke 22:15; Phil. 1:23).

Verse 18: Because we wanted to come to you—I, Paul, again and again—but Satan hindered us: This gives proof of the sentiments of the previous verse. The apostles' determination had been thwarted. In using the word *wanted* they were not merely saying in a general sort of way that the visit was attractive ("I want to take a trip to Europe"). To use the language of government, it was their policy. *I, Paul,* partially analyzes the *we.* It reveals the dominant personality in the group, the one who would be the chief target for any slanderous attacks. It need not imply that the others were reluctant. Repeatedly Paul was "all set to go" but "Satan threw up a roadblock" (the metaphor is used again in 3:11). The obstacle was human rather than an event in nature. The devil uses sinful men as his agents. The Thessalonian authorities might have forbidden the return of the preachers, or at any rate of their leader; or the Jews might have raised problems which detained them. Without doubt, the desired journey was a subject of prayer (cf. 3:11) —which is an answer to those who would limit prayer to "spiritual" matters. What Paul himself sought to avoid (1 Cor. 9:12) Satan for the moment accomplished. (Cf. 2 Cor. 2:11; 12:7.)

Verse 19: For what is our hope: The operative word is *for.* In Paul's swift thought he omitted a sentence. The result is something like this: "(Our keenness to return to you is natural and to be expected.) For . . . ." (See discussion on 2:1.) The explanation is given in the form of a rhetorical question and answer. There is no verb in the Greek, which allows for a certain elasticity of thought. As the reference is to the Lord's coming, a future tense would be fitting. But it would hardly be right to speak of what "will be" our hope then: "hope that is seen is not hope" (Rom. 8:24–25). The meaning is: "What is our hope (which will be realized) before our Lord Jesus at his coming? What will be our joy or crown of boasting then?" It is hardly necessary to say that Paul did not place his hope of his own salvation in the Thessalonians. His hope was for them, not in them. At the Second Advent, Paul would rejoice that the Thessalonians had endured to the end in steadfastness (cf. 1:3) as he had hoped they would, and his joy then would be a continuation of his joy over them now (3:9). (It must not be thought that hope is a weak term, with the suggestion of "I hope they will, but I have my doubts." He could make some very strong statements about the future without any suggestion of "hoping against hope," as in 4:13–18.)

The *crown of boasting* is a phrase which goes back to the Greek Old Testament (Prov. 16:31; Ezek. 16:12; 23:42). The imagery is that of the athletic contest in which the winner was given a chaplet or wreath to wear on his head (1 Cor. 9:24–25). Paul was confident that he would not have run his Thessalonian race in vain (cf. Phil. 2:16). His crown (not the royal but the victor's) would consist of his Thessalonian converts: a crown to be proud of. This reflects the spirit of an evangelist who does not boast of his own achievements. It is all due to the grace of God, who chose them (1:4), called them (2 Thess. 2:13–14; cf. 1 Thess. 2:12 and discussion) in spiritual power (1:5; 2:13) and keeps them (5:23): "He . . . is faithful, and he will do it" (5:24). The collection of "scalps" with which the modern cynic charges evangelists is far removed from the humble thanksgiving and confidence of the apostle Paul and his colleagues.

The *coming* of the Lord is, to transliterate the Greek, his *parousia*. The basic meaning of the word is "presence" (1 Cor. 16:17; Phil. 2:12), and it shades off into "presence begun," "becoming present," that is, "coming" (Phil. 1:26). The corresponding verb is used in John 11:28, "The Teacher is here." The noun took on a technical sense to describe the visit of a king or emperor. To this day novelists with a royal theme speak of a man "being ushered into the presence." It is but a short step to limit this meaning to the Presence or Second Advent of our Lord. (See Matt. 24:3; 1 Cor. 15:23; 2 Thess. 2:8; 2 Pet. 3:4; 1 John 2:28.) The subject is a serious one, and Paul treated it seriously. It is theological and practical (cf. 4:13–18).

In the question *Is it not you?* (which in the Greek is interjected in animated style between the words *boasting* and *before*), a single word *(kai)* has been left untranslated. The meaning is either "even you (the people we are accused of abandoning)" or "you also (in addition to other Christian groups)" (cf. Phil. 4:1). In either case the Thessalonians are very much included!

Verse 20: For you are our glory and joy: The final summary statement. The thought is: "(It is certainly you.) *For* . . . ." (Cf. v. 19 and 2:1.) For *glory* see the discussions on 2:6 and 12. Paul meant that the preachers' reputation or renown was to be found in the Thessalonians. There is an analogy in Paul's statement that the Corinthians themselves "are our letter of recommendation" (2 Cor. 3:1–2; cf. 1 Cor. 9:1–2). There is an interesting parallel between the divine and the human glory. Just as the glory of God reveals God, so the "glory" of the preachers reveals them as they really are. This is another aspect of their answer to calumny. *Joy* equals cause of joy.

(2) A mission inaugurated (3:1–5)

The suspense was more than they could bear. Timothy was sent to deal with a situation in which afflictions were in danger of becoming temptations, in spite of the fact that the church had already been told that afflictions are native to the Christian.

Verse 1: Therefore when we could bear it no longer, we were willing . . . : The phrase describes the breaking-point and its consequence. *Therefore* draws an inference from verses 17–20 and is reinforced by the statement of inability to endure. The *we* naturally oscillates: all three preachers found the situation intolerable; and two of them, Paul and Silvanus, decided to remain at Athens and they sent the third, Timothy, to Thessalonica. This seems the best explanation of the use of *we*. It is inconceivable that Timothy was aloof and detached while his two senior colleagues were breaking their hearts. Timothy was emotional too (see on 1:1).

The order of events must be determined from the present epistle in conjunction with the Acts. Paul had left Silas and Timothy at Beroea and had gone on to Athens. On arrival he urgently summoned them to join him (Acts 17:14–15). They did so, and Timothy was sent to Thessalonica (1 Thess. 3:1–2) and Silas to some other part of Macedonia (Acts 18:5). Paul left Athens and went to Corinth (Acts 18:1) where he was later joined by Silas and Timothy (Acts 18:5; 1 Thess. 3:6). The present epistle was written from Corinth.

It is to be observed that the man who was willing to "endure anything rather than put an obstacle in the way of the gospel of Christ" (1 Cor. 9:12) and who taught that "love bears all things" (1 Cor. 13:7) now seems to have fallen below his own standards. But the inconsistency is more apparent than real. The love of Christ inspired him to endure incredible hardship. It was love for the Thessalonians which made him toil at his labors to earn a living (2:8–9). It was love for them which made his present position unendurable. Love endures; and sometimes love, if it is love, cannot endure because of the anguish of uncertainty and of separation. There is a difference between enduring for someone beloved and enduring because of him. A mother will endure anything for her child, but to see him poised between life and death rends her heart. She will endure her suffering for him; she cannot endure his suffering for love of him. (Cf. 2:7.)

We were willing: This is more than mere acquiescence. The eager desire and the "policy" crystallized into a decision *to be left behind at Athens alone.* Paul and Silvanus, senior men though they were, felt a touch of desolation, expressed partly by the plural *alone* and partly by the verb. It is the same as that used by Martha, who complained that her sister was trying to leave her on her own to carry on the work of "serving" (Luke 10:40). Paul and Silvanus did not blame Timothy, as Martha blamed Mary, but they had the same feeling of being "left." How they wanted to go with him!

Verse 2: And we sent Timothy, our brother and God's servant in the gospel of Christ—an eminent position. In other connections Paul addressed Timothy as his *teknon,* a word which is variously translated by "child" or "son" (1 Tim. 1:2, 18; 2 Tim. 1:2; 2:1). This was appropriate when the apostle was speaking to his spiritual child. But he wanted Timothy to stand high with the Thessalonians, and by calling him *brother* he associated him with himself and thereby enhanced his authority—and in an atmosphere of affection. To this day listeners detect a difference when a bishop, instead of saying "one of my clergy" or "one of my staff," says "my brother."

Timothy was *God's servant.* But what sort of servant? Modern textual critics prefer the reading which gives "God's fellow worker." Such a daring expression is more likely to be original that a substitute. For elsewhere Paul called Timothy "my fellow worker" (Rom. 16:21) and Apollos and himself God's "fellow workers" (1 Cor. 3:9). In a sense it might be said that Timothy had two masters, but it would be nearer the truth to say that he served God through his aid to Paul. It is a bold rendering to speak of any man being "God's helper." God's need of human "help" must be carefully defined.

In any case Timothy's "help" is *in the gospel of Christ.* The farmer "works with" God in agriculture. If God ceased his activity there could be no harvest, and if men refused to work there would not be a harvest. Work is a divine ordinance and husbandry is under divine tuition (Gen. 2:15; 3:17–19; Isa. 28:26). Timothy's work was not the general work of food production. It was restricted to *the gospel,* though this is no narrow limitation. It affects the whole of personality and is not merely food for the body. It lasts longer because it is for time and for eternity.

In the last analysis there is no essential difference between the gospel of God, the gospel of Christ and our gospel. (See discussion on 1:5; 2:2, 4, 8–9; 2 Thess. 1:8; 2:14.) The gospel of God is no mere theory (even if true) about his nature. Even if it is a theory or statement, his nature is not quiescent. The gospel of God has as its heart the fact that "God sent forth his Son" (Gal. 4:4). The gospel of Christ preaches the word of the cross, Christ crucified (1 Cor. 1:18, 23; 2:2), and exults in his love and sacrifice (Gal. 2:20) to God (Eph. 5:2) in complete obedience to his Father (Phil. 2:8). This is indeed "our gospel" and "my gospel" (Rom. 2:16; 16:25; 2 Tim. 2:8). Wherever we start, whether with the gospel of God or the gospel of Christ or our gospel, we have to include sooner or later the same facts, the same mercy, and the same invitation. Paul's language means that Timothy was working "in the sphere of the gospel of Christ" which here covers both evangelism and pastoral care. For he was sent *to establish you.*

To establish you in your faith and to exhort you: A weighty task for such a man as young Timothy. The figurative use of *establish* is illumined by the literal. Children on the shore are fond of digging channels in the sand. The tide comes in and the water flows into the gulf. In spite of all the "repair operations" the sides keep caving in. By contrast a ravine of rock stays fast: "a great chasm has been fixed" (Luke 16:26). Timothy had the task of turning any sand into concrete. Simon (more fitting than Peter here?) had a similar ministry (Luke 22:32). It is remarkable that God chooses men in their weakness to strengthen others. Timothy seems to have been of a timid nature (1 Cor. 16:10–11). Peter was unstable (Luke 22:33–34). Paul must have been in a weak state (after being stoned) when he was "strengthening the souls of the disciples" (Acts 14:22). Notice the association here and in the Thessalonian passage (3:2–3) of the three concepts —strengthening, exhortation, and tribulation or affliction (same word, *thlipsis*).

But it is God who strengthens (Rom. 16:25; 2 Thess. 2:17; 3:3). How then could Timothy have been expected to do it? He had been sent *to exhort* (cf. discussion on 2:3, 11), and it meant that he had to speak and teach (cf. Acts 20:2; Titus 1:9). He would not merely tell his listeners of the desirability of the good life or bark out orders to "behave." One subject was always uppermost in his mind. Like Paul he would base his "persuasion with authority" on the mercies of God in Christ (cf. Rom. 12:1; 15:30; 1 Cor. 1:10). He would apply the Word, which has its effect (Isa. 55:11). It is thus possible for a man like Timothy and for God to strengthen the church. Therefore Timothy was indeed "God's helper." Paul understood this when he prayed to return to Thessalonica and remedy the "defects" in the faith of the Christians there (3:10).

In your faith: The phrase is best left at the end of the verse, where it appears in the Greek. The idea is that Timothy should strengthen the Thessalonians by exhortation "in the interests of your faith." (Cf. 2 Cor. 1:6, "in the interests of your comfort," literal.) Thus if a man asks by whom he is to be strengthened, the answer is threefold: God does it; the preacher or teacher does it; and he himself does it. Faith grows in response to God's Word through the minister, and if a man's faith increases (that is, if he believes more earnestly), he is himself strengthened. In other words, "he does it"—but the glory belongs to God. However little faith is, if it is genuine faith it can grow because it has vitality (see Matt. 17:20; cf. 13:32). Strengthen your hearts (Jas. 5:8)!

Verse 3: That no one be moved by these afflictions: Everything turns on how the "movement" is brought about. The verb in question is not found elsewhere in the Greek Bible and its meaning is obscure. As far back as Homer it was used of dogs wagging their tails and so came to mean "to fawn on." In the story of Odysseus we read of animals refraining from attacking men, and jumping up and down, fawning on them and wagging their tails. "As when dogs fawn around their master on his return from a banquet, for he always brings them scraps to still their hunger." [1] This picture fits in with the thought of the epistle. Morale is tested and may be low "in these afflictions," (notice the "in") and advantage may be taken of the church. The opponents (the Jews?) approach the Christians, fawning on them and looking for a morsel. A change in the method of persecution is suggested, even if only temporary. Not violence (Acts 17:6) but guile is visualized (something different from 2:14–15). The "morsel" which the "tail-wagging" persecutors look for is of course the abandonment of the Christian faith. The Thessalonians must not let themselves be "fawned upon."

You yourselves know that this is to be our lot: A variation on a persistent theme. The writers constantly appealed to the Thessalonians' knowledge in confirmation of what was being written (1:5; 2:1, 5, 11; 3:4; 4:2; 5:2). No thought of "fate" is to be discerned in *our lot.* The thought is that "we are in position for this," just as Paul was "at his post for the defense of the gospel" (Phil. 1:16; cf. Luke 2:34— "set for the fall and rising of many"). The *this* is a loose reference to the *afflictions* in the preceding phrase; "to be afflicted is our lot." The *our* ("we" in the Greek, as part of the verb—"we are placed") means Christians generally. Ultimately it was God who put Paul in particular "in position" for the defense of the gospel, and it was God who put Christians in general in position to be afflicted. A possible rendering is "we are appointed for this (i.e., to be afflicted)." Attention is thus

---

1. Homer *Odyssey* 10. 214–19. Cf. 16. 5–10; 17. 302.

drawn to the divine control, which is brought out otherwise by saying that "it is necessary for us to (we must) enter into the kingdom of God through many afflictions" (Acts 14:22). Divine appointment implies necessity for humans. Behind the appointment lies the love and wisdom of God. The possibility of suffering is an encouragement to constant prayer and to a constant dependence on God. If a sensitive Christian knows that the blow may fall at any moment, then he is always looking to God to sustain and deliver him. The spiritual life is fostered "moment by moment." And mature Christians grow in experience whereby they may aid their brethren who are younger in the faith (cf. 2 Cor. 1:3–7).

The "being fawned upon" of this verse anticipates the temptation of verse 5.

Verse 4: For when we were with you, we told you—prophecy, fulfillment, experience. The missionaries had not merely "put it on the record" by giving a single warning (and thus giving themselves an alibi, so to speak), but had repeatedly prepared the church for its future. This is an example for the modern pastor and counselor: he should teach basic doctrine to new converts and also prepare them for coming battles. In saying that *we* are on the road to affliction, the authors were thinking of Christians generally. There is a touch of divine predestination in *we were to,* similar to our Lord's statement that "the Son of man is to be delivered into the hands of men" (Matt. 17:22). It is no novelty to the instructed Christian (1 Pet. 4:12–14), who knows that affliction produces the experience, character and confidence of the veteran, who is proof against "sudden wild alarms" (cf. Rom. 5:3–5; for similar language, see 2 Thess. 3:10). The preachers were practical realists as well as pastoral theologians and evangelists. The influence which is built up by a minister is partly due to his wise foresight and being proved right. If he is tempted to say, "I told you so," he should exhibit the same love as Paul did.

Verse 5: For this reason, when I could bear it no longer: Paul is the chief sufferer of verse 1 (cf. 2:18). He was obviously the moving spirit in the sending of Timothy. The *reason* is the certainty of affliction.

I sent that I might know your faith—Paul's main concern. The separation was distressing but his motive was not merely to relieve his own anxiety. He wanted to find out the state of their *faith.* Note the basic and inclusive term for the life of those who have responded to the gospel. Without faith we have at best a mere formality. With real faith there is also worship and work. The aorist tense of the verb *know* implies "to get to know," "to find out."

For fear that somehow: The phrase introduces two fears, one referring to the past and the other to the future. The past is unalterable; the future is open, even though the *labor* is in the past: "for fear that our labor might turn out to be in vain" (when we hear the news). It would prove to be in vain if Timothy arrived after the Thessalonians had passed the point of no return, or if they had not yet passed it but Timothy could not prevent its occurrence (cf. Gal. 2:2). (For *labor* see discussion on 1:3.) There is a sense in which it is never in vain (1 Cor. 15:58): "Well done, good and faithful [not successful] servant" (Matt. 25:21, 23). Note that the tempter takes advantage of an existing situation. In times of affliction some Christians are a sitting target.

(3) Good news reported (3:6–10)

Timothy's return and report was a gospel in itself, inspiring new life in the hard-pressed preachers. They could not adequately express their thankfulness for their new joy. They prayed the more ardently that they might visit the Thessalonians again and complete their ministry among them.

Verse 6: But now that Timothy has come to us from you, and has brought us the good news: Life from the dead! The mission (3:2, 5) was successful. Timothy had "found out," had exhorted, and had strengthened the church. He brought news of the essentials, of their *faith and love* (cf. Gal. 5:6; 1 Thess. 1:3), and of the subsidiary and personal blessings, the undying remembrance *(you always remember)* of the preachers and the longing to see them again—a yearning which was reciprocated. A little imagination can easily reconstruct the scene of Timothy's arrival with his glowing account, his messages *from you,* his detailing of incidents, and his mentioning of names.

Has brought . . . the good news: The phrase translates a single Greek verb usually restricted to the meaning "preach the gospel." It was indeed "gospel news" because it concerned the gospel, but it does not here mean that Timothy evangelized his colleagues. It is in fact a daring use of the verb figuratively. The news was so momentous, it brought such relief to the apostles' sense of desolation and concern, that Paul chose the greatest illustration at his command to express his joy. His burden rolled from his back as his sin had done when he first believed. John Bunyan has described how when Christian reached the Cross his burden rolled "till it came to the mouth of the sepulchre, where it fell in, and I saw it no more. Then was Christian glad and lightsome, and said with a merry heart . . . ." *The Pilgrim's Progress* reflects authentic Christian experience, and Paul chose the joyous reception of the gospel as an illustration of his feelings at the news brought by Timothy. On at least one other occasion Paul was to use the "big illustration." There is only one possible illustration of the universal significance of Christ, and that is Adam. There is only one possible illustration

of the blessing which he brings, and that is the scale of Adam's
condemnation. And even this fails—it is not big enough ("much more"
Rom. 5:15, 17).

Verse 7: For this reason, brethren, in all our distress and afflictions:
The blessed impact of affliction on affliction. Timothy came from an afflicted church (vv. 3–4) with good news for afflicted men. For Paul and
Silvanus were hard pressed. The *distress* exercises its compelling power
over them, forcing them into circumstances against their will. It may
be need of money or external constraint, or perhaps overwork at the
trade of tentmaking. The *affliction* suggests a pressure or a "squeeze."
The corresponding verb is used of a path which has been "squeezed
thin" and has a narrow gate to match it (Matt. 7:14). The source of
the pressure is personal (2 Thess. 1:6–7) and the "rest" from it means
relaxation. The pressure is "off." The thought is permitted that in the
severity of *affliction* the mind is narrowed—not in the ordinary sense
of becoming narrow-minded but restricted to one thought: the impact
of persecution. The afflicted man is "cabin'd, cribb'd, confin'd, bound
in." [1]

We have been comforted about you through your faith: The news
from Thessalonica braced them. The faith of the church was the great
concern of the preachers (3:2, 5). To learn that it was sound and
strong encouraged them *in* (their) *distress and affliction* and to face it.
For the word *comforted* see discussion on 2:3, 11; 3:2. We need not
think that Timothy set out deliberately to "persuade with authority."
His report in itself would do that. The *reason* is the faith, love, remembrance and longing of verse 6.

Verse 8: For now we live, if you stand fast in the Lord: This elabo-
rates the reason for the comfort (v. 7). The "big illustration" is continued, for the gospel can be interpreted in terms of "comfort" (Luke
2:25; 2 Thess. 2:16—*paraklēsis)* and of "life" (Rom. 6:23). The implication is that *distress and affliction* (v. 7) are a form of death. It is not
implied that if Timothy had brought bad news the preachers' life in
Christ would have come to an end. The modern interpreter would illustrate by "a shot in the arm." Paul chose the reception of the gospel, but
it is no more than an illustration.

There is still an element of the hypothetical. "We go on living if *you*
go on standing. . . ." There was still room for growth (v. 10). "To
stand" is the opposite of collapse. If men are not to "sag," they need
"backbone." Hence Timothy was sent to strengthen the Thessalonians
(v. 2). (For the concept of "standing," see Rom. 14:4; 1 Cor. 16:13;
Gal. 5:1; Phil. 1:27; 4:1; 2 Thess. 2:15.)

---

1. William Shakespeare, *Macbeth,* Act 3, Scene 4.

Verse 9: For what thanksgiving can we render to God: Here is the Christian paradox. Timothy worked; the Thessalonians continued to exercise faith and love and thereby inspired joy; but God, not the church, was to be thanked. The *joy* was of the utmost purity because it was *before our God.* The writers were fully aware that God knew about it and that they were in his presence. *For* is either parallel to the "for" of verse 8 or the thought is: "(This is overwhelming.) For what. . . ." The *can* is important. It means that the apostle felt the hopelessness of the task of giving to God an adequate or corresponding thanksgiving. This is implied by the verb *render,* which appears as verb and noun in Luke 14:12–14. When you give your reception or banquet, invite the poor: they cannot invite you back to a similar function and make a return to you on the same scale. There is a lesson here for all who have received a blessing, particularly that of answered prayer. They should notice the answer as an answer and should give thanks—or rather they should "return thanks." Thanksgiving is the only "repayment" to God which can match the scale of his giving. Paul found that he could not make his thanksgiving "big" enough.

Verse 10: Praying . . . that we may . . . supply what is lacking in your faith: Prayerful joy and joyous prayer. The participle links on to "the joy which we feel" of the previous verse. The prayer is that of petition. It went on *night and day* like the work (2:9). It was the background of their conscious hours and they were constantly lifting their hearts to God. We see here an intensity of feeling, a frequency of practice, a seriousness of purpose, and a concentration of thought in prayer. It was not a hasty "saying their prayers" once or twice a day. The deep emotion did not create a moral and spiritual blindness. Realism persisted and thought could still be given to *what is lacking in your faith.* The "deficiencies" remind us that man the sinner "falls short" of the glory of God (Rom. 3:23; but cf. 5:2). Faith also can "fall short" of certain qualities. It may be weak or incompletely instructed or forgetful. But if it is true faith it joins us to God in Christ. Salvation turns not on the perfection of faith, but its reality. It is a case of the mustard seed again (see 3:2 and note).

To *supply* renders a verb which is used of mending fishing nets (Matt. 4:21; Mark 1:19). The translation is thereby suggested: Paul prayed that he might see the Thessalonians again and "mend the gaps in their faith." It would involve unfolding the unsearchable riches of Christ, leading the disciples into the unexplored territories of the Christian faith (Eph. 3:8); in more pedestrian terms, teaching the content of Christian truth and the obligations of Christian discipleship. Paul could not wait for the visit to materialize, but proceeded at once with his instruction in the fourth chapter.

5. The Preachers and the Thessalonians: Both Parties as Subjects of Prayer (3:11–13)

Hitherto Satan had prevented the preachers from visiting the church again. Prayer was therefore offered that the divine providence would bring them to the Thessalonians. The news had shown that their faith and love had remained constant. The only possible prayer was therefore for increase—that it might "abound."

(1) Prayer for the preachers' journey (3:11)

It was not that they did not know the road. They needed the divine providence to ensure that they actually traveled on it.

Now may our God and Father himself, and our Lord Jesus, direct our way to you: Divine sovereignty in control of a journey! The significant *our* implies a personal relationship, the doctrine of adoption (Rom. 8:15; Gal. 4:5–7) and the disciple's pledge. The characteristic *himself* (cf. 4:16; 5:23; 2 Thess. 2:16; 3:16) is a repudiation of deism, the theory that God created the world and then left it to be self-working. The title *Lord Jesus* identifies the historical Jesus with the ascended and exalted Lord. The close association of Jesus with God is remarkable (cf. discussion on 1:1). From the early days of the church he was regarded as Savior and had a place in men's prayers (Acts 7:59–60). In providence also he was believed to be present and active. (What is implicit here in the Thessalonian text is explicit in Colossians 1:17, "In him the universe is a system"—literal). Most striking is the fact that the verb is singular though the subject is plural or at least dual. In structure the sentence is the expression of a wish ("O that God . . . and Jesus may direct. . .").

God is more than a signpost or a kindly bystander who gives us directions for our route ("go east three blocks and then turn right"). The verb *direct* is used in the expression "to guide our feet" (Luke 1:79) and "direct your hearts" (2 Thess. 3:5). The *way* is a journey and the *direct* is the opposite of Satan's hindrance (2:18) though the same metaphor is preserved. We should see therefore the overruling providence of God which (or rather "who" himself!) facilitates the journey to Thessalonica of the preachers who, though they do not know the details of God's master plan, are yet deeply aware that they are in his hands. It might be that the way would open for them to disengage from their immediate involvement; it might be that some turn in human affairs would bring them to the city (as the opposition to Paul and then the court case brought him later to Rome—at government expense); or even that the weather and conditions of travel generally would help them on their way. (A stranded traveler might lament his predicament and then meet in his hotel the very man who could open doors to his final goal.) Doctrine and religious experience are thus united. The prayer that God in Christ, the object of faith and obedience, who is known in prayer and worship, would lead them on their way is a charter to all those devout souls who seek his guidance and help in such ordinary matters as a journey. The verse corresponds to the first part of verse 10.

(2) Prayer for the church's growth (3:12–13)

The prayer was not for any kind of love, no matter what. They already had Christian love. The preachers prayed that it might overflow. Even this had a further purpose, that the Lord might so hallow them that the divine scrutiny would find no defect at the Second Advent.

Verse 12: And may the Lord make you increase and abound in love to one another and to all men, as we do to you: A greater prayer than the previous one for the preachers' journey. Another visit could be only temporary; Paul looked to the Second Advent. He prayed that through their experience of the Lord the Thessalonians would exercise love with greater thoughtfulness and imagination, with greater intensity and wider range, linking a deeper emotion to a growing purposefulness. He prayed that their love, like the sea coming in to a tidal river, would flow strongly up river, rising to the top of the banks and overflowing into the fields on either side. The warm "family love" or "love of the brethren" is to be directed to the non-Christian also. The love exercised toward the unbeliever may be a "one-way" traffic. He may answer kindness with kindness, but as an unbeliever he is out of his depth. It takes "all the saints" in the interplay of their fellowship with one another to grasp the love of Christ, and he does not yet belong to them. Even the individual believer does not by himself comprehend the breadth and length and height and depth of Christ's love, for every other saint has his own story to tell of the Lord's mercy—ever the same but always with exquisite variety (cf. Eph. 3:17–19). (See 2 Thess. 1:3 for the answer to the prayer.)

Paul was a dynamic rather than a static personality, pressing on rather than standing still. He was no mere discontented critic but a pastor with large ambitions for his converts. They had reached a high standard, but Paul wanted "more and more" (4:1, 10), though not mere intensity (Phil. 1:9–11; cf. Phil. 4:17). Though he had converts he wanted to win "more" (1 Cor. 9:19). Paul "pressed on" in his sermons: "until midnight"; "still longer"; "until daybreak" (Acts 20:7, 9, 11); and likewise in his search for language to express the inexpressible divine love. He spoke of "surpassing grace" (2 Cor. 9:14); the "immeasurable greatness of his power" (Eph. 1:19); the "immeasurable riches of his grace" (Eph. 2:7); "an eternal weight of glory beyond all com-

parison" (2 Cor. 4:17); the "unsearchable riches of Christ" (Eph. 3:8).
In a sense Paul gave up the impossible task—God's gift bursts the
bounds of any story, baffles the subtlest expositor, outsoars every scale
of values, is inexpressible (2 Cor. 9:15). His power at work within us by
comparison reduces our largest petitions and our broadest concep-
tions to an infinitesimal point (cf. Eph. 3:20). The love of Christ
surpasses knowledge. Paul thus recognized the hopelessness of his
search for adequate language and the impossibility of knowing what
surpasses knowledge. Yet he could still pray that men might know the
love of Christ, for he knew it in his own experience. And the cross is its
measure (Eph. 3:19; Gal. 2:20).

The words *make you* must not be taken in the sense of "make you
against your will" ("If you don't, I will make you."). The prayer was
offered that they might love more and more, and if the answer came it
would be due to the Lord. Perhaps "inspire" would suit instead of
"make." (For the wider love cf. Matt. 5:43–48; 2 Pet. 1:7.) The
preachers set the example (cf. discussion on 1:6).

*Verse 13: So that he may establish your hearts unblamable in
holiness:* The purpose of the prayer of verse 12. For *establish* see on
3:2 and for *hearts* see discussion on 2:4. Observe the parallelism between "strengthening you" (3:2) and "strengthening your hearts" (3:
13). The latter emphasizes the inner life. If the Thessalonians were to
love more and more in a continuous development, their inner attitude
("hearts") would become constant, "fixed" (Luke 16:26) and sustained. There would be no cessation, no fluctuation. Character would
be formed and settled. They would be in a state of *holiness* wherein
no flaw would be found.

This must not be interpreted as secular love. It began as *love to one
another* (v. 12), which means the mutual love of believing men. The
purpose is ideal and some would say that it is unattainable in this life.
Even so the goal is sound. The *holiness* which is "separation unto God"
is not that of "sacred" objects like church ornaments or communion
vessels, which are dedicated to God and are used in worship and
nothing else. It is an ethical and spiritual holiness, the constant love
of believing men (with all that "believing" implies) for their fellows
in Christ and for all men. (Cf. 1 John 4:7–8.)

The adjective *unblamable* is proleptic. We should render thus: ". . .
your hearts (so that they may be) unblamable . . ." (For the hope,
cf. 1 Cor. 1:8; Phil. 3:21; for the prayer, cf. 1 Thess. 5:23.) This is a
question of Christian character or sanctification. It does not conflict with
justification by faith.

Before our God and Father, unto whom all hearts are open, all
desires known, and from whom no secrets are hidden. All hypocrisy
and all merely nominal Christianity is thus ruled out. (Cf. v. 11.)

At the coming of our Lord Jesus with all his saints—when the God who tests apostolic hearts (see discussion on 2:4) will test the church members also. (Cf. Rom. 14:10–12; 2 Cor. 5:10.) The joyous hope of the Second Advent (4:17) is tempered, though not diminished, by its serious aspect. It is to be understood as the judgment of justified men, for whom there is no condemnation (Rom. 8:1). Their lives will be assessed. In Christ, God is eternally "for us" (Rom. 8:31–34). *Saints* may include angels.

Verses 12–13 correspond to the second part of verse 10 and especially to "what is lacking in your faith." Faith must work itself out in the love, the Christian love, which is holiness.

III. MATTERS PRACTICAL AND HORTATORY
(4:1–5:24)

After preliminary recognition of progress made by the readers in their walk with God, the preachers recalled the instructions which they had originally given. God willed the sanctification of the Thessalonians which, in view of the contemporary situation, was expounded as a sexual abstinence. Love of the brotherhood did not need to be mentioned, but restless excitability and idleness were to be avoided. Some distressing misconceptions about the Second Advent were cleared away and watchfulness advocated. This was to be a means of mutual encouragement for which a theological foundation was suggested. Exhortations of an ethical and spiritual nature followed in some detail, culminating in prayer for the readers.

1. Holiness—A Divine Requirement (4:1–12)

The Thessalonians already knew that holiness was required of them. They were obligated to act on their knowledge by abstaining from all illicit sex. Sex indeed was itself to be regarded as within the sphere of holiness rather than of heathen passion and selfish excess. The readers knew that God would judge in these matters, for holiness was the very air which Christians should have breathed from the time of their conversion. The giver of the Holy Spirit was not to be slighted. They were already manifesting Christian love. They were urged to continue in this more and more, to refrain from feverish speculation and a disinclination to work, to preserve the peace of the church and to remember the importance of "public relations."

(1) Preliminary encouragement (4:1–2)

A foundation was laid by a reminder of the commands given by the preachers during their visit. The commands had been received and obeyed: the readers' walk was pleasing God. This was recognized—for their encouragement. Now they were urged to "abound" in it the more.

[93]

Verse 1: Finally, brethren, we beseech and exhort you in the Lord Jesus: They were to make continued effort in view of the Second Advent. Dr. Margaret E. Thrall, following A. N. Jannaris, has shown that in *loipon oun* (translated *finally,* RSV), each particle reinforces the other. We ought in consequence to render by "therefore." [1] The topic, though new, grows out of the preceding paragraph. *Beseech* calls for an answer. For *exhort* see discussion on 3:2. *In the Lord Jesus* covers both verbs: challenge, persuasion and authority are thus combined.

That as you learned . . . more and more—a flying start! The readers had already accepted the apostles' teaching about the manner of their Christian "walk" (KJV) to which they were obligated (2:12 and discussion) and which would please God (cf. 2:4 and discussion), and they were acting on it, as the writers told them for their encouragement. Their spirits must not flag, nor should they merely continue. Their love for one another and for all men, and their obedience to God, should become even more dedicated, more detailed, deeper. More spiritual victories must be won. They must become ever more sensitive to the demands of the divine will.

Verse 2: For you know . . . : "(This is no innovation, suddenly sprung on you.) For you can identify the charges which we gave you" and can disentangle them from our narrative of the facts of the gospel. We might expect "which the Lord gave through us," which would not have been wrong. The point of the expression is that the apostles did not utter a series of naked demands. "You do this. We tell you to." The words were not spoken in a vacuum. In the absence of air, even the sound of words would have been absent. But the "air" in this case was —the Lord. Everything was said by the preachers, everything was heard by the Thessalonians, "in Christ." This is not the last word on this famous formula but it is applicable here. In the absence of that atmosphere it is doubtful if the instructions would have been accepted.

(2) Sex (4:3–8)

God's immediate requirement was holiness in matters of sex. This was its point of impact at the time. The negative emphasis was due to the prevailing social conditions and the religious practices of heathenism. The rights of the present or future husband were to be respected. Looming over human behavior and human rights was the judgment of God. He who gave the Holy Spirit had called for holiness from the time of every man's conversion. He was not to be slighted.

Verse 3: For this is the will of God, your sanctification: Not the whole of God's will (cf. 5:18), but God's will in its immediate application to the Thessalonians. They had accepted the teaching and their "walk"

1. Margaret E. Thrall, *Greek Particles in the New Testament: Linguistic and Exegetical Studies* (Leiden: E. J. Brill, 1962), pp. 25–27.

was pleasing God (v. 1); they knew the specific instructions (v. 2). Now came the detailed application, not only "through the Lord Jesus," but as *the will of God*. A somewhat similar Greek construction (1 Pet. 2:15) prompts the suggestion that we interpret thus: "For this is the will of God, that you should abstain . . . that each of you should know. . . ." *Your sanctification* is then in parenthesis, with this result: "This is the will of God (he wills your sanctification) that you should . . . . " To be sanctified, hallowed, consecrated thus involves at least an abstinence. There is a genuinely negative aspect to Christianity. Some deeds must not be done by Christians. In the broadest sense *immorality* implies all deviation from the moral law, but it has become restricted to sexual looseness. Here it means illicit sexual relations of every kind.

In the Septuagint, *sanctification* is redolent of the cultus: only the holy can approach God. Its basic idea is that of separation, to be set apart for God. All Christian believers are, in principle, holy ("the saints"), but some are more holy than others in that they have less of "the world" in them and that they walk more closely with God. It is thus possible to grow in holiness, and the growth involves ethical obedience to God. It presupposes the atonement (Heb. 10:10, 14) and is the moral outworking of the Christian's call. It is thus to be "pursued" (Heb. 12:14; cf. Rom. 6:19, 22). It is the mark of a living Christianity, and though it is a moral and spiritual goal for men, it is a divine achievement in men. It is due to God (5:23), to Christ (1 Cor. 1:2, 30), and to the Holy Spirit (Rom. 15:16; 1 Thess. 4:8; 2 Thess. 2:13; 1 Pet. 1:2).

It must be emphasized that holiness or sanctification is more than sexual correctness. But in the Christian life there is often one danger to which an individual or a group may be exposed. With some it may be sheer materialism; with others gossip. Some speak of their "besetting sin" or even of their "Achilles heel." Our Lord understood this: "If your right eye causes you to sin . . . " (Matt. 5:29–30). James spoke of a man who "fails in one point" (Jas. 2:10). With the Thessalonians the danger was sex. Public opinion regarded promiscuity with indifference and, if challenged, might even refer to their (pagan) religious rites in justification. (See on 2:3.) Holiness affects the body as well as the mind or soul. This derives from the Christian doctrine of personality. Man is not a soul living in a body—so that what happens to the body is of no consequence; man is an animated body. Body and soul form a unity. It is in accordance with this that the Bible teaches the resurrection of the dead rather than the immortality of the soul—which is Greek and not biblical thought. It is odd to reflect that "John Brown's body lies a'mouldering in the grave, But his soul goes marching on" might have come straight out of Plato! It is significant that the "enlightened" heathen, when converted, had to be taught their Christian duty with regard to marriage, and in some detail. This anticipates verse 5.

Verse 4: That each one of you know how to take a wife for himself in holiness and honor: This translation is a great improvement on the KJV. The word translated *wife* is literally "vessel" and has a wide variety of meanings. Scholars have been divided as to whether it here means the husband's "body" or his "wife." Against "body" is the fact that the verb means "to acquire" and not "to have acquired, to possess." A man can hardly acquire a body, but he can acquire a wife. In what sense?

It might seem at first that Paul was thinking of a bachelor seeking the hand of a lady in marriage. But Oepke suggests, with a delicacy which matches that of the apostle, that the marriage is already established. Paul was suggesting that in marital cohabitation the husband must constantly woo his wife and in a manner which honors her and does not treat her as the object of mere lust. This spirit will accord with God's ordinance (Gen. 1:28) and will be within the life of holiness. If this standard is maintained, "each one of you" will "know how to take his own vessel repeatedly." It may be right to argue that the Christian wife is the "weaker vessel" (1 Pet. 3:7) of God; but she is still "his" wife. The use of the term "vessel" reminds the husband that his wife belongs to God. Let him therefore "take her" as God commanded and not as lust directs.[1]

Verse 5: Not in the passion of lust like heathen who do not know God: It ought to be the passion of love. There is a decisive difference. In the passion of lust any woman will suit or the actual wife is treated as if she were any woman. In the passion of love only one woman is desired, the wife. And it is the wife as wife, not merely as woman, because she is the sole object of the tender love of the husband. (Cf. Rom. 1:26; Col. 3:5.) The implied construction is: ". . . not (taking her) . . . as the heathen (do) who . . . ." Notice the close connection between religion and ethics: knowing, or not knowing, God affects personal relationships.

The *heathen who do not know God* is an expression which goes back to Jeremiah 10:25 (the LXX Greek is almost identical; cf. Ps. 79:6—Ps. 78:6, LXX). The meaning is not "those (particular) heathen who do not know God (though some may know him)"; but "the heathen, who (by definition) do not know God." The point is important. It is in direct contrast to all those enthusiasts who are trying to persuade the modern church to listen to and learn from "other religions." Christians have indeed much to learn and in humility they ought to be teachable. But there is no truth in any non-Christian religion, moral or spiritual, which is not already in Christ. "Hear ye him!" It might be that in certain given circumstances a modern heathen might show a humility which put an

---

1. See Oepke, *Das Neue Testament Deutsch*, p. 170. Cf. Tobit 8:1–9.

individual Christian to shame. But this is a call to return to Christian discipleship and its already known standards. The failure of Christian obedience does not imply any superiority of "other religions."

The parallelism in the Old Testament texts cited between "knowing God" and "calling on his name" suggests that vital religion is implied, not theoretical knowledge. Men do have the knowledge of God available, but they suppress it or distort it (Rom. 1:18–23). This is strictly knowledge "about God." It is enough to condemn, but it reveals nothing of his saving purpose. (Cf. Acts 14:15–17; 17:30; 1 Cor. 1:21; Gal. 4:8–9; Titus 1:16. For ignorance, cf. 1 Cor. 15:34; 1 Pet. 2:15—the ignorant will talk!) Failure to know God is culpable. Its final judgment, "I have nothing to do with you" (Matt. 25:12, literal), is the judicial acceptance of the settled attitude of unbelieving men.

It is ironical that when some Christian leaders are advocating an irenical, "listening" approach to "other religions," the will and testament of Mr. Nehru, prime minister of India, forbade religious ceremonies after his death on the ground that he did not believe in them and rejected the shackles of religion and tradition that bind and constrain and divide and suppress. Consult again Galatians 4:8–9! It is Christ who makes men free (cf. John 8:31–36).

Knowledge about God is not to be despised. Without it we cannot preach Christ. But to carry conviction, the preacher must himself know God as well as know about him; and to be converted a man must believe the preached statements in some form, however elementary, and must trust Christ. Faith involves both credence and commitment; a sincere acceptance of the truths of the gospel (or why yield to Christ?) and a handing over of oneself to him. Acts 10:34–35 is no charter for "other religions" as such.

Verse 6: That no man transgress, and wrong his brother in this matter: Holiness requires that a man should not overstep the mark (by adultery or fornication) and thus (in the matter of sexual behavior) defraud his brother of his exclusive conjugal rights (1 Cor. 7:4; the RSV's "rule" means "have authority") or of the virginity of his future wife. The thought runs on naturally from verses 3 to 5 and is continued in the "uncleanness" of verse 7. There is hardly likely to be any reference to dishonesty in business, which would require a plural, "in (business) matters." How heinous if the defrauded brother were a Christian! (Cf. 1 Cor. 6:8.)

Because the Lord is an avenger in all these things, as we solemnly forewarned you: A motive for obedience. Christians should obey because God demands it; because they are not their own (1 Cor. 6:19–20); because gratitude should inspire it (Luke 7:47); because baptism implies it (Rom. 6:1–4); because holiness is both the atmosphere and the territory of the believer (1 Thess. 4:7); and because a disobedient

Christian is a living contradiction (v. 8). Behind these motives stands the divine sanction. Disobedience has consequences.

The immediate allusion is to Psalm 94:1 (but cf. Deut. 32:35; Rom. 12:19; Heb. 10:30). The *avenger* is not motivated by petty spite or malice, still less by temper. God is the upholder of the right and the last word is with him. (See discussion on 1:10.) This raises the whole question of the wrath of God in relation to the Christian. Either the sex offender turns out not to be a Christian at all, in which case he is still under wrath (Eph. 2:3); or he is an example of "sin in believers." If he is indeed a believer, we must remember certain factors in interpreting the apostle's words. Christ intercedes for him (Rom. 8:34, cf. 8:1; Heb. 7:25; 1 John 2:1). Christ is our deliverer from wrath, and God has not destined us for wrath (1 Thess. 1:10; 5:9); through him we shall be saved from wrath (Rom. 5:9). Even so the Christian has to be reminded of the supremacy of the right, and God vindicates it by the process of discipline. The divine judgment, for the Christian, takes the form of education, training, discipline, chastening (1 Cor. 11:30–32; 2 Cor. 6:9; cf. Heb. 12:5–11). What would be condemnation for the finally impenitent is discipline for the disobedient believer. It may take place in the present life or in the assessment at the Day of Judgment (Rom. 14:10; 1 Cor. 3:15; 2 Cor. 5:10). This ought not to come as a surprise to the Thessalonians. They had been warned, and warned with great seriousness.

Verse 7: For God has not called us for uncleanness, but in holiness: This is the all-inclusive purpose of God's call. The reference to the call was a reminder of the solemnity of the occasion of their conversion. (See on 2:12.) God was speaking to them and they knew it. He was calling them to the closest fellowship with himself—the Holy One of Israel (Isa. 43:3)—and they yielded. As members of the people of God they were holy. But holiness is not mechanical; they must become holy (cf. Deut. 7:6; Lev. 11:44–45; 20:26). Perhaps the best comment is 1 Peter 1:15–16 with its similar association of God's call, God's holiness, and God's demand for holiness.

Holiness includes morality, but it must not be regarded as secular morality. It is conceivable in theory (though unlikely in practice) that a man might keep the moral law perfectly. Even if such a man could be found, he would not thereby be holy. This is the glaring weakness of humanism. Holiness means walking with God. "Can two walk together, except they be agreed?" (Amos 3:3, KJV). The appeal in verses 6 and 7 is to conscience, not to a calculation of punishment or reward.

The prepositions should be given their due stress. God called us (at conversion; cf. 2 Thess. 2:14) not for the purpose of, with the object of, uncleanness but "in the sphere of holiness." The latter suggests the territory from which the gospel call was sounded and the atmosphere in which it was given.[1] Notice the same phrase in verse 4. Married life should be consciously lived in the same context as conversion.

Verse 8: Therefore whoever disregards this, disregards not man but God, who gives his Holy Spirit to you: He is swimming against the tide. The "setter aside" is like an executor who reads a will and then deliberately acts contrary to its provisions (Gal. 3:15); who knows a law and substitutes another of his own making (Mark 7:9; cf. Heb. 10:28); who knows the grace of God and offers instead the condemnation of law (Gal. 2:21). Only here he sets aside God. (Cf. Luke 10:16.) He is swimming against the tide because, if he is an authentic Christian, he is working against the Holy Spirit (note the "Holy") whom God gives to the individual believer. The allusion is to Ezekiel 36:27; 37:14.

Another metaphor is yet more appropriate. Such a man profanes the temple (Acts 21:28), for he himself is the temple of the Holy Spirit (1 Cor. 6:19; cf. 1 Cor. 3:16–17). (The adjective of the verb which we have above rendered by "profane" is used in association with "unclean" in Acts 10:14, 28; 11:8.) Marital looseness in the world conflicts with one of the institutions of creation (Gen. 2:24). If it occurs in the church of genuine believers, it does not undermine the authority of God—God is still God—but it sets him aside in the perpetrator's own estimation, goes against the whole thrust of the sanctifying Spirit, and defiles the man himself. This is the inference which is strongly drawn by the word *therefore.*

(3) Love, peace, and work (4:9–12)

Already taught by God, the readers needed no exhortation to love of the brotherhood. They were urged to continue in this more and more, and to set certain aims before themselves. They should live a quiet life, attend to their own affairs and work for their living. This would avoid giving the church a bad name for being parasites.

Verse 9: But concerning love of the brethren you have no need . . . one another: They did not need *to have anyone write* to them for the best of reasons. They were taught by God and in obedience were exercising love (v. 10). See on 3:12. The expressive word "God-taught" (a single word in the Greek) might at first suggest that apostolic ministry was not needed. But the continuous infinitive implies that the Thessalonians did not need anyone to "keep on writing" to them. They had learned the lesson. This pushes the question further back. Would they have been "God-taught" if the apostles had not visited them? The answer is that they would not. Two points follow. God's teaching is mediated: it may come through the Bible or the preacher, or through both. So far we have

---

1. Cf. with caution, Nigel Turner, *Grammatical Insights into the New Testament* (Edinburgh: T. & T. Clark, 1965), p. 121.

what might be termed the human level. There have been men in the history of the church who were skilled in doctrine but hardly knew God. Hence we must add to the human teacher, even such a teacher with the Bible in his hands, the mysterious influence of the Holy Spirit. The truth which has been heard or academically received is "driven home to the heart" by the Holy Spirit. Until that is done a hearer is "man-taught."

The text has affinities with Isaiah 54:13, which is quoted in John 6:45. The latter suggests the "drawing power" of God's teaching. It is a characteristic of the new covenant. When God writes his law upon men's hearts there is no need for men to teach one another to know the Lord. They already know him. This language of the prophet Jeremiah corresponds to what has been said about the ministry of the Holy Spirit (Jer. 31:33–34). Paul was himself so divinely taught (1 Cor. 2:13; cf. 1 John 2:27).

Notice the parallel "patterns of approach" in verses 1 to 3 and 9 to 11. First it is stated that the readers are already fulfilling a general Christian duty ("walking" and pleasing God; love of the brethren, vv. 1, 9); then they are exhorted to continue doing it "more and more" (v. 10); finally specific duties are set forth (holiness in sex, the quiet life, their own affairs and work). It is a mark of pastoral tact to appreciate and encourage before drawing attention to a defect, and perhaps also a sign that the writer was "God-taught" (Matt. 12:20; cf. Isa. 42:3). It accords with verse 8.

Love of the brethren concentrates more than "brotherly love" (KJV) does. The warm love which characterizes brothers in the best examples of "brothers after the flesh" (not the prodigal and the elder brother of Luke 15:25–30) should be present in the church, with added content. The "family atmosphere" is Christ.

Verse 10: And indeed you do love all the brethren throughout Macedonia: Not a parochial but a provincial love! Christian love can be exercised "at a distance." The obvious examples are prayer and contributions to meet necessities. The early Christians were linked not only by "belonging to the same organization"—a static concept— but by an active interest and love.

But we exhort you, brethren, to do so more and more: This is loving and pastoral discontent rather than unloving criticism. The discontent is that of the man who must always be "pressing on" and who calls his fellow Christians to join him. See further on 3:12. For *exhort* see on 2:3, 11; 3:2.

Verse 11: To aspire to live quietly is an unambitious ambition. The original of *aspire* is "to have as one's ambition" (cf. Rom. 15:20) and so "to make it one's aim" (2 Cor. 5:9). It is implied that there is a deliberately chosen goal and effort devoted to its realization. The word is here somewhat similar in meaning to that translated by "endeavored" in 2:17 (see note). It is not the "ambition" seen in politics or sport.

To live quietly is an elusive word. It hardly means "quietism," for the Thessalonians had given themselves to aggressive evangelism (1:8). Nor can it mean inactivity, like those who "rested" on the sabbath (Luke 23:56). Paul wanted his readers to work. It savors of some kind of freedom from disturbance. Those who "rested" were free from a bad conscience. The men who "were silent" (Luke 14:4) would have caused "trouble" if they had spoken, as undoubtedly they were still maliciously watching our Lord to see what he would do (cf. Luke 14:1). In a different spirit any possible disturbance was ended as recorded in Acts 11:18; (cf. Acts 11:2; 21:14). The woman who refuses to be silent and without submissiveness insists on teaching men rather than learning from them will occasion disturbance (1 Tim. 2: 11–12). Peace or "rest" after war means freedom from disturbance rather than complete inactivity (Judg. 3:11, RSV and LXX).

It may be inferred from 2 Thess. 3:11–12 that the disturbance was due to meddlesomeness. (Work is opposed to idleness and "quietness" to being busybodies.) Idlers, absorbed in religious discussion and the like, may have made impossible demands on the church, and on being refused too much "charity" may have interfered in its affairs (cf. 5:12– 13). The result is a touch of humor, possibly unconscious. Meddlers have to be told to make it their aim, their ambition—to keep their mouths shut! It is an honorable activity! If they heeded the exhortation, there would be no need to tell them to *mind your own affairs*.

And to work with your hands, as we charged you: The charter of dignity for manual labor. At that time men did not "like" work any more than they do now, especially when there were slaves to do it. But from the Christian point of view, work is not beneath the dignity of a free man. It may be conjectured that most of the members of the church were ordinary working people (cf. 2 Cor. 8:1–4) rather than men of the professional class. This accounts for the reference to *your hands*. It is not manual labor as such which was advocated. The preachers, who may have seen the situation in its earlier stages or may have foreseen it and therefore *charged* the church to work, were asking the individual members to maintain a sturdy independence. They were not "exalting the proletariat" at the expense of the professional. After all, Paul did speak of "Luke the beloved physician" (Col. 4:14), and whatever the status of doctors in the ancient world they were hardly manual laborers.

Verse 12: So that you may command the respect of outsiders, and be dependent on nobody: A paraphrase, with the underlying metaphor lost. Literally the Greek means "so that you may walk decently in your dealings with outsiders." (For the Christian "walk" see 2:12; 4:1, and discussions.) Whereas the readers had been earlier urged to walk in a manner worthy of God, they were now reminded of the impression that the same walk would make on non-Christians. "Public relations" are important. (Cf. Matt. 5:16, a text which Theodor Zahn regarded as summing up the Sermon on the Mount.) The same idiom is rendered "let us conduct ourselves becomingly" in Romans 13:13. Whatever the immediate circumstances, there is a Christian style or gait, even a Christian gesture, which should mark the Christian's walk.

The *outsiders* correspond to the *others* ("the rest") (v. 13). The *outsiders* are outside the Christian fellowship—but are not shut out. They have the gospel invitation to come in. The *others* are those who have not taken up the Christian privileges—though they may have them if they will start at the beginning, with repentance and faith. The two groups, *outsiders* and *others,* are identical but viewed from slightly different standpoints. We cannot, and sometimes we must not, judge whether an individual is inside or outside, but in principle there is a clear-cut distinction between the Christian and the non-Christian. The New Testament does not teach that all men are saved and that they merely need to be told about it.

The literal rendering of the last clause is "and have need of nobody (or nothing)." The Greek *(mēdenos)* is ambiguous, as it is impossible to tell whether it is masculine or neuter. If it is masculine, the readers were being warned against being parasites; if it is neuter, it picks up the thought of working with their hands and so advocates financial independence. The latter is slightly preferable.

2. Advent Perplexities Answered (4:13–5:11)

The church had obviously been sorrowing because hope had mistakenly been abandoned for recently deceased members, who, it was thought, had by their death lost the blessings of the Second Advent. On the contrary, they would be with the Lord no less than those who survived until his coming. The Thessalonians were well aware of the suddenness of the Advent and had no need of instruction about times and seasons. They should await the Lord's coming with alertness and sobriety. This was conduct which should be expected of those who had already been illumined. Alive or dead they were destined for the salvation of living forever with the Lord who had died for them. This should mean mutual encouragement and edification.

(1) The Christian dead suffer no disadvantage (4:13–18)

Sorrow for the Christian dead had obscured the Christian hope. When the Lord came, the dead in Christ would be resurrected and would be with him. The Advent was pictured in vivid colors but the main—and practical—point was the presence of the dead with the living Christians in closer fellowship with the Lord forever. The readers should encourage one another by dwelling on this theme.

But we would not have you ignorant, brethren: This is a polite and tactful approach favored by Paul. (Cf. Rom. 1:13; 11:25; 1 Cor. 10:1; 12:1; 2 Cor. 1:8.) Its spirit would be better rendered by "We do not wish you to be unaware (uninformed, in the dark)," or even "to continue to be in the dark." Note the warm *brethren* which tends to disarm any possible objection to being regarded as "ignorant."

Concerning those who are asleep: The euphemism has a diverse effect. For the "outsider" the word is but a shroud to cover the finality of death. For Christians it implies a later awakening.

That you may not grieve as others do who have no hope gives the purpose of the new teaching. Notice that knowing and believing Christian doctrine has practical consequences for the believer. Christian morticians comment on the behavior of non-Christians at funerals: they exhibit the absence of hope. Paul was anxious to put a stop to certain attitudes which were marks of the deficiencies of the readers' faith (cf. 3:10 and discussion). He therefore wrote "in order that you may not go on grieving. . . ." The distinction between Christian and non-Christian is brought out in the sharp contrasts of Ephesians 2:12. On the one side we have Christ and on the other, separation from Christ, in the world, without God, having no hope (cf. 5:6).

Verse 14: For since we believe that Jesus died and rose again, even so, through Jesus, God will bring with him those who have fallen asleep: The work of Jesus ensures that believers are always with him. The young church was clearly worried about an unexpected event, the death of believers before the Parousia. (For meaning of "Parousia," see on 2:19.) Would they lose its blessings and glories? Far from it. For "if we believe (as we do) that Jesus died and rose again, so also (we believe that) God" will not withhold from them the blessings of both the resurrection and the Parousia. The thought is vividly compressed. The "belief" is of the heart as well as of the head (Rom. 10:9–10). Jesus died and rose for the purpose of exercising lordship over dead as well as over living (Rom. 14:7–9). He is not the Lord of mere corpses!

The words *through Jesus* are pushed forward in our translation (RSV) to follow immediately after *even so*. The thought then dominates all that follows. In a sense it is no doubt true that it is all *through Jesus,* though the result is somewhat cumbersome. It is not natural to speak of God, through Jesus, bringing people with Jesus. The Greek order is: "so also (as well as raising Jesus) God those who fell asleep through Jesus will bring with him." It is plain that God will bring with Jesus those who fell asleep through him. To fall asleep through Jesus corresponds to "dying to the Lord" (Rom. 14:8). The famous Johannine text, "I am

the way" (John 14:6) is thus illustrated. There is a road through life
—and it is Jesus. There is a road through death—and it is Jesus. And
God is not at the end of the road. He is present at every point. It should be
observed in addition that he is not absent from the Parousia. It is not
said from where God will bring those who had fallen asleep, and it is
not really necessary, for they were sleeping in Jesus.

Verse 15: For this we declare to you by the word of the Lord: The
foundation for "this" is a statement of Jesus. ("This" is the latter part of
the verse, introduced by "that we who are alive.") The whole verse is
the language of Paul, which he inferred from a word of the Lord which
he proceeded to quote (vv. 16–17a). "This" anticipates verse 15b and
"the word of the Lord" anticipates verses 16–17a which should be introduced by "that." (See on next verse.) The thought is that "we are
saying this *as involved in* a word of the Lord" (the Greek preposition
is *en*). The word of the Lord is an independent, noncanonical, "unknown" saying of Jesus, standing on the same level as that recorded
in Acts 20:35.[1]

*That we who are alive, who are left until the coming of the Lord,
shall not precede those who have fallen asleep:* No advantage attaches
merely to survival. We know now that Paul himself cannot be numbered
among the survivors. At the time of writing the question was open. It
is by no means certain that Paul believed that the Lord would come
before his own death. He knew the uncertainty of life just as much as we
do. The second chapter of the Second Epistle is at least a warning to
us against hasty conclusions. And we can trace the course of his swift
thought in the language. *We* means "those like ourselves who are not
among those who fell asleep in Jesus." This is explicitly shown by the
words which follow at once, *who are alive,* "who go on living." Then,
as if the thought struck him that there might be further deaths, he
added "who survive until the Parousia." He had already written *we* with
some emphasis and it was too late to alter it. The whole expression thus
means the church on earth at the time of the Parousia, viewed from
Paul's standpoint (cf. 2:19).

*Verse 16: For the Lord himself will descend from heaven with a cry
of command, with the archangel's call, and with the sound of the trumpet of God:* This is typical apocalyptic language, in which grandeur *the
Lord himself* is seen to dominate. *For* is the Greek *hoti,* which means
"because" or "that." The former has influenced our translators (RSV),
though "that" is more suitable if a "word of the Lord" (v. 15, discussion) is here reproduced. It need not necessarily be an exact quotation.

In interpreting such a passage as this we ought to bear in mind certain principles which are sometimes forgotten. God's thoughts and ways

---

1. See Joachim Jeremias, *Unknown Sayings of Jesus* (London: S.P.C.K.,
1957), pp. 4–5, 64–67.

are not ours: they are infinitely higher and different (Isa. 55:8–9). We may therefore expect to be out of our depth with such a subject as the Parousia; not everything can be rationalized in accordance with our own philosophies. The New Testament speaks of "a new heaven and a new earth" (Rev. 21:1) in a direct quotation (Isa. 65:17; 66:22), and Paul knew the prophetic context, and seems to reecho it. (Cf. Rom. 10:20–21 with Isa. 65:1–2; a fragment of Phil. 2:16 with Isa. 65:23, LXX; 2 Thess. 1:8 with Isa. 66:4, 15.) It is by no means certain that the laws of nature as we know them will be operative, unchanged, in the new heaven and the new earth, yet in the nature of the case Paul had to use the language appropriate to the present earth and its laws of nature. This should be at least a partial answer to the mockery about "saints flying through the air." And it means a modification of James Moffatt's view that the statement, "we shall always be with the Lord" (v. 17), is all that we have left. He has assumed that our modern scientific outlook, which is admittedly different from that of the first century A.D., will be applicable at the Parousia. We do not know. But Moffatt's emphasis is right: to be forever with the Lord is "everything."

Not only are God's thoughts and ways higher than ours; we can begin to understand them only when we have ceased to be the "natural" man (1 Cor. 2:14). All of our Lord's teaching about receiving the kingdom of God as a little child is relevant here (Matt. 18:3; 19:14; Mark 10:14–15; Luke 18:16–17). A childlike (not childish; cf. 1 Cor. 14:20) faith can quicken the intellect. Even when the apostle had abandoned childish ways, he knew only "in part" (1 Cor. 13:11–12).

And in the Thessalonian text under discussion he was writing "in part," because his purpose was practical. His aim was to give enough reasons of a doctrinal nature to end the grief concerning those who slept in Christ. He used current apocalyptic pictures but subordinated them to Christ. He did not set out to give a complete timetable or a rationally satisfying synthesis.

The event will take place in an "instantaneous moment" (1 Cor. 15:51–52; Matt. 24:27; Luke 17:24) in which the whole church, living and dead, will be "changed." The survivors cannot therefore forestall those who have fallen asleep (v. 15).

The descent of the Lord from heaven must be understood and expounded with great care. It will not be the first time that he has descended. The identical Greek verb is used in John 3:13 and 6:33–58 several times, and in Ephesians 4:9–10. A "long journey through space" is not indicated for a new mode of the presence of Christ. He who is Lord of time and space could not enter time and space by means of a journey through space. The point is that he will be manifested personally in power and great glory, and the word "descend" was the only one available in the world view of the time. (Cf. Acts 1:9–10.)

The *cry of command* is the "context" of the descent, and it is expounded by the following two phrases, *the archangel's call* (cf. Jude 9) and *the trumpet of God* (cf. Joel 2:1). The emphasis is on the *command* rather than on the *cry*. Lothar Schmid cites Herodotus in illustration (Hdt. IV. 141). The Egyptian stood on the river bank and uttered his call. Histiaeus obeyed the first summons, though its content was not stated by Herodotus because Histiaeus already knew it—a fine commentary on all those exhortations to "keep awake" (cf. 1 Thess. 5:6). We know what the *command* will say when it comes! [1] The few apocalyptic details create the atmosphere for the resurrection (John 5:28) and the End.

And the dead in Christ will rise first: A logical rather than a chronological priority. It is all "in the twinkling of an eye" (1 Cor. 15:52), but the dead must rise *first* if the living are to be "together with them" (v. 17). The "change" affects the living and the dead. The phrase *in Christ* is generally taken adjectivally to describe *the dead*. Some, however, link it adverbially with the verb: they rise in Christ. The meaning is hardly seriously modified, though a side glance at 1 Corinthians 15:22 is suggestive. It seems unlikely that the formula *in Christ* is to be interpreted instrumentally, "through Christ." [2]

There is a puzzle in the thought that the descending Lord has with him the Christian dead (v. 14) and that they also are resurrected. Are the Christian dead in two places at once? This is really the wrong question. They are not to be visualized as "traveling," and there is no reason for the crude idea that God will assemble the scattered dust of each dead Christian.[3] The dead are in Christ, and as Paul can only be writing "in part," we cannot completely visualize the process. This is a case where faith must leave the "how" to God. Paul's language, however, not only regards the Christian dead as being in Christ always; it safeguards the biblical doctrine of the body. Christians will not be disembodied spirits in heaven. Paul's illustration of the seed (1 Cor. 15: 35–38) will be understood by any man who has dug up potatoes. The original seed is a squashy mess and its life has passed into the new crop. The implication is that the new body of the resurrected Christian is continuous with the old but not identical with it. It will resemble the body of Jesus after his resurrection (Phil. 3:20–21; cf. 2 Cor. 5:1–5). And when the living are simultaneously "changed," their glorified bodies will likewise be continuous with their earlier ones. Their "spiritual body" (1 Cor. 15:44–49) will be ready for behavior which would

---

1. Lothar Schmid in *Theological Dictionary of the New Testament*, 3:657.

2. See footnote to v. 15. Blass-Debrunner-Funk leave the question open (para. 272). The Latin Vulgate renders "et mortui qui in Christo sunt," "and the dead who are in Christ."

3. See J. A. Schep, *The Nature of the Resurrection Body: A Study of the Biblical Data* (Grand Rapids: Wm. B. Eerdmans, 1964), p. 195.

be abnormal, to say the least, for a mere body (cf. John 20:19; cf. 1 John 3:2).

The dead in Christ includes those who had already fallen asleep (vv. 13–14) at the time of writing and is thus tenderly aimed at healing the sorrow of the Thessalonians. But it is not limited to these. Paul could not have failed to realize that some Christians might die between the "now" of his writing and the "then" of the Parousia. *The dead in Christ* is thus a comprehensive term to cover all the Christian dead at the time of the Second Advent. This will affect our interpretation of the next verse. "We" must be more than the preachers and the church of the Thessalonians (cf. 5:10).

Verse 17: Then we who are alive, who are left, shall be caught up together with them in the clouds to meet the Lord in the air: Not unwillingly! The description of the survivors is the same as in verse 15 (see note). At that stage how could the apostle avoid saying "we"? "You" or "they" would have been too detached. The destiny of an apostle is the same as that of the whole believing church.

We . . . shall be caught up: A forcible or sudden seizure is suggested. (The Greek verb *harpazō* means "to snatch.") The suddenness is obvious but the "force" must be interpreted with care. It is the supreme example of the Lord's power to "draw" men (John 12:32). They are already in his hand and no man can snatch them out of his hand (John 10:28, cf. 29). At the Parousia he will snatch them out of the world. Other biblical uses of the verb prompt some interesting reflections. The bridegroom will take to himself his bride (cf. Judg. 21:21, LXX). The sower will gather the fruit of the good seed from the mixed harvest. He will snatch the (full grown) seed, the sons of the kingdom, out of the world (cf. Matt. 13:38; contrast v. 19). It is not without significance that the verb is used in nonbiblical literature to describe the action of a magnet.

The "rapture" (to use traditional language) is described in four phrases. It is to be *together with them.* This means coincidence in time and place (cf. 5:10). The fellowship of the church will be complete and the Christian dead not forestalled (v. 15; cf. 2 Thess. 2:1). It will be *in clouds* (the Greek has no "the"). The mystery and majesty is not withheld from the church (Luke 9:34; 21:27; Acts 1:9), for this is the beginning of glory (Rom. 8:30; Col. 3:4). The cloud is a veil rather than a vehicle—a veil of glory. (See on 2:12.) The purpose of the rapture is *to meet the Lord,* "our" purpose no less than that of him by whom "we shall be caught up." If not, we should have to consider the question of reluctant Christians. Similar language is used in Matthew 25:1, 6; Acts 28:15. The expression reflects the civic custom of a public welcome for a distinguished visitor, which is most apt. It is something like Luke 15:20 in reverse. The fourth phrase, *in the air* (*eis aera*) is really the source of the "up" which goes with "caught." It might be better to translate by "we shall be snatched airwards," as no indication is given of how far into the "air" the church will be taken. Three ideas are combined: the magnetism of the Lord; the eagerness of the church for his coming; and the corporate welcome. Ephesians 2:2 suggests that the Lord is indeed the Lord and will invade alien territory.

Some remarkable parallels with Exodus 19:16–18 should be noted, especially in the Septuagint version: cloud, trumpet, meet, descend. Both passages point to the majesty and glory of God. But the one is the giving of the law for the earthly life of the people; the other is the manifestation of grace at the climax of the earthly pilgrimage. In the one the people tremble and are warned against drawing near to God (v. 21, LXX); at the Parousia they come closer to the Lord—forever. Paul found this to be a source of comfort and the end of sorrow.

And so we shall always be with the Lord: Here is the end of the matter. The practical purpose has been served by a doctrinal statement. *And so* means "and thus," that is, "with this introduction." The prospect is a comfort to the bereaved and to the frightened; it is also a test of discipleship. The man who does not rejoice at being forever with the Lord should examine his faith.

It is no doubt possible for exponents of a full-blooded realized eschatology to believe that after death the believer will be with the Lord forever. But they seem to leave the course of history without a satisfactory end. Will it go on forever? Will there be a church on earth forever? Or will it break up piecemeal with the death of individuals? Without the Parousia death is perilously near to having the last word instead of being put out of action forever. Without the Parousia alien rule will not be put out of action, the kingdom will not be delivered to the Father and it will not be inherited by flesh and blood (1 Cor. 15: 23–28, 50). Without the Parousia the course of history will be like a road which ends in a wilderness, a river which degenerates into a swamp. And the wilderness and the swamp "have no future."

Verse 18: Therefore comfort one another with these words: Of course! The *words* as written and the arguments they express should be used as a *comfort* to the sorrowing, an appeal and an exhortation to the flagging, a stimulus to the listless. Note that an emotion (sorrow) is to be dispelled not primarily by another emotion but by teaching. The Christian intellect is the answer to an un-Christian emotion. Speech has mighty possibilities. There is ample room in the church for the teacher and his office, but the apostle did not limit the work to an official office-bearer. He visualized the whole church buzzing with conversation about things divine. In such a situation the humblest member (cf. 1 Cor. 1:26–29) may have a ministry of grace (Eph. 4:29).

Every member may be a Barnabas, whose characteristic it is to give encouragement to others (Acts 4:36).

(2) The speculative have no prior information (5:1–3)

The readers knew that the Lord would come with the suddenness of a thief in the night. Men who urged that all was peaceful and secure implied the possession of knowledge that the Lord was not yet at hand. Sudden destruction would undeceive them.

Verse 1: But as to the times and the seasons, brethren, you have no need to have anything written to you: They had already been instructed (cf. 3:4; 2 Thess. 2:5), no doubt on the lines of Acts 1:7. *Times and seasons* are usually distinguished thus: *Times* means periods of time, time as measured on the calendar or the clock, time in its quantitative aspect. *Seasons* points to the quality of the time. They are what Stauffer calls "smaller temporal units" within the total stream of time and they have their own characteristics.[1] *Season* may mean the "proper time" (Luke 12:42) or "right time" (Rom. 5:6). It may savor of "opportunity" (Gal. 6:10; Heb. 11:15). A variation is "critical time," "time charged with significance" (Matt. 16:3). Perhaps the richest meaning is to be found in Jesus' lament over Jerusalem. They did not recognize the significant time, the decisive time, the time which called for decision, the opportunity, of their visitation (Luke 19:44). *Times* is thus relevant to the question, "How long before the Parousia?" *Seasons* is appropriate to "What sort of critical times will be associated with the Parousia?" The Thessalonians needed no letter of instruction on this subject, which is a sign of their robust Christian sanity. Nor did they need a letter about love of the brethren (4:9). An excellent combination.

Verse 2: For you yourselves know well that the day of the Lord will come like a thief in the night: Their knowledge was precise and clear-cut on this point. (Cf. 3:3 and discussion.) *The day of the Lord* is found first in Amos 5:18. It represented a popular idea that God would intervene to establish Israel against all nations. Amos moralized the idea: God would indeed intervene and vindicate his own righteousness. The prophets looked forward to God's final visitation, to the day when he would judge and redeem (Joel 3:14, 18). "In the latter days" the kingdom of God will be established (Isa. 2:2–4). Such "day" or "days" mark the furthest limit of the prophetic vision. The Old Testament hope is fulfilled in Christ. The promise of the Spirit (Joel 2:28–32) was recognized by Peter as being implemented "in the last days" (Acts 2:16–21); and he went on to speak of Jesus of Nazareth.

The day of the Lord has in fact come. It has come in Christ. Yet in

---

1. Ethelbert Stauffer, *New Testament Theology* (London: SCM Press, 1955), p. 76.

another sense it has not yet come. The last days have been inaugurated in the life, death, and resurrection of our Lord; but they will be consummated at the Parousia. In principle God has given his people "all things" with Christ (Rom. 8:32), but we await their full enjoyment until the Second Advent. This is the "day" to which Paul referred.

It is like the *thief* in its suddenness. This accords with Mark 13:32–37. The simple illustration goes back to Jesus (Matt. 24:43; Luke 12:39; cf. 2 Pet. 3:10).

Verse 3: When people say, "There is peace and security": This is the attitude of public opinion, spoken or unspoken. (With the Hebrew people, thinking involved saying—in direct speech—and Paul was a Hebrew; cf. Jas. 1:13.) This is the fool's paradise of absorption in innocent activities (Matt. 24:37–39; Luke 17:26–30); the sin of the false assumption which neglect of God implicitly makes. For *peace* see discussion on 1:1.

Then sudden destruction will come upon them: As sudden as the thief and as inescapable as a snare or spring trap (cf. Luke 21:34). (These activities are not innocent.)

As travail comes upon a woman with child: The sudden pain of labor. Even when it is expected (and a woman expects labor just as a Christian expects the Parousia), it is sudden when it comes.

And there will be no escape, as with the trap or snare. Paul was thinking of the "people who say." The denial is emphatic. There is no question, no possibility, of their escape. (Cf. Luke 21:36.)

(3) All should be on the alert (5:4–11)

The Thessalonians, as children of the light, were not in such darkness that the coming of the Lord would surprise and overwhelm them. They should therefore avoid the characteristics of night. They should not be unconscious like sleepers nor drunken like revelers. They should rather be marked by an alert expectation in thought and a sobriety in life; by sober expectation without fantastic speculation. For they had a sure hope. The Lord who had died for them intended to keep them with him forever. They had therefore the means to encourage and build one another.

Verse 4: But you are not in darkness, brethren, for that day to surprise you like a thief: A direct contrast to the "people" of the previous verse, who are in the darkness not so much of ignorance (as they may have been warned) as of moral and spiritual estrangement from God. They are still resting in "peace and security" when the day is, so to speak, "switched on." (The aorist tense justifies the metaphor.) The thought is now of surprise. But alert Christians will not be surprised. The Greek verb behind *surprise* is used in John 1:5 (cf. 12:35) of darkness "blanketing" the light—like a sea fog pouring in over the harbor and covering a maritime city. The situation is now reversed. The unbelievers, already in darkness, will be "blanketed" by the day! It is an apt comment on the prophetic words of Amos: the *day* is *darkness* (Amos 5:18–20)!

The reading, "like thieves," transfers the metaphor from the day to the Christians. It is not intrinsically impossible; in some contexts it could be vivid ("the householder switched on the light, to find the burglar working at the safe"). It is an ancient reading—the attestation is good —and the change is not un-Pauline (cf. 2:7, 11, 17 and discussions). But it is incongruous, and recent textual critics (Aland, Black, Metzger, Wikgren) regard *like a thief* as "virtually certain." (Cf. Rom. 13:11–14; 1 Cor. 3:13; 4:5.)

Verse 5: For you are all sons of light and sons of the day—and therefore not surprised. In Hebrew idiom, a "son of" anything shares his "father's" nature, and the idiom has passed over into the Greek Testament. (Cf. Luke 16:8; Eph. 5:8.) All the New Testament passages which speak of God or of Christ as light are relevant here (cf. 2 Cor. 4:6), and *all* the members at Thessalonica (note the encouragement!) belong to Christ. The light of the Parousia will be no new thing to them; it will be more and more of what they already have. It will always surprise them in exciting their wonder and admiration (1 Pet. 2:9), but they will not be caught unawares by the Day as they are *sons of the day.* They look forward to it as the introduction to their life with the Lord forever (4:17 and discussion). They belong to the day, just as they belong to Christ.

We are not of the night or of darkness: The same truth in changed form. The Hebrew idiom gives way to Greek, and the person is changed from the second to the first. "We Christians" are not "men of night," and we do not belong to the night. The meaning of this is shown with great dramatic force in John 13:27–30. Satan entered into Judas. . . . He went out at once. It was night. Paul identified himself thus with his readers and so prepared the way for the exhortation which follows, which is for all Christians, not only some Thessalonians.

Verse 6: So then let us not sleep, as others do, but let us keep awake and be sober: A practical inference drawn from the previous verse. Paul was calling his readers to join him in a course of action. To *sleep* means to be morally and spiritually insensitive. (Cf. Eph. 5:14.) The sleeper does not hear the fire alarm, and is thus helpless in the face of danger. In speaking of *others* the apostle meant "the others," the totality of non-Christians. The same is true in 4:13. To *keep awake* is to be on the alert. To *be sober* is in contrast to the spiritual drunkenness which is not dead drunk (this would be sleeping) but has lost self-control. There should be no "woolliness" in their thinking, no devotion to excess, no self-assertiveness. (Cf. 5:2 and discussion; "you know with precision.") They should continue to be concerned with divine realities, not with inebriated imaginations; they should be ready for activity, not lazy stupor. Faith, hope, and charity should be their program and spiritual warfare. (Cf. v. 8; 2 Tim. 4:5; 1 Pet. 1:13; 4:7; 5:8 and context.)

Verse 7: For those who sleep sleep at night, and those who get drunk are drunk at night: A literal fact to illustrate a spiritual truth. There is a side glance at "the others" in verse 6. (Cf. Matt. 24:48–51; Acts 2:15.)

Verse 8: But, since we belong to the day, let us be sober, and put on the breastplate of faith and love, and for a helmet the hope of salvation: A description of soldiers under arms on guard against surprise. They were not in the dark (v. 4); their true home was the day—and the Day. They should continue in sobriety (v. 6 and discussion). *Put on* is an aorist participle and may be taken (as RSV) closely with the hortatory main verb: "let us put on . . . and be sober." (RSV reverses the order.) It seems better to render: "let us continue to be sober ("us" emphatic in contrast to the people of v. 7), seeing that we have put on . . . ."[1] It would ill become "us Christians," ready as we are (cf. 5:2), to become undisciplined. The metaphor of armor goes back to Isaiah 59: 17, LXX; cf. Wisdom 5:18; and is not infrequent in the Pauline writings. (Cf. Rom. 6:13; 13:12; 2 Cor. 6:7; 10:4; Eph. 6:11, 13–17.) The *breastplate* consists of *faith and love.* The *helmet* is *hope* which is directed toward *salvation.* It is no mere hope. It is negative (from wrath v. 9) and positive as it means new and eternal life (cf. Rom. 6:23). It may be enjoyed now (2 Tim. 1:9) as well as in the future (Rom. 5:9). (See 1 Thess. 2:16 and discussion.) It will be observed that Paul's use of the figure of armor is not mechanical. Like a modern preacher he could retain an illustration and at the same time modify it. For the triad of faith, hope, and love (1 Cor. 13:13) see 1:3 and discussion.

Verse 9: For God has not destined us for wrath, but to obtain salvation through our Lord Jesus Christ: Of course not! Otherwise he would not have elected, called, and taught us (1:4; 2:12; 4:9). The thought is (beginning with v. 8): ". . . the hope of salvation. (This is no vain hope.) *For* God has not destined us . . . ." (See on 2:1.) (For *destined* or "appointed" cf. Acts 13:47; 1 Tim. 1:12; 2 Tim. 1:11; 1 Pet. 2:8. *Wrath* has been considered in the discussion on 1:10 and 2:16.)

To obtain salvation: We are not born with salvation. Notice its content in 2 Thessalonians 2:13–14.

Through our Lord Jesus Christ: The best comment is Acts 4:12. The way of salvation is unique, given and compulsory. This is admittedly Petrine but it accords with Pauline thought. (For unique, cf. Rom. 5:15–19; 1 Cor. 8:6; Eph. 4:5; 1 Tim. 2:5. For given, cf.

---

1. Cf. Turner, *A Grammar of New Testament Greek,* 3:157.

Rom. 3:24; 1 Cor. 1:4; Gal. 1:4. For compulsory, cf. Acts 17:30; Rom. 10:16; 2 Thess. 1:8; 1 Pet. 4:17.) *Jesus* points to the historic figure, *Christ* to the purpose of God, and *Lord* to its accomplishment. See discussion on 1:1.

Verse 10: Who died for us so that whether we wake or sleep we might live with him: The visible tip of the iceberg. Underneath lies the whole doctrine of the atonement, "the word of the cross" (1 Cor. 1: 18). *Wake* and *sleep* are not used in the sense of verse 6 but of natural life and death (cf. 4:13). The ingressive aorist of *live* suggests the rendering: "that we might gain life." His resurrection is assumed without explicit statement. "Because I live, you will live also" (John 14:19). *Live* means "be alive," not "dwell" ("he lives with, i.e., dwells with, his mother"), though the latter is true in fact. The readers would be reminded of the preachers' visit (Acts 17:3).

Verse 11: Therefore encourage one another and build one another up, just as you are doing: The ministry of conversation. *Encourage* renders the same Greek verb as *comfort* in 4:18. Due weight should be given to the basis, *therefore*. *Build* is thought by some to refer to Paul's doctrine of the church (e.g., Eph. 2:20–22) but he was referring to individual members. Each separate Christian is a temple of the Holy Spirit (1 Cor. 6:19; contrast 3:16 with its "corporate" temple). To *build* or to edify is (to change the metaphor) to increase the spiritual muscle of a man (1 Cor. 8:1; 14:4, 17). The readers did not have to start from the beginning. They were already in the light of day (vv. 4–5, 8) and giving one another comfort and encouragement. It is again a mark of pastoral tact that Paul should mention this (cf. 4:1, 10), *just as you are doing.*

3. Ethical Exhortations (5:12–15)

In view of the hitherto prevailing restlessness, the church members were asked to pay greater regard to their pastors, who were toiling among them in pastoral care and admonition. The nature of their work should call out Christian love. There were duties to be mutually discharged among the members and the good of all should be sought.

(1) Duties toward pastors (5:12–13)

The pastors were spending themselves in the care and teaching of their flock. Such important work should inspire both respect and love. An earlier attention to this might have saved many tears.

Verse 12: But we beseech you, brethren, to respect those who labor among you and are over you in the Lord and admonish you: The church was here asked for a definite response. The ministers are described more by function than by office. Their "toil" (1:3; 2:9; 3:5 and discussions) was not a separate activity; the term reveals the strain of supervision and admonition, for only one group is in view. Every man who exercises authority in the church, whether by office or influence, should take note that it is *in the Lord:* it is he who is the head of the church (Eph. 1:22; 4:15; 5:23; Col. 1:18; 2:19; and especially 1 Cor. 11:3), and there is no hierarchical "chain of command" which denies the access of the humblest member to the Head himself. History has shown that sometimes the pew is wiser—and nearer to the Lord—than ecclesiastical authority. Both sides, "rulers" and "ruled," need to bear in mind that it is "in the Lord." Those who *admonish* appeal to the conscience and the will rather than to the pure intellect; in this they may be roughly distinguished from teachers, as the giving of admonition is the work of the shepherd or pastor (cf. Eph. 4:11). In practice the same man may discharge the duties of pastor and of teacher, but the duties may be distinguished.

Verse 13: And to esteem them very highly in love because of their work: The pastors had claims even if they did not assert them. Human personalities may seem incompatible but *in the Lord* the true pastor commands (not the best word!) respect for the self-sacrificing toil of his *work.* As *work* (*ergon*) also means "function," a characteristic work, the fact that it is spiritual should commend itself to those who are truly *in the Lord.* On their side the latter should be moved by love (which is not an emotion but a commanded activity—Matt. 22:39; John 13:34) to give respect to their pastors.

Be at peace among yourselves: A program for the whole church for all their time on earth. The danger point is reached whenever it is necessary to *admonish* (v. 12). Hence comes the need to abide *in the Lord* (cf. John 15:4) and to *love.* (Cf. Mark 9:50; Rom. 12:18; 2 Cor. 13:11.)

(2) Duties toward church members (5:14–15)

Needs were matched by duties: admonition for the idle, comfort for the fainthearted, help for the weak, long-suffering toward all. Retaliation was ruled out: the good of all should always be sought by all.

Verse 14: And we exhort you, brethren: Here is persuasion with authority once more. The repetition of *brethren* suggests that the address is still to the church (cf. 4:18; 5:11), but *admonish* shows a special application of the exhortation (cf. v. 12). *Those who labor among you* would have to take the lead.

Admonish the idle—with tact, in order to keep the peace. The lesson had to be reinforced (2 Thess. 3:6–12). Like troops who are not in battle order or like ships in disarray, church members who are not "at their post" (i.e., "on the job") give a bad impression to unbelievers, especially if they are constantly looking for handouts. We have something to give!

Encourage the fainthearted: To do this would be following the example of the preachers (2:11 and discussion). The *fainthearted* are those whose spirit is all but broken and who are on the verge of "giving up." The word is used (Isa. 54:6, LXX) of a forsaken wife. A male example would be Elijah (1 Kings 19:4, 10). The best treatment would be the so-called T.L.C. (tender loving care) prescribed for the depressed, combined with Christian truth.

Help the weak: Help must be given physically, mentally, morally and spiritually. (Cf. Rom. 14:1; 1 Cor. 8:7–13; 9:22.) The *help* is best given by personal interest, sympathy, and presence rather than merely by sending a message or even by giving an order for groceries to be delivered. The church has traditionally had passengers as well as robust members of the crew.

Be patient with them all: The emphasis is on time rather than on pain. We "endure" pain but "wait with patience" until a desired point of time is reached. (Cf. Acts 26:3; and others suggesting an absence of real pain: Matt. 18:26, 29; Heb. 6:12, 15; Jas. 5:7–8.) Patience is a characteristic of love (1 Cor. 13:4). Many a minister can produce examples of members who cause him no pain but take hours of his time. He does not need endurance but infinite patience. (Cf. Gal. 5:22.)

Verse 15: See that none of you repays evil for evil: This is the unceasing responsibility of the group for its individual members—without being busybodies (2 Thess. 3:11). (Cf. Matt. 5:9, 38–41; Luke 6:29; Rom 12:17; 1 Pet. 3:9.) The text means: "See to it, (all) you people, that no individual pays back (to any individual) evil for evil." The method would be the creation of a Christian public opinion by preaching, teaching, and living in which pastors and any members who knew the situation could tactfully intervene. The address to the church at large again suggests that the organization of the ministry is still fluid.

But always seek to do good to one another and to all: This is reciprocity without hindering universality, and with no exceptions (*always*). The church was to turn in upon itself and outward toward the world. It is striking that Paul the former persecutor could use a verb meaning "pursue" or "persecute." (*Seek to do* equals pursue.) (Cf. Acts 22:4; 1 Cor. 15:9; Gal. 1:13; Phil. 3:6.) Did he want his readers to put the same intensity into altruism as he had put into his persecution? Did the former legalist want them to display the same zeal for the welfare of others as Israel had done for herself in the pursuit of the righteousness of the law (Rom. 9:31)?

4. Spiritual Exhortations (5:16–22)

The sharp, staccato commands in this section admit no exceptions. Always the readers were to rejoice, pray, give thanks; to encourage spiritual utterance; to test everything and keep the good; to avoid every kind of evil.

Verse 16: Rejoice always—for it is always possible. Paul recognized that joy at times could arise out of circumstances like the arrival of friends (1 Cor. 16:17), and that in spite of the *always* the Christian life could know sorrow (Phil. 2:27–28; 3:18). The waters of the surface may be ruffled but the depths are still. "The secret [intimacy, familiar converse] of the Lord is with them that fear him" (Ps. 25:14, KJV). Joy, like love, is commanded and is not purely emotional nor ultimately dependent on external circumstances. It is "in the Lord" (Phil. 4:4) and is derived from him (John 17:13), a permanent possession (John 16:22). It is the gift of God to believers (Rom. 15: 13), a mark of the kingdom (Rom. 14:17), and the fruit of the Spirit (Gal. 5:22). (Cf. Luke 2:10; 24:52; 1 Thess. 1:6; 3:3–4.) We see here the paradox of the persecuted.

Verse 17: Pray constantly: The complement to keeping awake (v. 6) and the antidote to temptation (Mark 14:38) and losing heart (Luke 18:1) is to pray. It may be private (Matt. 6:6) or corporate (Acts 12: 12). Its method is described in Philippians 4:6. For *constantly* see discussion on 1:2. Not to cease praying (Col. 1:9) means deliberate thought and persistence (Acts 1:14; Rom. 12:12; Col. 4:2).

Verse 18: Give thanks in all circumstances: Here is the true optimism. This is sometimes a test of spiritual ingenuity, as some circumstances do not obviously inspire thanksgiving. However adverse they may be, we can always give thanks either that it is not always like this, or that it will not be. There are always the permanent grounds for thanksgiving, for God has qualified us to share in the saints' allotted place in the light (cf. Col. 1:12 in spite of 1 Tim. 6:16). And we can always give thanks *in all circumstances* that an opportunity has been given to us to "go on fighting the good fight of faith" (1 Tim. 6:12).

For this is the will of God in Christ Jesus for you: The apostolic exhortation rests on the divine will. *This* includes the three (vv. 16–18): the life of joy, prayer, thanksgiving. The Christian has before him the supreme example (Heb. 10:7) and the knowledge that the will of God is perfect (Rom. 12:2). How could he think otherwise? It is *in Christ Jesus*. The will of God is not a "naked" will: it is the will of one who is the Father of our Lord Jesus Christ, whose nature in Christ has been made known. God's will is thus known, desirable and practicable: in Christ who strengthens we can do all things (cf. Phil. 4:13). Paul had been appointed to know God's will (Acts 22:14). To do God's will was meat and drink to Jesus (John 4:34) and he did it completely (John 17:4).

Verse 19: Do not quench the Spirit—as they were in danger of doing. Either the idle claimed spiritual authority and others therefore resisted the "Spirit" excessively, not making a distinction between a false claim and a genuine manifestation of the Spirit, or an overemphasis on sobriety may have led to a cold disapproval of fervor. (Cf. 5:6, 8; 5:14; 2 Thess. 3:6–11.) The gifts of the Spirit are varied (1 Cor. 12:4–11; cf. Rom. 12:6–8). Those who were "aglow with the Spirit" (Rom. 12:11; cf. Acts 18:25) might invite criticism from the more "sober" through a confusion of deep spirituality with idle excitability.

Quench is a word appropriate to the extinguishing of a fire (Heb. 11:34; cf. Matt. 12:20). Timothy was reminded to "rekindle the gift of God" (2 Tim. 1:6). John the Baptist associated the Holy Spirit with fire (Matt. 3:11; cf. Acts 2:3). The church would have been harmed by the discouragement of men with gifts of spontaneous utterance (cf. 1 Cor. 14:26). We retain the same metaphor today when we speak of "pouring cold water" on a man's ideas. To *quench* the Spirit is undoubtedly to grieve him (Eph. 4:30).

Verse 20: Do not despise prophesying: One form of quenching the Spirit. Prophesying is the intelligible utterance of the will of God, and its purpose is to build, to stimulate, and to comfort (1 Cor. 14:1–5). Teaching is derived from knowledge; prophecy comes from revelation: the distinction is not absolute but is useful. In principle any one of the Lord's people may prophesy (Acts 2:18), though some in New Testament times were specially recognized as prophets (1 Cor. 12:28–29; Eph. 4:11). Prophets possess a gift (1 Cor. 12:10) and are themselves a gift to the church. The main task of prophecy is proclamation (1 Cor. 14:24–25), but prediction is not ruled out (Acts 11:27–28; 21:9–14). There is a subtle distinction between the New Testament prophet and the prophetic preacher of today. Both base their utterances on revelation, but today the revelation is mediated through the written Word.

Verse 21: But test everything; hold fast what is good—as God tests his apostles (2:4 and discussion). This should be interpreted in the light of verses 19–20. It is not a charter to the person who automatically criticizes everything merely because of an ingrained sourness. The church should be alert to detect error but always be ready to be persuaded. It would be a poor use of the "prophetic consciousness of the church" merely to criticize the preacher's grammar or gestures. If Christians *hold fast,* they will keep the truth in mind, they will prize it as a pearl of great value (Matt. 13:45–46; cf. Phil. 3:7–8) and of concentrated and supreme worth, and will obey it.

Verse 22: Abstain from every form of evil: However evil is classified, the rule is absolute. The exercise of private judgment must not be abused but must be turned inward as well as outward. Jesus is Lord (Matt. 7:21–22; 1 Cor. 12:3), and even the man who tests the prophets (cf. 1 John 4:1) should obey him. That man is not an exception and he must not make exceptions (Matt. 5:19; Jas. 2:10). Evil has many forms. There are many "kinds" of evil, from the gross sins to a refined form of envy or jealousy, and it enters into every activity of man. *Every form* suggests its inventiveness.

The Greek word behind *form* (*eidos*) is translated by "appearance" in the KJV, which is in line with "we walk by faith, not by sight" (2 Cor. 5:7). The sentiment is sound (cf. 2 Cor. 8:21) though it has its dangers (Matt. 23:5). *Eidos* may possibly take the meaning of "appearance," or "sight," but its natural meaning is to be preferred. It is the philosophic word for "species" ("genus and species") and is used on the popular level for "kind" or "sort." There is evidence from the papyri to support this. Keep away from every kind of evil! (Cf. 4:3.)

Verses 21–22 may reecho a frequently quoted but "unknown" saying of Jesus, "Be approved money-changers." The Christian should reject the counterfeit but retain that which rings true. Test every spiritual coin: keep the good, and keep clear of every kind of fake! [1]

5. Prayer for the Readers (5:23–24)

The substance of the prayer was the readers' complete sanctification, maintained even in the white light of the Second Advent. Its foundation was the faithfulness of him who was ever calling them onward.

Verse 23: May the God of peace himself sanctify you wholly—with no substitute and no deficiency. This is a wish with regard to the future and hence is a prayer. All our services and prayers would be of no avail if *God . . . himself* were absent. The apostle prayed that his readers might be holy through and through. They were not to be passive (v. 22) but ultimately holiness comes from God, who trains his people in their spiritual pilgrimage. He can act with vigor: "the God of peace will smash . . ." (Rom. 16:20, author's translation; cf. 15:33; Heb. 13:20). For *peace* see discussion on 1:1, and for *sanctify* see discussions on 3:13; 4:3. To *sanctify* is to make holy. If Christians are to grow in holiness and to become holy through and through, they must be at peace with one another (5:13) and must love one another (3:11–13). (Cf. 2 Thess. 2:16–17; 3:16.)

And may your spirit and soul and body be kept sound and blameless at the coming of our Lord Jesus Christ: This is a further elaboration of a long program and a complete achievement. The idea is: ". . . kept, blamelessly intact (when manifested) at the coming . . . . " There is no need to ask by whom they were to be kept. For *blameless* see

---

1. Cf. *Theological Dictionary of the New Testament*, ed. G. Kittell, 2. 375. See also Joachim Jeremias, *Unknown Sayings of Jesus*, pp. 89–93.

discussion on 2:10; 3:13; and for *coming* (Parousia), 2:19; 3:13; 4:15 and discussions. For so august an occasion the full title is appropriate—*Lord Jesus Christ* (1:1 and discussion). Observe the intimate *our* amid all the grandeur.

Spirit and soul and body have sometimes been taken as evidence for the tripartite nature of man. But Paul was not giving an analysis of the human constitution; he was praying that the whole man might be kept. This covers the mental and spiritual life of the believer: not only rational thought but also piety and righteousness, i.e., love to God and love to man, growth in holiness and in moral character; and the body as well (4:3). Given the fact that the *body,* as part of the unity of personality, must be sanctified and kept, but not the body alone, then it was all but inevitable that Paul should have used the terms *spirit* and *soul* for the sake of completeness. It would be as dangerous to take this as an argument for the threefold nature of personality as it would be to take Mark 12:30 for a fourfold. Heart, soul, mind, and strength were not meant to be a precise and exhaustive analysis.

Paul's terms, taken in the reverse order, mean: the body, in its vitality, of a willing and purposing self, and the mind open to God through the Holy Spirit. We speak today of "body and mind." The unbeliever has a mind, but fellowship with the divine is closed to him (1 Cor. 2:14). The believer has a mind, and with it he prays and knows God. The difference is that through the Holy Spirit his mind has been quickened. Paul called such a quickened mind *spirit*. This point is indicated by such studies as those of Dr. Robert O. Ferm of the psychology of conversion.[1] A study of the mind in conversion is by no means an activity of a rationalist! A rationalist may attempt it but a Christian psychologist has the more sympathetic understanding from his own experience. He studies the mind—and with Paul could call it *spirit*.

Verse 24: He who calls you is faithful, and he will do it—otherwise why continue to call? We heard God's call at our conversion and we still hear it, not merely as a vivid memory but because God goes on calling us. See on 2:12; 4:7. *Faithful* means trustworthy, loyal. God does not call his people to an anticlimax, still less to disaster. He will indeed keep them. He not only speaks; he acts.

---

1. Robert O. Ferm, *The Psychology of Christian Conversion* (Westwood, N.J.: Fleming H. Revell, 1959).

IV. FINAL REQUESTS AND BLESSING (5:25–28)

Prayer was sought and greeting given. The letter was to be read publicly. It ended as it had begun—with grace.

Verse 25: Brethren, pray for us: Is this appeal, exhortation or command? Most likely it was all three. It was an appeal from the heart of a fellow-believer (or rather "believers") amid all the strains and dangers of an itinerant life together with the care of all the churches (1 Cor. 4:8–13; 2 Cor. 4:7–12; 6:4–10; 11:23–33). It was persuasion with authority, for it was of apostolic origin and the readers ought thus to aid their beloved preachers (3:6). The "authority" merged into loving command: they ought to support the preaching of the gospel. The meaning is not "offer a prayer for us." It is rather "go on praying for us." (Cf. v. 17; 2 Thess. 3:1–2.)

Verse 26: Greet all the brethren with a holy kiss: Everyone is included, even the idlers (v. 14). The *kiss* is *holy* because it is within the circle of the holy, the saints (cf. 1 Cor. 1:2), and because it expresses Christian love. It comes from the writers, through (presumably) the elders (v. 12), to the members. The kiss eventually became liturgical, part of the liturgy or regular order of service of the Lord's Supper or Eucharist. It survives in some forms to the present day— the kiss of peace. Its suitability depends on the solemnity of the occasion.

Verse 27: I adjure you by the Lord that this letter be read to all the brethren, in order that all might know of his Christian love and admonition. The change to the singular, *I* (not "we") *adjure* you, strikes a solemn note (cf. 2 Thess. 3:14). In modern language it is almost: "I put you on your honor in the sight of the Lord." The motive of the apostle may be judged best by the preacher who has diligently prepared a message to meet a known need, only to find that the persons to whom it was addressed were not in church that day.

Verse 28: The grace of our Lord Jesus Christ be with you: The circle is completed. The letter began with *grace* and so it ended. See on 1:1. Again there is no verb. But whereas the letter began with "grace to you" here we have *with you.* If Paul meant any significant difference

[120]

in the change of prepositions, we might see their suitability. At the
beginning he was hoping to refresh their spirit with an access of grace;
at the end, after writing fully and dealing with problems, he left grace
with them. It can only mean that the epistle itself is a "means of grace."
Holy Scripture, like the Holy Communion, is a means of grace.

2 Thessalonians

INTRODUCTION

2 Thessalonians

Some matters of introduction are common to the First and the Second Epistles to the Thessalonians. Some account of the city of Thessalonica itself and the story of the visit of Paul, Silvanus, and Timothy and the planting of the church there will be unchanged, whether we are thinking particularly of the First or the Second Epistle. The reader is therefore referred to the Introduction to the First Epistle.

EXTERNAL EVIDENCE

The external evidence for the Second Epistle is somewhat better than that for the First. Polycarp of Smyrna lived approximately A.D. 69–155, and in his Epistle to the Philippians he almost certainly quoted from our Second Epistle. His words (11. 3, 4), as they survive in a Latin version, read thus: *De vobis etenim gloriatur in omnibus ecclesiis . . .* ; and *et non sicut inimicos tales existimetis.* The former, "For concerning you he boasts in all the churches," refers to Paul and is strongly reminiscent of 2 Thessalonians 1:4. The present tense, "he boasts," is the same as Paul's own words and looks like 'a quotation. The latter, "and do not consider such men as enemies," recalls 2 Thessalonians 3:15. Too much weight should not be laid on possible echoes in Ignatius and the Didache or Teaching of the Twelve Apostles, though some words in the Epistle of Barnabas seem to be indebted to the language of Paul rather than to that of popular piety. Like the First, the Second Epistle is included in Marcion's Canon and in the Muratorian Canon. It is quoted by Irenaeus, Tertullian, and Clement of Alexandria. Again like the First, it is present in the Syriac Vulgate and Old Latin Versions.

INTERNAL EVIDENCE

A number of scholars have taken the view that the Second Epistle is to be placed before the First. Their detailed arguments have been dealt with by W. G. Kümmel, [1] and only two points are necessary for

1. W. G. Kümmel, *Introduction to the New Testament* (London: SCM Press, 1966), p. 186.

our present purpose. In words of deep feeling Paul told his readers how he longed to see them again (1 Thess. 2:17–3:10). This passage could not be in any letter other than the first one after Paul had left the church in Thessalonica. In the Second Epistle the apostle urged the members to hold fast to the traditions which had been taught either through their speech or letter (2 Thess. 2:15). The speech must have been all that was said orally during the visit; the letter must be First Thessalonians.

More serious are objections raised against the authenticity of the Second Epistle on the ground of the internal evidence. It has been said that the eschatological teaching of the Second conflicts with that of the First. In the First the Parousia will come suddenly and unexpectedly; in the Second there will be preliminary signs. This difficulty is not insuperable. For one thing, both positions are present together in apocalyptic literature: suddenness and preliminary signs are not felt to be embarrassingly incompatible. And Paul seems to have taught both. After telling the Thessalonians that "the rebellion comes first" and describing the activities of the man of lawlessness, he pointedly asked them: "Do you not remember that when I was still with you I told you this?" (2 Thess. 2:5). He had obviously told them of the preliminary signs. In the First Epistle he told them that they knew that "the day of the Lord will come like a thief in the night" (1 Thess. 5:2). Sudden destruction will come but they will not be surprised by that day (vv. 3 f.). How did they know? Either the Jewish Christians in their membership told them from their knowledge of apocalyptic literature or the apostle Paul did so himself. The former seems unlikely, and in any case how did Paul know that they knew? Was it because Timothy had reported it (1 Thess. 3:6)? It all seems very involved and implies that Paul only told the church half of the apocalyptic message. It is much more reasonable to suppose that Paul had already given his readers the full apocalyptic teaching. Suddenness and signs contained no embarrassment for him. The argument against authenticity on the ground of incompatibility of apocalyptic teaching therefore breaks down. In either case Paul was drawing on his previous teaching to fulfill a practical purpose. In the First Epistle he encouraged his readers by the thought that the day would not catch them unprepared, in the Second by showing that the day could not have come already (2 Thess. 2:2). In each case it was necessary to refer to only the relevant part of his teaching.

It is perhaps worth reflecting that "suddenness and signs" are part of the stuff of human life and we are not troubled by them. The impatient child asks why the train does not start. "Any moment now," says his mother. "The engine must be coupled on first," says the father. Or consider a clergyman visiting a man who is desperately ill in hospital. "He cannot last much longer," says one. "The pulse must weaken a bit more," says another. When the expected end comes, even though it is expected it brings something of a shock.

Some scholars have been so impressed by the literary resemblances that they have regarded the Second Epistle as standing in a relationship of literary dependence on the First Epistle. This carries with it the implication of non-Pauline authorship.

Resemblance of epistolary outline can be conceded. But granted similarity of outline, it is to be observed that any linguistic repetition in the Second Epistle rarely appears in the same position in the outline. The agreements are not usually of great length and the author of the Second Epistle uses the material with some freedom. Indeed there is more new material than old. In at least one place the Second Epistle explains the First (cf. 2 Thess. 3:6–15 with 1 Thess. 4:11 f.; 5:14). The Second Epistle in fact is more intelligible if it is regarded as genuinely written by Paul. He was not averse to repeating himself (Phil. 3:1). Far from being an attempt merely to cool the overheated expectation of the Thessalonians, the Second Epistle embodies the double purpose of giving encouragement to the fainthearted and warning to the idlers. The vocabulary and the spirit are Pauline. It is of some significance that it was belief in the Pauline authorship which led Harnack to formulate his theory of two Thessalonian churches and thus to avoid the literary judgment that the Second Epistle is a forgery (see on 2:13).

The situation suggested by the Second Epistle is but a later stage of that suggested by the First. The Second may therefore be dated soon after the First: a matter of weeks rather than months.

THEOLOGY

The theology of the Epistle must now be considered. If it is genuinely Pauline, it might be argued that all the theology of the First Epistle can be carried over into the interpretation of the Second. It is an understandable position and without a doubt it is adopted by many a preacher. Nevertheless, we shall find it worthwhile to examine the Second Epistle entirely on its own, to see what results are yielded.

We begin with the complex of sin-wrath-judgment. The words "sin" and "wrath" do not appear in the letter but they are surely implied. If we were deliberately to rule them out even as concepts, we should find it difficult if not impossible to interpret the apocalyptic passage 1:5–2:12. It speaks of punishment and penalty as well as of judgment, and it is not for all. It is for those who do not know God and who do not obey the gospel. Why, it might be asked, is the punishment not for the Thessalonians? It is because they have received the gospel, the remedy for sin. The sin of men excites the wrath of God, and it culminates in judgment for those who spurn, who refuse the forgiveness of sin.

The man of lawlessness is obviously a man of sin, for law clarifies, defines, and gives precision to sin. He can hardly argue that he did not know what sin was. He is lawless, not in being without a knowledge of the law, but in acting contrary to the law, the known will of God. It should be noticed that the man of lawlessness sums up in himself the essence of sin. He "opposes" (2:4). This is precisely what the sinner does. The attitude of the flesh, of the unregenerate, is enmity toward God (cf. Rom. 8:7). This came out in the life of Saul of Tarsus (Acts 26:9; 1 Tim. 1:13). The lawless one "exalts himself," which is again the characteristic of the sinner. The Pharisees scoffed at Jesus, but God knew their hearts and did not like what he saw. "For what is exalted among men is an abomination in the sight of God" (Luke 16: 15). The lawless one exalts himself in "proclaiming himself to be God." This is implied by the sinner's self-glorification, because glory is for God alone (Matt. 5:16; 6:2; 1 Cor. 10:31; cf. Isa. 42:8). The lawless one concentrates in himself all sin: sin gives practical denial to God's authority, is sceptical of his goodness, argues with his wisdom, repudiates his justice, flatly contradicts his truth and despises his grace. It was a sound instinct which prompted the variant reading, "man of sin."

Detailed study of the passage will confirm all this. Why otherwise should the man of lawlessness be destroyed by the Lord Jesus? How otherwise can we interpret the references to "the activity of Satan" and "unrighteousness"? Judgment and salvation are meaningless apart from the concept of sin.

But there is another factor in the Epistle, divine love and grace. It is the love of God and the love of Jesus (2:13, 16; 3:5) and it is associated with "eternal comfort" (cf. Luke 16:25). Grace is from the Father and from the Lord Jesus Christ (1:2; 1:12; 2:16; 3:18). Its result is peace (1:2; 3:16).

This is more than a mere idea. Paul does not tell us much explicitly but he has given us certain keyholes through which we can see into his mind. "The steadfastness of Christ" (3:5) must imply the incarnation, and if the Lord will "guard you from evil" (3:3), he has at least an attitude to it. If the Lord Jesus is to come "from heaven" (1:7), it is pertinent to ask how in the thought of the apostle the incarnate Lord reached heaven. Room is left for the death, resurrection, and ascension. It may be argued that this is reading into the text. How else would Paul have thought of the matter? Again, why should we assemble to meet the Lord at his coming? Why not be impartial spectators? It is because our life depends entirely on him and his gospel (1:8; 2:1). The mediation of Jesus is not here expressed but it is suggested.

The "terms" of the gospel are surely faith, which is the true response to it. This is implied by the importance which faith has in the Epistle (1:3 f., 10 f.; 2:10–12; 3:1 f.). Reference should here be made to the introduction to the First Epistle for observations on faith and on calling (2 Thess. 1:11; 2:14). This, and "accounting worthy" (1:5, 11), cohere with the doctrine of justification by faith.

Christian duty includes growth in faith and love and endurance (1:3 f.), and in the experience of the love of God (3:5); thanksgiving and prayer (1:3; 2:13), with the author as the example as well as the teacher (1:11; 3:1). Inner faith is to be expressed in word and deed (1:11; 2:17) without ceasing (3:13). Gossip is to be avoided and a livelihood earned (3:11). Holiness is the divine purpose (2:13). The teaching already received is to be held fast (2:15; 3:6). All is in the context of the church (1:1, 4), the fellowship of which is to be a reality (3:6, 14 f.). Christians must not be deceived but must keep the mind of Christ (2:2 f.); but they need not and should not rely on their own strength (3:3).

This pattern of the plan of salvation is not so elaborate even as that in the First Epistle, still less than that in the Epistle to the Romans. But the broad outline or framework is the same. The details of Christian truth can be added without doing violence to the apostle's thought. In other words, he could have written the Second Epistle.

The doctrine of God accords with that in the First Epistle. He is the living God, for prayer is offered to him, and the language of the apostle assumes the sovereignty of God (1:3, 11; 2:13, 17; 3:1–3). He hears and he acts: not all the possible answers to prayer are "spiritual." It is by the exercise of his power that he delivers his servants from evil men. He works not only "externally" but in human hearts as well (as above). He is righteous in judgment (1:5 f.), which is mediated through the Lord Jesus (1:8). He is the only God (2:4). He loves (2:16; 3:5) and he elected to salvation and glory (2:13 f.). He called and he calls (1:11; 2:14). He is God the Father and God our Father (1:1 f.).

In Christology, due weight must be given to the title Lord Jesus Christ (1:1 f.). Christ is closely associated with the Father. Grace and peace come from the Father and the Lord, and from the Lord without mention of the Father (1:2; 2:16; 3:16, 18). "The steadfastness of Christ" (3:5) implies the incarnation, though the Lord is now in heaven (1:7). From there he loves his elect; and from there he will come to be glorified in his saints (1:10) and to execute the judgment of God (1:5–8), destroying the lawless one (2:8). As the dispenser of judgment and the central point of his people's assembly, he continues the work of mediation implied by his gospel (1:8).

The Holy Spirit is mentioned once (2:13) in a significant context. God receives thanksgiving, the Lord loves, and the Spirit works in holiness. This is not the formulated doctrine of the Holy Trinity, but it could be part of the material for it.

Once again we have a letter from the apostle Paul in which he used the relevant parts of his deep knowledge for practical and pastoral purposes. He did not tell all he knew, and it was not necessary for him to do so. But he did say enough for us to recognize that what he wrote came from the mind and heart of the apostle to the Gentiles.

OUTLINE

2 Thessalonians

COMMENTARY

2 Thessalonians

I. GREETING (1:1–2)

The conventional but Christianized form of the introduction used in the First Epistle is repeated with a slight addition.

Full comments have already been given on 1 Thessalonians 1:1, to which reference should be made.

God our Father: Does this differ from "God the Father" of the First Epistle (1:1)? It depends on who uses the words, and on the circumstances. An unbelieving historian or philosopher who was discussing theology might refer to "God the Father" when dealing with the influence of Christian doctrine in the history of thought. Paul himself might have so spoken in his approach to a thoughtful man who was seeking an exposition of Christian truth before committing himself to Christ. Our Lord spoke of "the Father" (Acts 1:7, cf. 1:4). In some situations the term "God the Father" can suggest a measure of detachment, either real as with the unbelieving philosopher or adopted for the purpose of discussion. When Paul used it to the Thessalonians we may be sure that *God our Father* was latent in his mind, bursting to come out—as indeed it did (1 Thess. 1:3; 3:11, 13). It could not appropriately be used always. Some preachers even object to the use of the Lord's Prayer at a service attended by non-Christians, as they cannot yet join in with "Our Father . . . . " The *our* slightly emphasizes the doctrine of adoption, the experiential intimacy and the Christian's pledge, and the fellowship or communion of saints who share a common Father. The Fatherhood of God is not universal, as men once believed, but is in Christ; it is not by nature but by grace. This is suggested (though the thought is not expounded) by the close association of *the Lord Jesus Christ,* before which the *in* is not repeated.

Verse 2: From God the Father and the Lord Jesus Christ, who are the source of *grace* and *peace.* This addition brings out explicitly what was only implied in the greeting in the First Epistle. At this point the source is one: the *from* which precedes *God* is not repeated before *the Lord.* It is true, though it is not here said, that God the Father is the eternal author of salvation and the Lord Jesus Christ the channel or Mediator. These human approximations draw attention to the work or "office" of our Lord in men's salvation. They do not mean crudely that "God thought of it" and "Jesus did it." Our Savior is the eternal Son of God and was in the counsels of the Father from all eternity. It is thus quite fitting for him to be regarded as the source of *grace* and *peace*. *God* is here preeminently *the Father* of *the Lord Jesus Christ*.

Reference should be made to the other Pauline epistles. It will be seen that the addition of the source became a regular feature of a Pauline introduction.

II. DOCTRINE AS GROUND OF ENCOURAGEMENT AND CHALLENGE (1:3–2:17)

Thanksgiving was due to God for the Thessalonians' spiritual growth. Their faith under pressure was an indication of God's righteous judgment. At the Second Advent fortunes would be reversed; they themselves would be vindicated and their oppressors punished. In the meantime they were the objects of the apostles' prayers. They need not be alarmed. The day of the Lord had not come and would not come before the rise of apostasy and the revelation of the man of lawlessness. His work was being restrained until his "Advent," when he would be destroyed with his dupes. Thanksgiving and challenge were reinforced with a prayer.

1. The Doctrine of Vindication (1:3–12)

The spiritual development of the Thessalonians called for continued thanksgiving. They had so grown in faith and mutual love, in spite of persecutions, that the apostles were boasting of them in the various churches. Their sustained Christian lives were an encouraging sign of God's righteous judgment. They would be deemed worthy of the kingdom of God and would be given relief at the Second Advent. Those who afflicted them would receive affliction and the punishment of destruction when the Lord Jesus came in power and glory. With this in view the apostles were praying for their spiritual welfare and future glory in the glorified Lord.

(1) Thanksgiving an obligation (1:3–4)

Paul and his companions recognized that thanksgiving was constantly due to God for a notable growth of faith and mutual love. It inspired them to speak with pride concerning the Thessalonians when they visited the various churches. Their faith had endured amid persecutions and afflictions.

Verse 3: We are bound to give thanks—an ethical duty as well as a spiritual delight. Some scholars see here a reply to the Thessalonians'

[135]

protest of unworthiness: the fainthearted had informed the apostles that they were not worthy of the kingdom or of the commendation given in the First Epistle. On the contrary, we must understand the answer, we ought to give thanks. This would account for the emphasis on obligation, but it is an assumption. There are times when a man is so impressed with the greatness of God's goodness that he feels that it calls for thanksgiving.

We are bound, literally "we owe," is the language of debt used to express obligation. The same word is used in Romans 13:8, where what is "owed" is mutual love. "We owe love" means that "we ought to love." (Cf. Rom. 15:1, 27.) Similarly disciples owe a mutual "footwashing" (John 13:14). Sometimes the "debt" is doubly due: we owe it anyway, as moral duty, and we may owe it in the sense that we ought to have paid it already. Thus, in the Lord's Prayer we pray "forgive us our debts" (Matt. 6:12). Such moral duty not done is called "sins" in Luke's parallel account (Luke 11:4). Paul's debt of thanksgiving was not a sin: he was paying at once! (Cf. 1 Thess. 5:18.)

Thanksgiving is thus a moral duty (cf. 2:13), though complete thanksgiving is sometimes beyond our powers. It can at least be attempted (1 Thess. 1:2; 3:9). "Ought," "can" and "do" summarize three lines of thought. Thanksgiving ought to be given; it will probably be inadequate; it can at least be begun. It is of great importance in the spiritual life, particularly in the life of prayer. It is hardly too much to say that the observance of answers to prayer and the offering of thanks for them is the condition of obtaining further answers (Phil. 4: 6). Thanksgiving should be constant, *always,* rather than spasmodic. In rendering it *to God* we recognize his hand in what seems to be a human matter. After victory in war men have been known to adjourn to the house of God for thanksgiving. The cynic may say that they won by their own efforts. He is partially right even though his spirit is wrong. But ultimately victory in a righteous cause must be ascribed to God. So it is with the church militant, in the "good fight" in which all Christians are involved (1 Tim. 6:12; 2 Tim. 4:7).

As is fitting: Thanksgiving was justified by the facts. The idea is thus more than a mere repetition. The thanksgiving was due to the divine obligation, but apart from the conduct of the Thessalonians Paul could not have given thanks *for you.* Two "human" facts are stated, *because* of which thanksgiving was *fitting.*

Your faith is growing abundantly: It was not static. If Paul were alive today and at work among young people he would have great sympathy with those who love the prefix "super." At any rate he seems to have coined the word, for "we are super-conquerors" (Rom. 8:37, literal) and he certainly reveled in the fact that God "super-exalted" his Son (Phil. 2:9). So here he delighted to magnify the growth of the

Thessalonians' faith. It was "super-growing." The obvious illustration is the mustard seed (Matt. 13:31 f.; Luke 13:19) which grows into a tree, though we need not limit ourselves to the luxuriant growth of vegetation. When faith is growing in the way in which Paul saw it grow, there is an increase in strength. Faith—or the believing man—can stand more strain. When faith has grown, it is mature and the believer has deeper insight into God's dealings with him. When faith is growing it is rising like the wind, and when its stiff breezes attain to gale force there is heightened mystery to attract the outsider and convince him of the depths of faith (John 3:8). It was a discerning spirit who suggested that in Christianity one of its great qualities—perhaps its greatest—is that you never know what it will do next.[1] When faith is growing it is waxing like the moon and has more and more light to shed on human problems.

The love of every one of you for one another is increasing: There was no exception in giving or receiving. Each member was a center of a radial outflow of love. What this meant in the life of the Thessalonian church can best be learned from a study of 1 Corinthians 13:4–8.

All this growth in faith and love was in response to the apostles' hopes and prayers. In some respects the Thessalonians' faith had been lacking (1 Thess. 3:10); now they were growing. There had been room for increase in mutual love (1 Thess. 3:12); now it was indeed *increasing.* The preachers marked it and gave thanks.

Further subjects of thanksgiving deserve notice: the election of the readers to salvation (2:13); their genuine conversion (1 Thess. 2:13) and its outworking in their lives (1 Thess. 1:2 f.). It is God who is to be thanked both for divine election and for human work. The following verse shows that Paul did not hesitate to give encouragement in recognition of human endeavor. Perhaps the paradox is resolved if we say that Paul can thank God and praise men for what they have done; but that the men in question do no more than thank and praise God: for them boasting is excluded (Rom. 3:27). We have here a mark of Paul's great sanity. It is possible so to emphasize that "it is all of God" that the saints are discouraged. Some people indeed seem to think that the only way to glorify God is to criticize the preacher and denigrate the pew. Paul preserved the balance: he praised and thanked God for everything and gladly recognized every honest endeavor to live the Christian life.

Verse 4: Therefore we ourselves boast of you . . . : A new note added to the chorus (1 Thess. 1:8 and discussion). To all the general talk was now added the apostolic approval, not only of faith but of faith under fire. At first we may feel that the word *boast* is unexpected

---

1. Cf. H. R. Mackintosh, *The Originality of the Christian Message* (London: Duckworth, 1925), p. 26.

on the lips of Paul. He held strongly that men should not boast in the presence of God. If they must boast they should boast of the Lord (1 Cor. 1:29–31). This allusion to Jeremiah 9:23 f. was repeated in 2 Corinthians 10:17. To do otherwise would savor of human effort (Phil. 3:3), and nobody should boast of men (1 Cor. 3:21). Boasting would suggest human self-reliance and even self-existence. It would imply that the ground of boasting had been produced by men, whereas it had been received from God (1 Cor. 4:7).

But life would be poorer and indeed sour if there were no encouragement and recognition of human achievement. The secular state frequently recognizes and rewards high endeavor and public service. Some states have an "honors list" at regular intervals recording the award of medals, decorations, orders of chivalry, titles, etc., referring to 1 Peter 2:14 to justify the custom. In the church a retired and honored servant of God is often appointed "minister-emeritus" or a layman is made a "life-deacon" or some other honorary official, without the necessity of constant reelection. On a celebrated occasion our Lord said in a parable, "Well done, good servant!" (Luke 19:17). Paul followed this precedent and commended the Corinthians (1 Cor. 11:2) and even boasted about them (2 Cor. 9:1–4). At times he seems to have come near to boasting about himself and his work (Phil. 2:16; cf. 1 Thess. 2:19).

Such boasting comes strangely from a man who would boast in nothing but the cross (Gal. 6:14)—or so it may seem to us at first sight. But it is not really so strange. We must see here not an apostolic inconsistency but a richness of thought and experience. The man who decided to know nothing except Jesus Christ and him crucified (1 Cor. 2:2) did not restrict himself to a limited field or sound no more than a single evangelistic note. He knew much in addition to the cross, but he knew nothing except the cross in the sense that he related everything to the cross. This is a sound clue in the understanding of his boasting. He boasted in nothing but the cross in the sense that every boast was related to the cross. If he boasted of the Thessalonians, it was because they were the triumphs of the cross, both in their conversion and in its outworking in their lives. If he boasted of himself and of his work, it was because he was a preacher of the cross (1 Cor. 15:10). He was the channel of power, not its originator; he himself was nothing—yet would receive his wages (1 Cor. 2:5; 3:5–9).

In the churches of God—where sympathy might be assumed and encouragement welcomed. The world would hardly be interested; the churches would. (Cf. 1 Thess. 2:14 and discussion.) Paul was still boasting of the Macedonians in 2 Corinthians 8:1–5.

For your steadfastness and faith: A single conception. The two abstract nouns are linked by one article, not two. Paul's thought of the "steadfastness-and-faith" of the Thessalonians suggests that *faith* does not exist in a vacuum. It has to persist, and if it is attacked it has to hold its ground. In simple terms the meaning is that the church members continued to believe even when to do so they had to go on enduring. For there were those who sought to knock the faith out of them—the *persecutions;* and life itself brought *afflictions,* a wider term than persecutions though including them. In affliction men are under pressure; the life is being squeezed out of them.

In the Christian life faith must continue always. We must meet persecution with steadfastness, standing unmoved under a rain of blows. We must "put up with" afflictions, but temptation must be resisted (Jas. 4:7; 1 Pet. 5:9).

Note the tenacity of the Thessalonians. They held on in *all* their *persecutions.* Never did they haul down the flag. And *the afflictions* had not stopped: *you are enduring.* (See further in the First Epistle 1:3, 6; 3:1–8.)

(2) Fidelity an encouragement (1:5–10)

The endurance of their faith under pressure was a plain indication of God's righteous judgment. For they would be deemed worthy of the kingdom for which they were suffering and would be given relief with the transfer of their affliction to their persecutors. They themselves would be vindicated when the Lord Jesus was finally revealed in power, for their oppressors, who rejected the knowledge of God and disobeyed the gospel, would be punished and banished from the divine presence and glory.

Verse 5: This is evidence of the righteous judgment of God: Human constancy, divine consistency. The thought is not obvious for the *evidence* is not on the surface. Suffering is often thought to be evidence of God's unrighteousness rather than of his righteousness. "Is it fair?" is the repeated cry. But here we have the suffering of Christians, which makes all the difference.

This summarizes the experience of the Thessalonians. It refers not to their steadfastness and faith alone, nor to their persecutions and afflictions alone, but to their steadfastness and faith amid persecutions and afflictions. Their trials were severe and they may be likened to a besieged garrison. The beleaguered troops were able to hold out because supplies were regularly brought in to them under cover of secrecy. God himself was sustaining them. God was on their side; God was "for them" (cf. Rom. 8:31) because they were already on his side—surely an aspect of the covenant. This was the heart of the *evidence.* The God who sustained them in the sufferings of faith would continue to sustain them up to and including the Day of Judgment. God upheld the right in Thessalonica; he would uphold it at the judgment—for the Thessalonians were justified, deemed righteous. They believed, and kept on believing under stress, because God inspired their faith. Their faith had been reckoned to them as righteousness (Rom. 4:1–5). It was the gift of God (cf. Rom. 5:17; 1 Cor. 1:30) and on the Day of Judgment God would recognize it. God's judgment is thus righteous.

In short the meaning is that God sustains their faith now and will own it at the judgment. Their experience is therefore a pointer to God's righteous judgment.

This insight is not the result of purely theological reflection. It sprang from Paul's own dealings with God. He too knew the sharp adversities of the Christian life and prayed to be delivered from them. But "my grace is sufficient for you, for my power is made perfect in weakness" (2 Cor. 12:7–10). (Cf. also Phil. 1:28.)

That you may be made worthy of the kingdom of God—the purpose of the righteous judgment. Paul did not mean that they would be refined by suffering in a sort of earthly purgatory and therefore be able to stand in their own purity at the judgment. Their persistent faith, sustained by grace, was a saving faith, and the purpose of the judgment was that they might be "deemed worthy"—a better translation. The eschatological justification by faith will be reaffirmed at the judgment. This inverts the usual order: it is usually said that justification is an anticipation of the judgment. Note the close association of the consummated Kingdom with the Advent and the Judgment.

For which you are suffering: The kingdom makes the sublime background to suffering. It is said that sailors have the look of "distance" in their eyes. They do not spend their time looking down over the side of the ship to the sea which it cleaves. Their eyes are often on the far horizon. So Paul would turn the thought of the Thessalonians away from that of "being hurt" to the fair prospect of the kingdom; they were looking away to Jesus (Heb. 12:2). At the back of his mind Paul may have been contrasting the present and the future experiences ("steadfastness of hope," 1 Thess. 1:3), and linking writers and readers in the common Christian privilege (Acts 5:41).

Verse 6: Since indeed God deems it just . . . . : The guarantee of the evidence (v. 5). The sustained faith of the Thessalonians could only be evidence of God's righteous judgment if his righteousness remained constant and was finally expressed in action. The evidence, as evidence, in all times depends on the righteousness. This is brought out by Paul's language and its hypothetical form. The translation of the RSV is not inaccurate but it does not bring out the condition. *Since indeed* renders *eiper,* a conditional particle which means "if really (as is the case)." The thought is: "If it is really true (as it is) that God . . . , then your persistent faith is evidence . . . ." It is not a big jump from "if really" to *since indeed,* because the condition is true in fact; it is not merely supposed. *Just* (which again is not wrong) renders the same Greek word as that behind "righteous (judgment)" of verse 5. A literal rendering would lose a certain simplicity but would reveal the flow of the apostle's thought. "This is evidence of the righteous judgment of God . . . —if it is really righteous with God (as it is) to repay . . . ."

The repayment seems at first to resemble the *lex talionis* or law of retaliation (Exod. 21:23–25), and it raises the question of whether God's punishments or rewards are always "of the same kind" as the sin or service. Certainly with rewards the principle holds to some extent. The reward of service is more service. The man who controlled a pound and by trading gained ten more was given the control of ten cities (Luke 19:17). But it is doubtful if the principle is to be applied mechanically. God has vast rewards for his people and they are far wider in scope than the negative "rest from affliction" of the next verse. Paul must be understood to be giving a particular case of a general rule. Affliction for unrepentant sinners and relief for the saints are examples of God's righteousness, which upholds the right. The persecutors will be punished and righteousness thereby upheld; the persecuted will be relieved and thereby enjoy the final salvation which comes from God's righteousness. God is righteous in the forgiveness of sins (Rom. 3:25 f.) through the cross no less than in the judgment of sinners—his righteous judgment (v. 5; cf. Rom. 2:5; 2 Tim. 4:8). Both Judge and judgment are righteous.

The word *repay* suggests giving back something in return for something, and is used in 1 Thessalonians 3:9 in connection with thanksgiving ("render"). There is at times a thought of obligation or expectation. Paul was obligated to give thanks and God expected it (1:3). We can hardly say that God is under moral obligation; even so, *repay* suggests a certain fitness in the act. Repayment in the sense of retribution is the prerogative of God (Rom. 12:19; Heb. 10:30; cf. Deut. 32:35).

Verse 7: And to grant rest with us to you who are afflicted: A repayment of another kind! The "repay" of verse 6 has two objects: God will repay affliction to the persecutors and rest to the Thessalonians. No doubt the translators of the RSV wanted to avoid the atmosphere of "repay" and so used the word *grant* instead. This avoids saying anything which implies that the persecuted deserved the *rest* or that Christians are entitled to their reward. All God's mercies, including *rest* and reward, are of grace. "Repay," however, recognizes that the *rest* (or reward, in another context) is related to Christian experience. All the treasures of heaven which believers will receive in Christ come from grace; some of them, also of grace, are in recognition of service and suffering. The *rest* is but one aspect of the heavenly "reward." It does not here mean a cessation of activity or a recovery of strength but rather a relief, a let up. In heaven the Thessalonians could relax! It will be more than relief; it will be glory (Rom. 8:18).

The phrase *with us* rings with warm Pauline feeling. The apostles are one with the Thessalonians in the fellowship of suffering and its outcome. (Cf. Phil. 1:29 f.; 1 Thess. 3:3 f. and discussion.) The two words occupy little space and may be compared with the touches on an oil painting whereby the authentic artist is revealed. This is the master himself! Notice how Paul was dealing with an existing situation and how vividly his words bring a picture before our eyes: "those who are now afflicting you" (v. 6) and "you who are now being afflicted" (cf. 2 Cor. 4:14).

When the Lord Jesus is revealed: More than a mere mark of time. The literal rendering is "in the revelation of the Lord Jesus." (Cf. 1 Pet. 1:7, 13; 4:13.) This may be interpreted as a secondary Hebraism: behind the Greek language lurks Hebrew syntax, as in Ephesians 6:19. "In opening my mouth" would mean "when I open my mouth." But in Romans 2:5 Paul was careful to say "wrath in the day of wrath and of the revelation of God's righteous judgment." Where the time element was to the fore he used the word "day." This at least should make us pause. It would seem that God's "repayment" is "involved in the revelation of the Lord Jesus." It is part of the unveiling of the Lord. The revelation is more than an exhibition, glorious though it will be. It will be a program. In it God's righteousness will be seen in operation and in a dual aspect. On the one hand it will mean judgment for the wicked, and in particular for the oppressors of the Thessalonians; on the other hand it will mean full salvation for the Christians, in particular the Thessalonians. We must thus see in Paul's thought here more than a note of time, "(the day of) revelation." Revelation includes the vindication of righteousness.

We should not read into the text anything which savors of spite or revenge. What will be done will be done by God and it is related to Christ. It will be done by one whose character is known. In the holy love of God there is no room for petty spite or malice. And there should not be in the Thessalonians or any other Christians. Persecutors not only cause pain to their fellow-men; they are fighting against God, against truth and righteousness. When Christians are finally vindicated they will not be vindicated merely as men but as representatives of God's truth and righteousness. If they were not Christians they would not be persecuted.

The Second Advent is referred to in the New Testament by three different nouns which may be anglicized as apocalypse *(apokalupsis)*, parousia, and epiphany *(epiphaneia)*. Apocalypse, the word here used in verse 7, means an unveiling or disclosure of what was hitherto hidden, unseen or unknown. Thus Paul could speak of "the revelation of the mystery which was kept secret for long ages" (Rom. 16:25) and of "how the mystery was made known to me by revelation" (Eph. 3:3). The gospel itself came to him "through a revelation of Jesus Christ" (Gal. 1:12). Christ has already been revealed, but he will be revealed again, and there are men who eagerly await the day: the Corinthians "eagerly wait for the revealing of our Lord Jesus Christ" (1 Cor. 1:7; cf. Phil. 3:20). The emphasis in the term "apocalypse" lies in the fact that the hiddenness is at an end. At present Christ is hidden and will continue to be hidden until God acts to disclose him. That act will be "the revelation of the Lord Jesus."

Parousia has already been considered (1 Thess. 2:19 and discussion; cf. 3:13; 4:15; 5:23; 2 Thess. 2:1, 8 f.). It is in marked contrast to an absence (cf. 2 Cor. 5:6) and it implies that "he is really here."

Epiphany (2 Thess. 2:8; 1 Tim. 6:14; 2 Tim. 1:10; 4:1, 8; Titus 2:13) is a word used by Aristotle for the "surface" of a solid body. It hardly therefore means "mere appearance" without the reality. Perhaps the best rendering would be "manifestation," a making subject to awareness, whether men choose to be aware or not. Whereas Parousia emphasizes the reality of the presence, epiphany points to the certainty with which believers see the Lord when he comes. If they are on the alert they will really see him—for there will be something to see.

The nuances of the three words thus suggest that the hiddenness of the Lord will be ended; that his presence will be in objective reality; and that his people will really see him in a way which transcends even faith (2 Cor. 5:7).

From heaven with his mighty angels in flaming fire: Origin, escort, scenery. If the Lord comes *from heaven* it is bound to involve revelation, for he is as hidden there as God is. He shares the mode of life of "Our Father who art in heaven" (Matt. 6:9). As the apostle was thinking of Jesus, the historic person (see on 1 Thess. 1:1), we must ask again how such a man got to heaven. Once more we must say that the ascension is implied, the exaltation to the right hand of God. (See on 1 Thess. 1:10.) The concept of revelation was in the mind of Jesus himself (Luke 17:30).

His mighty angels is linguistically possible, though a literal rendering would be "angels of his power." (Cf. Luke 18:6, where "the judge of unrighteousness" is translated by "the unrighteous judge.") The Book of Enoch (61:10) speaks of "all the angels of power," though it is doubtful if Paul deliberately quoted.

Angels were present at the giving of the law (Acts 7:53; Gal. 3:19; Heb. 2:2; cf. Deut. 33:2, Ps. 67:18, LXX—68:17, RSV). It is therefore not unfitting for angels to be present at the judgment (Matt. 16:27; Mark 8:38; Luke 12:8 f.). But their role is subsidiary; they have no independent command; they are "ministering spirits sent forth to serve" (Heb. 1:14). In the gospels they appear from time to time as heralds of God's action, and occasionally they served Jesus directly. They ministered to him at the Temptation (Matt. 4:11; Mark. 1:13) and under severe restraint at the Passion: our Lord accepted angelic aid to help him through Gethsemane (Luke 22:43) but would not summon their legions to prevent his arrest (Matt. 26:53). But how will the angels serve the Lord at the judgment?

It could be that they are witnesses, much like the spectators in court at a modern trial, if this is a reasonable inference from Luke 12:8 f. But this is too passive. They are agents of judgment or rather of the judge. He will separate men one from another (Matt. 25:31–33); but it is the angels who will gather together the elect (Matt. 24:31; Mark 13:27) and the angels who will eliminate the evildoers (Matt. 13:39–42, 49 f.). They are obviously agents of the judge. Through them he does his work. It should be observed that this final separation implements the choice already made by men (John 3:19–21).

The angels will have to be *mighty* if they are to carry out their task; but they are "angels of his power," not their own. They are mighty only as the Lord gives them might. "His power" ought to be retained in translation or at least in exposition, if only for the sake of the Thessalonians. At the time of writing they were suffering from persecutors. Their position resembled that of Jesus at the time of his arrest. The same could be said of their enemies as of his: "This is your hour, and the power [*exousia* here] of darkness" (Luke 22:53). But the positions would be reversed with the coming of the Lord. The power which would be manifested would be his.

It might be asked if the presence of angels at the Second Advent has any valued meaning today for Christians. Some would assert that they are no more than "paint" taken from an apocalyptic can to give color to the scene. We may readily admit the existence of a large can of apocalyptic paint. But Paul used it sparingly. The angels can have significance and in two ways. First they make manifest the power of the Lord. If Christians suffering from the power of evil men suddenly see the Lord's angels mightily gathering in his people, including themselves, and eliminating the power of evil, they will know in actual fact that the Lord is on their side. The position would be manifestly reversed. Secondly the angels enhance the dignity of the Lord. In many walks of life the higher a man goes the more people he has to obey him. The number of people "under" him (cf. Matt. 8:9; Luke 7:8) is almost a status symbol. So the angels who speed to do the Lord's bidding in the power which he has given to them are signs of the surpassing glory which is his.

Paul has written with restraint, omitting sensational and ghastly details which could have been drawn from apocalyptic literature. He did not say that the Thessalonians would look from on high and see their enemies in hell, and recognize them and rejoice (Assumption of Moses 10:10; cf. Enoch 27:3). He concentrated on the fact of judgment in the presence of the awaited Lord for the practical encouragement of his readers.

It should be observed that the apostle speaks of Jesus in a spirit in which the Psalmist can speak of God. "Bless the Lord, O you his angels, you mighty ones who do his word" (Ps. 103:20). This is one of the many unobtrusive pointers to the deity of Christ. Similarly the revelation of the Lord Jesus will be *in flaming fire,* a reminiscence of the judgment of Isaiah 66:15 and of the burning bush of Exodus 3:2. The Septuagint rendering gives "in a flame of fire" whereas the phrase in the epistle is "in a fire of flame." The difference is not serious. The latter appears in Siracides (Ecclesiasticus) 8:10; 45:19. The fire is characteristic of the divine presence and of the retribution. The presence is unmistakable (cf. Acts 2:3) and the retribution may be felt: it is more than unconscious degradation.

Verse 8: Inflicting vengeance upon those who do not know God: This is the personal judgment of the Lord, not the impersonal action of the flame. Shall not the judge of all the earth do right (Gen. 18:25)? *Vengeance* must not be understood in the sense of revenge, on the lines of the human and sinful "getting one's own back." It means punishment or retribution. There are three main theories of punishment. The deterrent says that society must be protected and "makes an example" of the man who has offended. The educative aims at reforming the criminal. Now if these two theories were all there is to be said about punishment, it would be open to anyone to suggest that now and again some innocent citizen should be given a dose of punishment to make it plain to all men what will happen to them if they break the law. Similarly any man who needed the "education" but who had not actually committed a crime could be sent to a penal institution for his own good. The suggestions are outrageous: punishment is for those who deserve it and for nobody else. This is reflected in the Septuagint version of Deuteronomy 32:35, "in the day of punishment I will repay [*antapodōsō*]." This is the "repayment" of verse 6 (see discussion). The retributive theory of punishment may include the deterrent and the educative in human legislation, but retribution is the essence of punishment. Without this element the door is left open for all the excesses of totalitarianism and of "corrective" institutions: a man could be sent to prison or concentration camp merely for discussing a policy, not for advocating it, and still less for carrying it out, on the ground that he was guilty of "deviation" and might be "dangerous." It may be argued that deviation is an offense of which he is guilty. This brings us back to retribution. It is for "those who do wrong" (1 Pet. 2:14). Deterrence and education can have no place in a final judgment. Without a clear understanding of retribution we shall not fully understand the meaning of the cross. We shall not plumb its depths anyway; but apart from retribution, we shall not go as far as the New Testament would take us. In the cross Christ bore the judgment of God.[1] Believers are saved from it (Rom. 8:1; cf. 1 Thess. 1:10; 2:16; 4:6; 5:9 and discussions).

Those who do not know God recalls 1 Thessalonians 4:5 (see discussion) though here the heathen or Gentiles are strikingly omitted. The reference can hardly be to the Jews as such, as the knowledge of God is by no means unknown in the Old Testament, and it was not always nominal. There were those who were acquainted with God (e.g., Ps. 36:10). Paul was speaking in general terms of those who were unwilling to know God (Rom. 1:28).

And upon those who do not obey the gospel of our Lord Jesus: These are the same people described differently. The two classes were not Gentiles and Jews respectively. The Thessalonians had both in their local church (Acts 17:4). To *obey the gospel* is to *know God,* and to know him in intimate acquaintance in contrast to knowing about him (Rom. 1:18–23) is possible only through obedience to the gospel. It should be noticed that the gospel is more than information, advice, invitation or call. It has the nature of a commandment. Men have not the sense of themselves to respond to Christ, and God in his mercy "commands men that all men everywhere should repent" (Acts 17:30; note the literal translation). When men are thus addressed by God in the power of the Spirit (cf. 1 Thess. 1:5), they recognize the authority of the Gospel and know that God is speaking to them. (Cf. Rom. 10:16, where "heeded" means "obeyed"; and 1 Pet. 4:17. For *gospel* see discussion on 1 Thess. 1:5; 2:2; 3:2.) Notice how Paul has "taken off" and is in full flight (up to v. 10). The Thessalonian airport (vv. 5–7) is behind and forgotten!

Verse 9: They shall suffer the punishment, as befits the general class to which they belonged and the character which they manifested. Those who refuse to know God and to obey the gospel belong to the general class of unbelieving evildoers. Irreligion involves immorality (cf. Gal. 5:19–21). Paul was not at this point restricting his thought to "those who afflict you" (v. 6). The *punishment* means the penalty: it is related to their attitude, character and deeds. The Greek word (*dikē*) means "justice" (see Acts 28:4). Evildoers merit justice; it is exacted from them when they "receive justice" as we say; and so they undergo it—as *punishment* (Jude 7).

It consists of *eternal destruction and exclusion.* Efforts to translate

---

1. Cf. Alan Richardson, *An Introduction to the Theology of the New Testament* (London: SCM Press, 1958), p. 77.

eternal (*aiōnion*) by "age-long" are not convincing. The same word is used to describe eternal life (Matt. 25:46; cf. Matt. 18:8 with Mark 9:43; and see Luke 16:26). This fearful doom is God's Amen to their persistent secular prayers. When the evangelist seeks to "introduce" them to God they refuse to meet him. When the Lord says "Come unto me" and "Follow me," they walk away. This attitude of mind and heart sets hard like concrete. Or it may be put another way.

Some seaports operate all the year round, like London or New York. Others are icebound during the winter. It is said that in a port like Montreal in Canada the authorities urge a captain to get his ship out of port when the freeze-up is imminent. He procrastinates; he wants to load even more cargo. In the end he cannot leave: his ship is frozen in. He has gained what he asked for. He refused to take the opportunity of getting away when he could. But now is the day of salvation. Eternal punishment thus marks two facts. God's patience is not for ever; and man's "ability" to repent is not unlimited. His repeated choice of godlessness ends in a settled character of godlessness. He does not want God. All the pleas and persuasions, all the blessings and blows of life, all the evidences and reminders of God's deep love in Christ have left him unmoved. What else can there be for him but that destruction which is *exclusion? Exclusion from the presence of the Lord* is what he has been seeking all his days. Now he has it. He has cut himself off from divine goodness and love and God judicially implements his decision. We might compare Romans 1:24, 26, 28; Revelation 22:11.

This is a legitimate interpretation of the text. But it ought to be said that the Greek, rendered literally, reads: "They will pay the penalty, (namely) eternal destruction (proceeding) from the presence of the Lord." The "from" indicates the origin of the destruction, not that in which it consists. The language is drawn from Isaiah 2:10, 19, 21 somewhat freely, as the prophet was thinking of men hiding themselves *from* the Lord. This allusion to the Septuagint recalls also the "inflicting vengeance" of verse 8. (Cf. 2 Thess. 2:8.)

It seems best to take the text as a "telescoped" or pregnant construction, as in the KJV. The destruction comes from the Lord and it consists in exclusion from him. And just as destruction actually is exclusion, so *the presence of the Lord* actually is *the glory of his might. Glory* stands for God revealed (see on 1 Thess. 2:12). The Lord in his might is in marked contrast to the Lord in the apparent weakness of his crucifixion and in the apparent weakness of his disciples, the Thessalonians. It will be clear to the condemned that he can carry out his judicial decisions. *Presence* is literally "face," a Hebrew idiom which has passed over into the New Testament. It would be linguistically wrong to overemphasize the aspect of "face"—even the sky has a face (Matt. 16:3, KJV); but it is hard to forget such passages as Revelation 1:7; 6:16.

How the face will look will depend on who you are, for "his servants shall worship him; they shall see his face" (Rev. 22:3 f.). But they will surely see it differently. For them it means the joy of the Lord forever; for the wicked it is devoid of hope.

The distinction should be kept in mind between *presence* in the sense of Advent (*parousia*—see discussion on 1 Thess. 5:23) and *presence* which translates the word *prosōpon*, "face."

Verse 10: When he comes on that day—the day of revelation (v. 7). (See discussion on 1 Thess. 5:2.) *On that day* appears at the very end of the verse in the Greek, and it may therefore be related to *glorified* and *marveled at*. The purpose of the coming is twofold, *to be glorified* and *to be marveled at*. This suggests that the punishment of the wicked is a by-product, as it were. Even at the judgment grace is preeminent: the Lord's people are precious to him.

The *glory* of verse 9 is picked up in the expression *to be glorified*, which is reminiscent of Psalm 88:8, LXX (Ps. 89:7, RSV; cf. Isa. 49:3, LXX). The Lord will come in glory and he is to receive glory: to glorify God is to recognize him in worship as God, righteous, majestic and mighty. Such ascription of glory to God is characteristic of the Old Testament; glory is now to be ascribed to the Lord Jesus. This is analogous to calling him Lord. (Notice the language of Isa. 45:23, LXX.) In quoting it Paul said (Rom. 14:11) that every knee would bow and every tongue confess—to God. In Philippians 2:10 f. he used the allusion to make reference to Christ. The change is of high significance, whether Philippians 2:5–11 is an early Christological hymn quoted by Paul or whether composed by him.[1]

The Lord is to be thus glorified *in his saints*. The vague *in* (Greek *en*) is susceptible of the widest interpretation. *His saints* (cf. 1 Thess. 3:13 and discussion), his holy people, will be the place where he is glorified; they will be the agents of his glorification, uttering his praises; and they will be the reason for it, in view of his work for them and in them. (Cf. John 17:10; Gal. 1:24.) J. B. Lightfoot suggests that the saints mirror the glory of the Lord, however imperfectly, just as the Son perfectly mirrors the glory of the Father (John 14:13; cf. Heb. 1:3).

The twofold purpose is expressed in roughly synonymous parallelism. Parallel to *glorified* is *to be marveled at*. "To marvel" renders a Greek verb which has the meaning "to admire" as well as to be astonished or to wonder. Admiration is strictly part of the aesthetic vocabulary. Truth is believed, moral act is approved and beauty is admired. But we read in IV Maccabees 17:17 that "the tyrant himself and his

---

1. See R. P. Martin, *Carmen Christi: Philippians ii. 5–11 in Recent Interpretation and in the Setting of Early Christian Worship* (Cambridge: University Press, 1967).

whole council admired their endurance"; and Jesus himself "admired" the centurion on the ground that not even in Israel had he found a faith so great (see Luke 7:9, NEB). The Lord, then, is to be admired; he is admirable, for "he has done all things well" (Mark 7:37).

The Lord is also *to be marveled at*. He is wonderful, just as God's deeds are wonderful (1 Pet. 2:9), corresponding to his marvelous light. We must picture men stepping out of a room of complete darkness into the blazing sunshine outside. They rub their eyes . . . . So in conversion men find the Lord to be one who brings surprises; and so it is in their pilgrimage as they make new and surprising discoveries of the unsearchable wealth of Christ (Eph. 3:8). So it will be *on that day*. The Lord is the surprising one. His people will be astonished. There may be an allusion in this verse to Psalm 67:36, LXX (68:35, RSV), "God is wonderful in his saints." Once more Paul has transferred the language to Christ.

If the parallelism is genuinely synonymous we should note that when we find the Lord wonderful we are glorifying him; and when we glorify him we are admiring him as one who always had surprises for us. Similarly *his saints* are *all who have believed,* and believers are his saints. The aorist tense would be well brought out here by rendering "all who (at their conversion) placed their faith (in Christ)." This corresponds to the original call (see 1 Thess. 4:7 and discussion). The *in* is used in the same sense as the *in* earlier in the verse.

At this point Paul was back in Thessalonica, preaching as an evangelist for conversions. His thought was moving swiftly from the last day to his days in the city. He therefore understandably omitted to express his thought completely and the result is an elliptical sentence. In full he meant: ". . . in all who believed—including you, *because our testimony to you was believed."* This was for their encouragement. They would be present in the throng of those who with wondering eyes would not be excluded from *the glory of his might* (v. 9) but would join in the praises of the Lord. They would be vindicated.

Paul's "theory" of preaching is striking. It is the giving of evidence, the telling of a story, rather than the development of an argument. Early proclamation was factual.

(3) Prayer a consequence (1:11–12)

Meanwhile the apostles were praying for their readers' continued worthiness and for the completion of every resolve and deed. This was to be for the glory of the Lord Jesus—and indeed for theirs in virtue of divine grace.

Verse 11: To this end we always pray for you, that . . . *:* Final perseverance ensured by divine means. *To this end* or "with a view to this" sums up the salvation of verses 5–10, with a special glance at the *worthy* (v. 5), which anticipates the same word later in the present verse. The prayer is in addition to the thanksgiving and the "boasting" (vv. 3 f.). Final perseverance is not mechanical: it does not mean that once a man has heard the call of God and has believed, he may be left alone as he will go to heaven anyway. He has the whole Christian life before him, with all its pitfalls and temptations. God's method of getting him across the ocean of life to the farther shore is pastoral. Apart from "the means of grace" such as private devotion and the life and worship of the church, God has other means. First there is warning. A mother who tells her child, "You will be burned," is not uttering an absolute prediction, though the form of the sentence looks like it. It is a caution, an alarm. The dire warnings of Scripture are designed to keep the believer in the way of salvation. A second means is that of prayer. Fellow Christians pray, as Paul prayed here. And in response God keeps his people unto the perfect day. This is illustrated in 1 Thessalonians 5:23 f. Paul prayed that his readers might be kept; and was sure that they would be.

That our God may make you worthy of his call—by working in them as well as over them (Phil. 2:12 f.). "Working out one's own salvation" does not mean "contributing" to what is all of grace. It has been likened to the work of a disciple, who is a learner who receives information, an observer who learns by watching the Master at work, and an apprentice who learns by actually doing the work himself. An apprenticed carpenter learns, not so much by lectures as by watching the skilled man and then trying his hand with hammer and nails and all the rest of the tools. And all the while the spiritual apprentice is thus working, the Holy Spirit is active within. For *make you worthy* see discussion on verse 5. The *call* came at the time of conversion (1 Thess. 4:7) and was continued throughout the Christian life (1 Thess. 2:12). God says "Up!" to us in a call which goes on until "that day" (Phil. 3:14). From the beginning the Christian life should be worthy of the initial call (Eph. 4:1). It is instructive to compare 2 Peter 1:3–11.

And may fulfil every good resolve and work of faith by his power: God working over them in providence as well as in them in experience. As he is *our God* (cf. "with us" v. 7), Paul was speaking out of his own experience. A delight in goodness, culminating in a *resolve,* has to be put into effect. We *fulfil* it when we do it. A *work of faith* (cf. 1 Thess. 1:3 and discussion) springs from faith and is carried out by faith. We *fulfil* it when we do it completely; when, in regard to it, a pastor does not have to say, "You were running well" (Gal. 5:7) or that we had put our hand to the plow and had then looked back (Luke 9:62). Fulfillment of a *work of faith* thus implies the overcoming of interruptions and of weariness (3:13). There may also be the thought that *by his power* the effect may be greater than intended or known.

Verse 12: So that the name of our Lord Jesus may be glorified in you:
This is the ultimate goal. The Greek is very close to that of Isaiah 66:5,
LXX, "that the name of the Lord may be glorified." "The name" means
God as revealed to men in distinction from God as he is in himself; it
means God manifested in his character, and standing in relation with
men. It summarizes all that men know of God and implies God as
known, present, and active. Now, significantly enough, *the name* is
transferred to *our Lord Jesus*. For *glorified* see the discussion on verse
10 and observe the parallels between *when he comes . . . to be glorified* and *so that the name . . . may be glorified*. The person and the
name are one. Notice a further parallel: he is to be glorified *in his saints*
and *in you*. This should have encouraged the Thessalonians—they will
be there—and inspired them to hold out, for by so doing they would
add to the Lord's glory. The ultimate purpose of the prayer (v. 11) is
thus that through God's blessing on their every good resolve and work
of faith the Lord Jesus may be glorified. The Thessalonians were already the glory of the apostles (1 Thess. 2:20); they could be the glory
of the Lord himself. The thought of this must surely banish any faint-
heartedness in disciples.

And you in him—at the receiving end also! The thought in full is,
"*And* that *you* (may be glorified) *in him*." The Greek would allow
the translation "in it (i.e., the name)" without any difference of basic
meaning. *In him*, however, is better as being more intimate, and it
accords with Paul's rich formula, "in Christ." It is more than "with
him." The Thessalonians, like the Corinthians, were members of the
Body of Christ and therefore "in" it (1 Cor. 12:18, 27). Now if
"glorify" means "to recognize a person for what he is," they will be
glorified in Christ in two ways. Men will say that they are in Christ
because they have put on Christ (Rom. 13:14; Gal. 3:27) as their
new clothing. This corresponds to imputed righteousness (Rom. 4:1–
12). And the churches of God will not forget: they will recognize the
Thessalonians as steadfast and faithful in persecution and affliction
(1:4). At the moment they had their cross; then they would have their
crown. And they would be forever with their glorified Lord (1 Thess.
4:17). If the Body is honored, the members share in the honor (cf.
1 Cor. 12:26).

According to the grace of our God and the Lord Jesus Christ: Grace
is the standard of measurement. The glory will be as great as the grace,
which indeed is the source of the glory. The Lord has his own glory,
that of the revealed Son, Savior and Lord. He has the glory of the
worshiping church, which acclaims him as Son, Savior and Lord. He
has the glory of those who acclaim him for what he has done in them.
The Thessalonians will have their own glory, the recognition of their
own steadfastness and faith. But their steadfastness was inspired by

hope in the Lord and their faith was due partly to the work of the preachers and partly to the power of the Holy Spirit (1 Thess. 1:3–5). Ultimately it was all therefore due to grace (see on 1 Thess. 1:1) and they will accordingly cast the crown of their glory before the throne and rejoice that the Lamb of God is worthy to receive it (cf. Rev. 4:9–10; 5:12).

A technical point arises here concerning the interpretation of the Greek. There is no article before the Greek word for *Lord.* This involves the translation "our God and Lord, Jesus Christ." On the other hand *Lord Jesus Christ* (without "the") is a fixed formula and the absence of the article does not matter. The issue is important: did Paul call Jesus God? He provides us with ample evidence for the deity of Christ, but did he explicitly refer to him as God? Support for the affirmative view is found in Romans 9:5 (RSV footnote *n*); Titus 2:13; cf. John 20:28; 2 Peter 1:1. As regards usage, however, Paul tended to use the term "God" for the Father and "Lord" for Jesus Christ, as in verses 11 and 12a. Simply to call Jesus God seems to ignore his humanity and the other Persons of the Godhead. Even so the difficulty of decision is testimony to Paul's high Christology. According to Oscar Cullmann we cannot exclude the possibility that the formula in the verse under consideration refers only to Christ.[1] Nigel Turner would go much further, and his words carry weight, for he is one of the greatest of living grammarians. In a section boldly entitled "Jesus is God" he suggests that special pleading is not guiltless of weakening the tremendous affirmations of the New Testament. The correct rendering of our text, he says, is "our lord and God Jesus Christ." [2]

If *the Lord* is the Septuagintal manner of translating the Old Testament Yahweh, and if Paul used *the Lord* as a title of Christ, then it is surely open to the same theological objection as the term "God." The Old Testament "Yahweh" or "Lord" must mean either the undivided Trinity or God the Father, either of which terms is inapplicable to Christ. Yet Paul applied *the Lord* to Christ. He knew, and his readers knew, that the Christ was Jesus—the man. It was not necessary to say everything all at once, every time. If, then, we can use *the Lord* of Christ, we can also speak of him as God. Such a passage as Philippians 2:11 surely requires no less.

2. The Doctrine of the Second Advent (2:1–17)

There should be no panic at Thessalonica through reports that the day of the Lord had come. It had to be preceded by apostasy and the revelation of the man of lawlessness. He was already at work and was

---

1. Oscar Cullmann, *The Christology of the New Testament* (London: SCM Press, 1959), p. 313.
2. Turner, *Grammatical Insights into the New Testament,* pp. 13–17.

being restrained until the time of his "Advent." The exercise of his
satanic power in false signs and wonders would deceive those who believe falsehood rather than the truth. Such deception would be God's
judicial act for the judgment of unbelief. Thanksgiving was renewed,
for the election of the Thessalonians demanded it. They were accordingly urged to stand firm and to hold fast to what they had been taught.
Thanksgiving passed into prayer for the readers.

(1) The keynote: no alarm (2:1–2)

By whatever means the report had come to them, whether spiritual
utterance, cool reasoning, or an alleged apostolic letter, the Thessalonians should not be driven out of their wits by thinking that the day of
the Lord had come.

Verse 1: Now concerning the coming . . . states the subject. The
coming and the *assembling* are united by one Greek article. Paul was
thinking of one event, not two. At the climax of history the Lord will
not be without his church, and his church will not be without him. For
coming, see the discussion on Parousia at 1:7 and its further references. The *assembling* recalls Matthew 24:31 and Mark 13:27, where
the word "gather" is the Greek verb corresponding to the noun *assembling.* Was Paul thinking of the church "gathering" or "being
gathered"? The latter, the passive sense, is implied by the texts in the
Gospels and it accords with 1 Thessalonians 4:17. Interesting confirmation is found in 2 Maccabees 2:7, "until God gather together a
gathering of the people" (RV footnote). In the previous chapter (1:27)
the prayer is offered, "Gather together our Dispersion." The language
of purely Jewish expectation and hope has been turned by Paul to
Christian use (cf. Deut. 30:3–4; and "dispersion" in Jas. 1:1 and 1 Pet.
1:1).

But *assembling* appears also in Hebrews 10:25, KJV, "not forsaking
the assembling of ourselves" ("to meet together," RSV). Here the
church gathers itself, or should do, for worship. The thought arises that
"going to church" is a miniature (we hesitate to say a rehearsal) of the
gathering of the saints at the last day. And many a preacher may be
tempted to tell his congregation that some cannot be trusted on earth
to gather themselves together—they rarely attend church—but that at
the end God will gather them. There is surely a warning embedded
here (1 Thess. 5:6).

To meet him: Converging on him. He is the rallying point for all his
scattered people in the one event (see above). For the "one event," see
1 Thessalonians 2:12, "kingdom-and-glory," and the discussion there.

We beg you, brethren: Paul requires an answer and expresses affection. (Cf. 1 Thess. 4:1; 5:12, where the same Greek verb is rendered
by "beseech.")

Verse 2: Not to be quickly shaken in mind or excited: No sudden shock; no constant fluttering. The former picture is that of being shaken "out of" one's mind (*nous*): not insanity but sudden panic. This involves two contrasts. They have received a kingdom which cannot be shaken but abides (Heb. 12:26–29). The subjects of the kingdom should match the kingdom and indeed its king, who is "the same yesterday and today and for ever" (Heb. 13:8). As Christians they have further the mind (*nous*) of Christ (1 Cor. 2:16). They should hold it fast.

Excited suggests the period after the initial shock has passed. The impact is followed by the feeling of disturbance, the continued uneasiness and apprehension. The verb is strikingly used in Matthew 24:6; Mark 13:7 ("alarmed"). Even wars, actual and imminent, should not occasion what in wartime is officially called "despondency." There is a "must" about events, which is not fate but divine sovereignty; and "the end is not yet." The situation was not precisely the same at Thessalonica but analogous, but the remedy was the same. Divine sovereignty would choose the time of the Second Advent, and it was not yet.

Either by spirit or by word, or by letter purporting to be from us: Ecstatic utterance, speech or argument, even apostolic pretensions should have been tested (1 Thess. 5:19–21; 2 Thess. 3:17). Apparently there had been nobody to "distinguish between spirits" (1 Cor. 12:10). A letter may have been foisted upon the congregation as Paul's or innocently but mistakenly attributed to him. On the other hand, there may have been no actual letter at all. Paul was considering every logical possibility to account for something for which he would not himself take the responsibility. The RSV relates *purporting to be from us* solely to the *letter* but it could be applied also to *spirit* and *word*. Some spiritual utterance or other expression of Paul's may have been "quoted." The point is that the apostle repudiates its content. The reference can hardly be to the First Epistle, which was more than *purporting*. Some parts of it, however, such as 4:13–18 may have been misunderstood.

To the effect that the day of the Lord has come, in a sense beyond that of Acts 2:16 f. (For *day of the Lord* see discussion on 1 Thess. 5:2.) Full force should be given to *has come.* It is more than "is imminent." The same verb is used elsewhere of the present in contrast to the future (Rom. 8:38; cf. 1 Cor. 3:22; Gal. 1:4). It would seem that the old anxiety had broken out again at Thessalonica in a more deadly form. They had worried that their deceased members would miss the blessings of the Parousia (1 Thess. 4:15). Now they were thinking, "We have all missed them." For if the day of the Lord had really come, it had come—and gone. For where was the Lord and why were they not with him? They must have missed it all. So they surely reasoned in their fashion. But could the Lord come unnoticed? Could the archangel and the trumpet of God be unheard? Somebody must have misled them (v. 3).

(2) The order of events (2:3–5)

Before the day of the Lord came there would have to be apostasy and the revelation of the man of lawlessness. Destined for destruction, he would prove to be an active secularist. Opposed to every object of worship, he would exalt himself with pretensions to divinity.

Verse 3: Let no one deceive you in any way: The manifold methods of evil. The deception is regarded as deliberate. In the thought of Paul deception could be brought about by sin (Rom. 7:11), the devil (2 Cor. 11:3, "the serpent"), fair and flattering words (Rom. 16:18), and by the self (1 Cor. 3:18). The warning against deception reechoes the teaching of the Lord (Matt. 24:4 f., 11, 24; Mark 13:5 f., 22; Luke 21:8).

For that day will not come: An example of ellipsis, which is not infrequent in the Pauline writings. Everything after *for* has to be supplied by the translator—it is not in the Greek.

Unless the rebellion comes first: The religious (not political) rebellion of non-Christians against God. *The* rebellion is the one already taught by the apostles to the Thessalonians (v. 5; cf. 1 Thess. 5:1). Paul was writing selectively and the readers would understand more clearly than we do, because they had received his teaching.

And the man of lawlessness is revealed, the son of perdition: He is associated but not identical with the rebellion. The revelation may accompany or follow the rebellion. Paul was here beginning to use the vocabulary appropriate to the Christian religion: *revealed,* mystery (v. 7), at work (v. 7—like the word of God, 1 Thess. 2:13), coming (*parousia,* v. 9), activity (*energeia*) and power (*dunamis,* v. 9, cf. Eph. 3:7), signs and wonders (v. 9, cf. Acts 2:22; 5:12), believe (v. 11). This has points of contact with the concept of antichrist, which embodies opposition in the guise of similarity (1 John 2:18). There is the Christian fellowship and there is such a thing as an unholy fellowship. It has all the activities of the genuine church, but all are steeped in falsity, sin, and hostility to the truth. Paul's use of Christian vocabulary accords with this.

The man of lawlessness is the concentration of evil, and as *the son of perdition* he is "destined for destruction." He is a sort of arch-Judas, who is described in the same way (John 17:12). The lawless man (for such is the meaning of the Hebraistic genitive) is well described: it suggests his deliberate hostility to the known will of God. "If it had not been for the law, I should not have known sin" (Rom. 7:7).

The identity of *the man of lawlessness* has not been disclosed. We can dismiss such figures as Nero or any member of the papacy up to the present time. He is a figure of the eschatological future and he can be identified only if the rebellion has already started. But has it? Some would say that it has and can point to the upsurge of secularism and atheism to prove it. But it may be doubted if even this is big enough. The world is capable of carrying its rebellion against God even further than it has done hitherto. Even if it were granted that the rebellion had started, it would be difficult to identify *the man of lawlessness*. There seems to be no obvious candidate. At the most we can say that the present mood of the world could become the rebellion.

We are not told who reveals him. The Christian vocabulary, as described above, would suggest that the evil one, the devil, deliberately imitates the life of the church. He therefore is the one who reveals— but only under the all-controlling power of God.

There is an apparent contradiction of 1 Thessalonians 5:2-3. The day will come like a thief in the night, with sudden destruction, but the rebellion must come first. These two positions are not irreconcilable as a matter of logic. For example, a woman's pangs are not unanticipated. But more important is the Semitic mind. It feels no embarrassment at what we should regard as sweeping statements. Its tendency is to make a general statement and then follow it with details. Thus "he came unto his own (home or property), and his own people did not receive him" —this is general enough. "But to all who did receive him . . . " (John 1:11 f.)—this is the subsequent "detail." (Cf. Gen. 2:16 f; 9:3 f; Exod. 12:10.) The same "contradiction" as Paul made is found in Mark 13. "Watch . . . you do not know when" (v. 33); "the end is not yet" (v. 7).

Verse 4: Who opposes and exalts himself against every so-called god or object of worship: He is the secularist *par excellence.* The opposer and self-exalter is one superhuman ("revealed") person, a mocking parody of Christ. The Greek behind "opposer" (*antikeimenos*) is used by Aristotle for "contradictory" propositions.[1] Paul made use of the verb to express the mutual antagonism of flesh and Spirit (Gal. 5:17), for the mind of the flesh is hostile to God (Rom. 8:7). When a wide door was flung open to evangelism there were many "adversaries" (1 Cor. 16:9). Active, relentless hostility is thus implied.

But the adversary not only wants to strike down any and every opposition; he *exalts himself* and does so *against every . . . god.* The latter phrase is from Daniel 11:36, LXX. Paul has inserted *so-called,* not because he was here attacking the gods of heathenism (cf. 1 Cor. 8:5) but to give his thought the widest possible expression. As a

---

1. Aristotle *Prior Analytics* 2. 15. 63b. 31.

Christian Jew he was the last person to speak of "every god." But he wanted to show the hostility of the man of lawlessness to every object of human worship, true or false. He would countenance no religion of any kind. Paul would not include the Lord God among gods in general. *So-called* is slightly unfortunate as a translation: he meant "every god that is said to be (i.e., recognized as) god." The attitude of the Almighty to all that is exalted is seen in Isaiah 2:11–17.

The *object of worship* includes images, etc. (Acts 17:23).

So that he takes his seat in the temple of God—the final insolent intrusion. *So that* introduces the natural consequence rather than the actual result of the opposition and self-exaltation. It emphasizes what the opposition tends to produce rather than what it actually produced. There is thus a causal connection between the drive against all religion and the ultimate blasphemy. The thought is: he opposes . . . and so exalts himself as to take his seat . . . .

In the background lurk such passages as Ezekiel 28:2; Daniel 11:36; Isaiah 14:13 and perhaps the remembrance of the attempt of the Roman emperor Caligula to erect a statue of himself in the Temple at Jerusalem in A.D. 40. But this is more than a statue; it is visualized as a personal act. This is sensed in Mark 13:14, KJV, "the abomination of desolation . . . standing . . ." (see Dan. 12:11), where "standing" is masculine though it should be neuter to agree with "abomination."

There is something permanent about *takes his seat*. It is parallel to our Lord's heavenly session. The "levitical drudges" of whom Moffatt speaks stand at their daily ritual services. Jesus Christ took his seat— because his work was done (Heb. 10:11 f.). It need hardly be added that the permanence exists only in the mind of the antichrist (see v. 8). The meaning of *the temple of God* should not be forced. We naturally think of the temple in Jerusalem but Paul could think of the church as the temple of God (1 Cor. 3:16 f.). The Greek in both passages is *naos*, the inmost shrine and abode of deity: it is the dwelling place of God (Eph. 2:21 f.). The point is that the antichrist settles down for permanent occupation of the place of God. It cannot be any denominational building *as such*, because his motive is to sweep away all existing religious institutions, gods and things alike. If a building is insisted on we could cite (without cynicism) in illustration the chapel of the United Nations. If, however, the church is meant, the text means that antichrist has taken it over and is its head. A feeble illustration would be Hitler's domination of the German church and the talk of "German Christians" in his new sense.

Proclaiming himself to be God: Explicit, ultimate blasphemy. Not "a god," for all gods have been banished. The proclamation is in deed rather than in word. We might render, "takes his seat . . . , thereby proclaiming himself . . . ." We have heard of the Reformation and the Counter Reformation. Here we see the Advent and the Counter Advent.

Verse 5: Do you not remember that when I was still with you I told you this: Paul shows confident, individual expectation. The form of words expects the answer, "Yes, we do." This may be due to the apostle's emotion or to his clear recollection. Note that he has changed from "we" to "I." Our feelings are like those of a man who listens to one side of a telephone conversation. The people "at the other end" understand better than he does. The Thessalonians would grasp the allusions. (Cf. 1 Thess. 2:9 for *remember,* with Acts 20:31; 1 Thess. 3:4; 2 Thess. 3:10 for *with you;* 2 Thess. 3:17 for *I.*)

(3) Secret activity temporarily restrained (2:6–7)

The man of lawlessness, still unrevealed, was secretly active though temporarily held back. The time would come when the restraint would be removed.

Verse 6: And you know what is restraining him now: Literally: "you know the restraining (factor)." This is more than a mere knowledge of identity. The gender of the participle is neuter. If a man says, "I know who the President is," he means that he can state his name; he can identify him. If he says, "I know the President," he claims personal acquaintance with him. The latter is the point here. The Thessalonians have some experience of the factor which is exercising restraint. This would rule out the activity of angels.

It is widely held that Paul was thinking of the Roman state, though his language was guarded for political reasons. It would be unwise to speak too loudly of what was going to be removed (v. 7). His readers would understand the allusion. He did not mean the Roman Empire as such but simply as the power of the state, which at that time happened to be the Empire. It has long ago declined and fallen, but the state is still with us in other forms. Paul had experienced its power, sometimes in operation against himself (Acts 16:19–24); somewhere about this time he knew its protection (Acts 18:12–17). His theory of the state is written in Romans 13:1–7, where bearing the sword corresponds to the factor of restraint, and authority to "the restraining (factor)." But Paul in that passage spoke of rulers and of the man "to whom [singular] taxes are due . . . ." (7). This reflects the personal "he who now restrains" of verse 7. Paul also knew of the forces of law and order in Israel: he had not been a student of the law for nothing. Consciously or unconsciously Paul was repeating the teaching of his Master (Mark 12:17; cf. 1 Pet. 2:13–17). If there is any thought of angelic powers, they were embodied in the state; and it was the state of which the Thessalonians had experience, not the angels.

An alternative theory regards the restraining factor as the preaching of the gospel and "the restraining one" (v. 7) as the apostle Paul himself. The latter is unlikely and the former might have been possible when the church was dominant in Christendom. The life of the church, its real moral and spiritual life, has its effect in social life. The more obedient Christians there are, the less is the need for policemen. But the church had not spread far enough (or deeply enough) when the epistle was written for this view to be tenable. If the theory is linked to the belief that the world must be evangelized before the end comes (Matt. 24:14), then the restraining factor is God. But would Paul refer to God by means of a neuter participle? Even if he could, it would seem that God keeps the door open for evangelism by the prevention of anarchy—which is the state once more, working as God's servant (Rom. 13:4).

So that he may be revealed in his time—the time appointed for him by God, not the time chosen by him. The man of lawlessness is straining at the leash, but he cannot come out into the open until God permits. The clause combines the result of the restraint with the purpose of God. The *time* is what is often called the "psychological moment."

Verse 7: For the mystery of lawlessness is already at work: The explanation of the previous verse. The secrets of God which man's unaided reason would never discover have been brought to light in the gospel. Hence *mystery* in the New Testament is a secret which has been made known in Christ—often called an "open secret." (Cf. Matt. 13:11; Rom. 16:25 f.; Eph. 3:3 f.; Col. 1:26.) The countermystery has not yet been revealed but it is at work in opposition to the word of God (1 Thess. 2:13). It is at work *already*. In one sense it always has been since sin entered the world. It is possible, however, that Paul had in mind "one last effort" of the evil one. Men seek explanations of horrible crimes of sex and violence, and the word "Why?" is frequently on their lips. The ultimate explanation is at present a *mystery*, beyond rational statement. The man of lawlessness is working under cover. (Cf. 1 John 2:18.)

Only he who now restrains it will do so until he is out of the way: The restraint is personal and of limited time. Paul's style here is animated and elliptical and the problem is where to mark the omission. All that the Greek gives is (in this order): only he-who-restrains now until from the midst is (removed). We can make a start by rendering "until he who restrains now is out of the way." The problem is what to insert between this and the prior "only." The RSV implies "only (he who now restrains it will keep on restraining it) until he who restrains it is out of the way." It might be simpler to take the whole verse thus: "The mystery of lawlessness is already at work (and it will be at work secretly) only until he who restrains it now is out of the way." (Verse 8: And then . . . will be revealed . . .) There may be a shift of emphasis but apart from that, the meaning seems to be the same. Evil is at work in secret, but under restraint; in due time the restraint will be removed.

It should be noticed that "the restraining factor" (neuter) of verse 6 has now become "he who restrains" (masculine). The state makes its impact in the person of its magistrates. *He who . . . restrains* expresses a class rather than an individual (cf. Eph. 4:28, "he who steals").

(4) The pseudo-Advent (2:8–10)

The lawless one would be revealed in his "Advent" when he would enlarge his secret work. His satanic power and false signs and wonders would deceive the unrighteous and unbelieving though the presence of the Lord in his Advent would counteract effectively.

Verse 8: And then the lawless one will be revealed: The end of legal restraint means limitless scope, world anarchy and the emergence of the lawless one. He can now reveal his hand and instigate all manner of evil.

And the Lord Jesus will slay him with the breath of his mouth . . . : His Advent speech. This is creation in reverse (Ps. 33:6—Ps. 32:6, LXX). The power of divine speech is remarkable, both to create and destroy. The destructive power is heightened by the "flaming fire" (1:7). (Cf. Rev. 1:16; 19:15; Isa. 11:4.) As the word for *breath* (*pneuma*) also means "spirit," it is perhaps not fanciful to connect with John 6:63, "the words that I have spoken to you are spirit and life." The same word can give life or death (cf. 2 Cor. 2:15 f.). *The breath of his mouth* is the judicial sentence. There is a faint approximation to this in the story of the king who spoke so sternly to one of his erring subjects that he died on the spot.

Parallel to this clause is the statement that he "will put him out of action (in the activities of v. 4) by the manifestation (*epiphaneia*) of his coming (*parousia*)." (For the meaning of these terms see the discussion on 1:7.) The two clauses are different sides of the same act: *slay* is no mere death but the cancellation of a ministry; the advent is not a silent scene of grandeur but a powerful and authentic (and unmediated) ministry of the word.

Verse 9: The coming of the lawless one by the activity of Satan—the counterparousia. He is the instrument of Satan. Notice the effect of the repetition as the verse begins: ". . . and his *coming*. The *coming* of the lawless one . . . ." The Greek is *parousia* each time. As the lawless one is not Satan himself, we can see a further analogy. Just as Christ is the Mediator between God and man, so the lawless one is presented as the mediator between Satan and perishing man. *The activity of Satan* is both the cause and the "standard" of the *coming;*

in spite of the Christian vocabulary (cf. discussion on 2:3), the power and signs match their ultimate author for they are steeped in falsity.

Will be with all power and with pretended signs and wonders: All power, no authority, no Holy Spirit. (Cf. Matt. 28:18; 1 Thess. 1:5; Rom. 15:19.) The miracles are real but done by the agent of a liar (John 8:44) for his own purposes (v. 10). The *pretended* does not mean that they are fakes but that they are supporting evidence for the enemy of the truth. (Contrast John 3:2.) *Will be* is a translation of the RSV according to the sense. The Greek gives a prophetic "is." *Wonders* merely excite admiration; *signs* are wonders with a meaning. *Wonders* at first stupefy and then, when we have become used to them, they leave us unimpressed. *Signs* point to the truth and call for decision. (To illustrate: years ago we used to speak of "the miracle of wireless telegraphy"; now we just say, "turn that thing off!") The lawless one is intelligent enough not to rely on mere *wonders*. The counterfeit is well planned.

Verse 10: And with all wicked deception for those who are to perish: The thoroughness of wickedness. No deceitful device is omitted. The Counter Advent is for the perishing and its attendant deception is aimed at them. The man of lawlessness is an evangelist with a burden for souls—to make them as himself, "a son of perdition" (v. 3). (Cf. Phil. 3:19.) He confirms the unsaved in their ruin and would trick believers if he could, for he is the last and the greatest of the false prophets (cf. Matt. 24:11–13). He may be recognized as a Counter-John-the-Baptist. Believers should fan the flame of their love, should endure, should test everything (1 Thess. 5:21) and in faith remember him who keeps them (1 Thess. 5:23 f.). This is not unrelated to the doctrine of election (1 Thess. 1:4; 2 Thess. 2:13). Note Mark's striking "if possible" (Mark 13:22).

Because they refused to love the truth and so be saved—the reason for their destruction. No new doctrine is here introduced. Preachers sometimes urge their hearers to love Christ, as if they were teaching justification by love. In the mercy of God it is faith which justifies; some hardened sinners cannot love even Christ—but they can throw themselves on his mercy. They love him after they have put their trust in him. Here, however, *to love the truth* is an aspect of faith. The three stages of faith suggested here are: to understand what the preacher or teacher says; to be interested; to love the Christ who has been described by the preacher as the one who receives sinners. *The truth* means "the truth embodied in Jesus" (Eph. 4:21; cf. John 14:6). A man is not justified by "signing on the dotted line"; and Christ is not preached if the words of the sermon have no propositional content to describe him. The former is purely intellectual; the latter would be the quintessence of vagueness. Christ must be preached in his truth and trusted in his truth—and *love* expresses the obedience to the commanded word, the gospel (1:8); a sustained obedience.

Salvation, then, is offered and refused. This is the first step downward toward the final destruction.

(5) The judgment of God (2:11–12)

In consequence, human deception would become God's judicial act. Men would believe falsehood and take pleasure in unrighteousness. In the fulfillment of the divine purpose they would be judged.

Verse 11: Therefore God sends upon them a strong delusion, to make them believe what is false: The second step downward, and the first stage of judgment. *God sends* expresses a constant principle which will come to fruition with the man of lawlessness. The *strong delusion* is the activity of error. The error is not dormant, like that of a man who believes that the crown of Britain is worn by a man and not a woman, but does not spend all his days in argument about it. They are astray and are active in getting others to join them. God does not deceive. Deception is the work of the lawless one (v. 10). What he sends is error-and-its-moral-consequences, its outworking: a cancer, not a bullet.

The "principle" to which reference has already been made is seen in Romans 1:24, 26, 28. God is in complete control and uses evil in the outworking of his ethical purposes. Through sin, sin is punished. Men have refused salvation and God gives them their manifest desire—to believe the lie. *To make them believe* does not mean to force them. God works out his moral and spiritual law: men become thoroughly deceived, not only rejecting the truth but finally blind to it, so as to believe the lie—the intended result. What happens all the time in human life will be seen on a grand scale when the man of lawlessness comes. Such men are ripe for judgment (Matt. 12:31 f.).

Verse 12: So that all may be condemned who did not believe the truth but had pleasure in unrighteousness: Final judgment. This is the ultimate purpose of God in relation to these men, and it depends on their deluded belief of what is false (v. 11). Observe their twofold description. They *did not believe the truth* but decisively rejected it. We expect Paul to say that they believed the lie (as he did in v. 11) but instead he wrote that they *had pleasure in unrighteousness*. To disbelieve the truth is not merely academic scepticism; it is a practical attitude and it affects the will. Men of this nature incline to unrighteousness, consent to it, resolve on it and delight in it. (Cf. Matt. 6:23; Rom. 1:32.) So faith is practical as well as theoretical; it delights in righteousness. Truth should be known, believed and done (1 John 1:6, KJV). (For the contrast between truth and unrighteousness, see Rom. 2:8, KJV; 1 Cor. 13:6, KJV, using iniquity for unrighteousness.)

The "delusion" may be illustrated by the following story. A public figure who had long mocked the Christian faith and had advocated free love and the casting off of restraint, came back in a time of national stress and danger to faith in Christ. He had been sharply awakened by the sheer evil in the world and his repentance and faith were touching. Some commentators regarded it as the escape of a weaker soul into mysticism because he could not face the dark future with its unpleasant changes; he longed for the easy and elegant past which was gone for ever, and he therefore turned to religion. A critic "prayed" that a like fate would not befall him.

This reaction completely fails to understand the meaning of repentance and faith, and prays—to be delivered from becoming a Christian. Could delusion be more deep-seated?

Paul's sanity no less than his spirituality has become apparent as he has dealt with the problem: the interval between "Watch" and "Not yet is the end" must be filled with missionary activity. Extreme apocalypticism is dangerous. It can either stop evangelism or identify secular events with the Parousia.[1]

(6) Renewed thanksgiving (2:13–14)

Once more the apostles recognized that thanksgiving was constantly due to God. This time, however, its grounds were not so much the human response as the divine election to salvation. God had called his elect Thessalonians through the apostles' preaching of the gospel.

Verse 13: But we are bound to give thanks to God always for you, brethren beloved by the Lord—in spite of possible disturbance or discouragement. (Cf. 2:2.) *We* is emphatic. Paul purposely recalled his earlier words (1:3, on which the discussion should be consulted, together with that on 1 Thess. 2:13). There is a slight change here from the expression in the First Epistle (1:4, see discussion), where the brethren are *beloved* by God. *The Lord* means Jesus (cf. Deut. 33:12). God loves his people and Jesus loves them, and the love of God is present in Jesus: the love of Jesus is the love of God.

Because God chose you from the beginning to be saved, through sanctification by the Spirit and belief in the truth: An adequate because divine ground of thanksgiving. In the earlier thanksgiving Paul was giving due recognition to a human activity (see on 1:3); now he is pushing his thought further back; in fact to *the beginning* in eternity. The ground of temporal thanksgiving is eternal election (see on 1 Thess. 1:4). It should not be unnoticed that for Paul election is for salvation, not only for service. God determined to save us, not only to

---

1. Cf. William Manson, *Jesus and the Christian* (Grand Rapids: Wm. B. Eerdmans Publishing Company, 1967), p. 225.

use us. (Cf. 1 Thess. 5:9.) *From the beginning* represents the Greek *ap' archēs*. There is a variant reading *aparchēn* (accusative) meaning "firstfruits." This is suitable to some extent (cf. Rom. 16:5, KJV, RSV) though it does not have the encouragement suggested by *from the beginning*. Harnack used the reading "firstfruits" to support his theory that two churches existed in Thessalonica, the First Epistle being addressed to the Gentile church and the Second to the Jewish. Apart from problems connected with the salutation, would Paul have countenanced such a division? It is extremely unlikely. (Cf. 1 Cor. 1:13; Eph. 2:14–16.) The Jewish converts (Acts 17:4) may well have been the firstfruits of Thessalonica, but hardly to the extent of forming a separate church.

Through sanctification takes the Greek preposition *en* instrumentally. Linguistically this is possible, with *en* being used like the Hebrew *beth*. Theologically, however, it is open to question: we have been saved by grace through faith (Eph. 2:8). And the same Greek phrase (without *by the Spirit*) appears in the First Epistle (4:7, see discussion) with the meaning "in the sphere of holiness." This suggests the interpretation: God chose you from the beginning for salvation in the sphere of the Spirit's consecration and faith in the truth (cf. 2 Thess. 2:12). The order of words corresponds to Christian experience. The Spirit operates and man believes. This is not reversing the order of justification and sanctification. (Cf. 1 Pet. 1:2, same Greek.)

Verse 14: To this he called you through our gospel: This does not refer to salvation as such but to the whole complex, "salvation in the sphere of the Spirit's consecration and faith in the truth." *He called* them in their conversion with a view to salvation. Without the call their election would not have been put into effect. *You* puts the focus on the Thessalonians; the scope is wider in 1 Thessalonians 4:7, where the meaning concerns the call of "us Christians." (For Paul's thought on God's call, see discussion on 1 Thess. 2:12; 4:7; 5:24; 2 Thess. 1:11.) Paul, however, was here taking his readers back to the visit of the preachers. They had heard the call, and responded to it, *through our gospel*, that is, through the gospel which we preached to you. (See further the discussion on 1 Thess. 1:5.)

So that you may obtain the glory of our Lord Jesus Christ: The final goal. This makes explicit what is involved in salvation (1 Thess. 5:9 f.). (For *glory* see on 1 Thess. 2:12. Contrast 2 Thess. 1:9.)

(7) Challenge reinforced with prayer (2:15–17)

The inference was drawn that the readers should stand firm and hold fast to what they had been taught in spoken word or epistle. Prayer was offered that the author of eternal comfort would lovingly comfort the Thessalonians and strengthen them in advance.

Verse 15: So then, brethren, stand firm: Have backbone! (See 1
Thess. 3:8 and discussion on "standing firm.") *So then* is inferential:
duty is reinforced by reason. With so much to sustain them—election,
calling, salvation and the hope of glory—they should "go on standing
firm," not "jump to your feet."

And hold to the traditions which you were taught by us: They were to
"keep hold" rather than "take hold"—they were already holding the
traditions. The grasp of some may have weakened but they had not
abandoned them. The word "tradition" has suffered because it has
been set against Scripture or used to supplement Scripture. In itself it
is a neutral term and it is found in the New Testament in both a good
and a bad sense. Take the bad first. The traditions of men involve
distance from God, futile worship, abandonment of the divine commandments in favor of the human (Mark 7:3–9). They involve a
philosophic speculation which can capture the mind because not rooted
in Christ (Col. 2:8). In fact the supreme tradition is sin, the ancestral
conduct handed down from generation to generation (1 Pet. 1:18).
The good tradition consists of the facts of the gospel (1 Cor. 15:1–8),
the facts of the gospel in the setting of the communion service (1 Cor.
11:23–26). It includes the claims of the gospel, its ethical requirements from believers. The supreme tradition is Christ himself: "As
therefore you received Christ Jesus the Lord, so live [walk] in him"
(Col. 2:6). Note the two-sided nature of tradition: it is delivered and
it is received. (Cf. 3:6.)

Either by word of mouth or by letter: Mainly the apostolic missions
or the First Epistle. (Cf. Acts 17:1; 1 Thess. 3:1–6.)

*Verse 16: Now may our Lord Jesus Christ himself, and God our
Father, who loved us and gave us eternal comfort and good hope
through grace:* Hope until the Parousia, comfort for ever. Christ and
the Father are distinguished (though a singular verb is used in v. 17).
The Father *loved us,* but so did the Son (see on 2:13). *Hope* is *good*
because it does not disappoint (Rom. 5:5). It will not be necessary
after the Parousia (Rom. 8:24). The *comfort* is *eternal* because Christ
is eternal. A little exercise of the imagination will show us the picture of
our Savior giving encouragement to his people if any of them are nervous by the solemnity of the Parousia and the Day of Judgment. What
will he say to them then? Perhaps Isaiah 43:1–2 (cf. 1 Cor. 3:15).
Through grace would be better rendered "in grace" (the Greek preposition is *en*). God gave us grace ages ago, in Christ (when he elected
us), and it is as sure as his appearing and his cross (2 Tim. 1:9–10).
When we open the gift, so to speak, we find "in grace" that we have
received as well *eternal comfort.* For all eternity we are free from
worry about our sins, not through human carelessness but because
they have been righteously dealt with, put away and forgotten.

Verse 17: Comfort your hearts, with eternal comfort operative in time. (For *hearts* see on 1 Thess. 2:4.)

And establish them in every good work and word: Fixed and firm in intellectual grasp, evangelistic testimony and moral and spiritual life. (For *establish* see on 1 Thess. 3:2.) More is meant than the remembrance of what they had been taught (v. 15) as the Christian life is more than credence. With such establishment comes a deeper awareness of salvation, and this is comfort. (Contrast 2:2.)

III. MISBEHAVIOR THE OCCASION OF ADMONITION (3:1–16)

The apostles asked for their readers' prayers. They had confidence in the faithfulness of the Lord and in the Thessalonians themselves, for whom a prayer was offered. In spite of the confidence there were certain problems of discipline in the church. Idleness showed a disregard of the Christian duties which had been taught. The preachers' example of economic independence should be followed. Some idle busybodies were urged to talk less and work more. If any member did not heed these instructions he was to be avoided yet admonished as a brother. The section ends with a prayer for peace in the community.

1. Request for Prayer (3:1–2)

The Thessalonians were asked to continue in prayer for the writers, that they might preach to others as effectively as to them, and that they might be delivered from the opposition of unbelieving men.

Verse 1: Finally, brethren, pray for us, that the word of the Lord may speed on and triumph, as it did among you: The apostles are merged in the word. They did not say, "Pray for us, that we may triumph." The thought is: "Keep on making us the subject of your prayers." (Cf. 1 Thess. 5:25 and discussion.) The prayer should be mutual, as Paul has just prayed for the readers (2:16–17). No doubt he needed their prayers for himself as an individual Christian, but he was thinking of *us* primarily as preachers and evangelists. (For *the word of the Lord* see 1 Thess. 1:8 and discussion.) Paul was expressing both the purpose and the content of the prayer. *Speed on* is literally "run" (cf. Ps. 147:15—Ps. 147:4, LXX). The preacher will think of the running word as living, active, having direction, and moving with speed. It does not necessarily imply that the preacher must talk quickly, but he should be quick to take any opportunity which comes. *And triumph* in English does not reveal the connection of ideas in the Greek —"and be glorified." (See the discussion on 1:10, 12, and cf. Acts 13:48, KJV.) Both the running and the glorification are seen as continuous.

There are people who are charged with bibliolatry, the worship of a book. For the most part the accusation is ridiculous, but it contains an element of truth. Glory is for the Lord and in a deep sense he is present in the word preached and in the word written. To that extent it is in order for the word to be glorified. It does not mean that men bow down to a printed page *as such*. It does mean that they recognize the presence of the Lord and glorify him where he is—in sermon and Bible.

As it did among you—and still does. There is no verb in the Greek. (Cf. 1 Thess. 1:5, 8; 2:13.) The word ran and still runs to them, and was glorified and is still glorified in their fellowship.

Verse 2: And that we may be delivered from wicked and evil men: If the preachers are silenced, the word is unglorified. This is coordinate in form with the purpose of the prayer in v. 1 but subordinate to it in sense. Apostolic freedom would mean that the word would go on running. The *wicked and evil men* may be Jews (1 Thess. 2:15 f.; cf. Acts 18:6, 12), though others may be in mind also. *Wicked* (*atopos,* out of place, absurd) may suggest an element of irrationality. Jesus did nothing of this nature (Luke 23:41). *Delivered from . . . evil* is an echo of the Lord's Prayer (Matt. 6:13).

For not all have faith: Here lies the reason for their character and their opposition. As a general statement it is almost a platitude to say that not all men are believers. Paul might be thinking that not all Jews are Christians.

2. Statement of Confidence (3:3–5)

They were certain that the Lord was faithful and in him they were sure of the members, for whose life of discipleship they then prayed.

(1) In the Lord (3:3)

Their confidence was in the Lord. He was faithful to his people. His loyalty to them would be shown in his gift of strength and in keeping them.

But the Lord is faithful; he will strengthen you and guard you from evil: The Lord is credible in word, dependable in person. Faith in him is not misplaced. Three factors are involved: the Lord's character (cf. Rom. 3:3; 2 Tim. 2:13), the apostle's prayer just offered (2:16 f.), and divine providence (1 Cor. 10:13). There is a pleasing analogy between 1 Thessalonians 5:23 f. and 2 Thessalonians 2:16–3:3. Paul prayed and then said that God "will do it" and that "he will strengthen you" (strengthen = establish). Strengthening is not to replace affliction but to overcome it (1 Thess. 3:2, 4, 13 and discussion). There is contact here with Johannine thought (John 17:15; 1 John 5:18). To *strengthen* speaks of the divine work within the believer and is thus subjective; to *guard* implies the outer working of providence. The

Christian may know nothing of it, beyond the bare fact that God is working. From how many evils have we been delivered by the secret mercy of God? As far as the believer is concerned God's *guard* is objective. For *evil* read "the evil one." "Evil" savors of a philosophic principle; "the evil one" accords with the thought and atmosphere of the New Testament. Notice how Paul asked for prayer for his own deliverance (v. 2) and expressed his own assurance by saying that the Lord would strengthen and guard *you.*

(2) In the Thessalonians (3:4)

They were confident that they were carrying out and would continue to carry out the Christian duties laid upon them.

And we have confidence in the Lord about you, that you are doing and will do the things which we command: No Lord, no confidence. If we detach *in the Lord* we can translate: *we have confidence* in you. This is the meaning, but to repeat *in* would be very inelegant. The confidence was felt because writers and readers alike were "in Christ." Just as the Lord is the medium of communication between Christians, so he is the atmosphere in which confidence can grow. Paul could give instructions or commands, and he could have confidence, because all parties were *in the Lord.* (Cf. 1 Thess. 4:2 and discussion.) Note the pastoral touch: Paul was careful to give encouragement by stating that they *are* already *doing* what he wants them to do. (Cf. 1 Thess. 4:1.)

(3) Its secret (3:5)

Christian obedience is not secular but springs from the heart. Prayer was therefore offered that hearts might be directed to the love of God and the steadfastness of Christ.

May the Lord direct your hearts to the love of God and to the steadfastness of Christ: Bon voyage! This is not a flippant comment. We wish people God-speed in social life when they are taking a journey, and that is the picture here. The same verb (*direct*) is used as in 1 Thessalonians 3:11 (see discussion), where Paul prays for a journey to Thessalonica providentially ordered and overruling Satan's roadblock (1 Thess. 2:18 and discussion). Only here the journey is not to Thessalonica but a journey of *your hearts* (= you. See on 1 Thess. 2:4) into *the love of God* . . . . Paul would have them know it, realize it ("as soon as I realized") and act on it, feel it and respond to it in conscience. To some extent they were doing it already, as Christians, but they were shown the prospect of a deeper experience at the end of a spiritual journey and indeed on the journey itself. They would learn afresh the love which God had for them. *The steadfastness of Christ* is the steadfastness which our Lord exhibited, his endurance (Heb.

12:1–2). The Thessalonians were to observe it, copy it, and reproduce it (Gal. 2:20). The secret of endurance is intimate (as implied by *hearts*) knowledge of God who loves (2:16).

3. Treatment of the Disorderly (3:6–16)

The members had received instruction from the preachers during their visit on the behavior expected of a Christian. All knew from apostolic lips and lives of the necessity of working to support themselves, but even so, some were idle and given to gossip. They were charged to spend their time in work. Failure to respond should mean a measure of isolation. Peace was sought from the Lord for the community thus divided.

(1) Withdraw (3:6)

The Thessalonians were solemnly charged to keep away from every fellow-Christian who lived in idleness and thus neglected the guidance already given to the whole church.

Now we command you, brethren, in the name of our Lord Jesus Christ: The idea is that of solemn authority rather than the medium of communication. (See on 1 Thess. 4:2.) Paul's words in Acts 16:18 are almost identical.

That you keep away from any brother who is living in idleness: Deeds may achieve what words cannot. Paul had already spoken (1 Thess. 4:11 f.; 5:14). The Christian brotherhood must now bring home to the culprits what the Lord's will was. The action was still within the fellowship, as excommunication was not in view. Paul may have felt also that it was wise to avoid the possibility of "infection." The KJV translation "that walketh disorderly" means a moral verdict on men who were not at their post, were not where they ought to have been—at work. The motive of "keeping away" is quite different from that of Peter in Galatians 2:12.

And not in accord with the tradition that you received from us: The idler was failing in a duty common to all. For *tradition* see on 2:15. Paul and his companions had delivered it and the Thessalonians had *received* it. They knew their duties.

(2) Imitate (3:7–10)

The apostles had already set the example. When in the city, they had toiled in their own support so as not to burden anyone, even though they could have asked for it. They should be imitated: they had laid it down that the man who refused to work should not eat.

Verse 7: For you yourselves know how you ought to imitate us:

They had seen the life in action. It was not a question of merely hearing lectures on the subject. (Cf. 1 Cor. 11:1.)

We were not idle when we were with you: As the apostles had been "among them" no subterfuge would have been possible. They must have left a lasting impression on the young church. Paul was fond of reminding his readers of what they knew already (see on 1 Thess. 3:3 for references).

Verse 8: We did not eat any one's bread without paying—complete economic independence. We may be sure that this was not combined with the surly spirit sometimes manifested by those who are proud of standing on their own feet.

But with toil and labor we worked night and day, that we might not burden any of you: Paul repeats his point. He had spoken similarly in the First Epistle. (See on 1 Thess. 2:9.)

Verse 9: It was not because we have not that right: This would anticipate any possible charge of parasitism. The preachers could have insisted on the support of the church, for they had the authority of Jesus behind them. "The laborer deserves his food" (Matt. 10:10) and "his wages" (Luke 10:7). (Cf. also 1 Cor. 9:14 and context; 1 Tim. 5:18.)

But to give you in our conduct an example to imitate: Paul provides a second motive. The apostles worked for their living to avoid causing hardship (v. 8) and to set an example. (Cf. Phil. 3:17.)

Verse 10: For even when we were with you, we gave you this command: Paul used his vivid memory to good effect. The recollection of detail is perhaps an indication of his deep love for his converts. (For similar language see 1 Thess. 3:4 and discussion.)

If any one will not work, let him not eat: The situation was to be handled by deed as well as word. In modern language, the church was to adopt a policy of sanctions. The shirker was not to be given his sustenance. This was a drastic and stern remedy and some might have detected an absence of charity. But Paul was concerned with the public image of the church, and there seems to have been a hard core of resistance to his teaching (cf. 1 Thess. 4:11 f.). The discussion on the earlier passage should be consulted. *Let him not eat* is a third person imperative.

(3) Admonish (3:11–16)

This was no mere theory. News had come of idleness on the part of some members and they were told to abandon gossip and set to work. The persistent parasite should be admonished as a Christian brother, marked out, but not driven out. Help from the Lord was sought in prayer.

Verse 11: For we hear that some of you are living in idleness, mere busybodies, not doing any work: Their Christian walk was no more than talk. For the use of "walk," as used in the Greek of this verse, for "conduct" or "life" ("walking in idleness"), see the discussion on 1 Thessalonians 2:12. Paul's play on words can be brought out by rendering "not busy but busybodies." For idle Christians, confidence among believers can become "confidences," and this is but a short distance from gossip, which becomes all the worse when mingled with theological speculation.

Verse 12: Now such persons we command and exhort in the Lord Jesus Christ to do their work in quietness: Not merely the "some" of v. 11 but all who are covered by the description. This is now the direct address, from apostle to member, which combines a straightforward *command* with "persuasion with authority" (see on 1 Thess. 2:3, 11; 3:2). For *in the Lord Jesus Christ,* see 1 Thessalonians 4:2 and the discussion concerning the medium of communication. We have seen *quietness* before in the First Epistle (4:11, discussion).

And to earn their own living: Literally, "to eat their own bread." This recalls verse 8 and brings out how the apostles should be imitated (v. 7).

Verse 13: Brethren, do not be weary in well-doing: Even in a religion of grace there is ample room for human effort. It springs from salvation and does not contribute to it—except as evidence that justifying faith is indeed alive.

Verse 14: If any one refuses to obey what we say in this letter: Paul is the realist. But his language is hypothetical and it may have been designed as a "threat," the effectiveness of which would remove the need for its implementation.

Note that man, and have nothing to do with him, that he may be ashamed: Precise instruction for complete isolation. But the door was not to be bolted against him. It is more severe than verse 6 and therefore may be more likely to bring the man to his senses. The whole church is addressed.

Verse 15: Do not look on him as an enemy, but warn him as a brother: Though isolated, he still belongs to the fellowship. It is evidently supposed that the erring member will take the initiative in speaking to other members of the church. They would hardly speak to him if they are having nothing to do with him. Paul was thus giving guidance on how to receive him. The meaning is not quite "admonish him as if he were a brother" because he still is a brother. Paul wanted them to keep that in mind as they admonished him. This is very important. Unbrotherly criticism may do more harm than good. Even admonition can be expressed in a spirit of love. Perhaps the best comment is Galatians 6:1. Mend him!

Verse 16: Now may the Lord of peace himself give you peace at all times in all ways: The ultimate healer of any rift is *the Lord . . . himself,* the author of peace, wholeness and unity (see on 1 Thess. 1:1; 5:23), for "he is our peace" (Eph. 2:14) continually in all its aspects. Whether the church will accept the gift depends on the vitality of its Christian faith. "The fruit of the Spirit is . . . peace" (Gal. 5:22).

The Lord be with you all—including the obstinate brother. There is no verb in the Greek. Paul may therefore be expressing a hope or prayer, or reminding his readers of a fact. But *may . . . give* early in the verse is a prayer—a wish with regard to the future.

IV. THE AUTHENTIC FAREWELL (3:17–18)

Paul himself wrote the final greeting in his own hand, the mark of authenticity in every letter. Grace was for the Thessalonians—all of them.

Verse 17: I, Paul, write this greeting with my own hand: The rest of the letter must therefore have been dictated. As we compare this with 1:1 we see who was the dominant personality among the three preachers.

This is the mark in every letter of mine; it is the way I write: The writing which differs from that in the body of the letter is a sign which authenticates the whole. Paul wrote it himself.

Verse 18: The grace of our Lord Jesus Christ be with you all: The benediction is the same as 1 Thessalonians 5:28 except for the significant *all.* Ultimately it comes to the same thing whether we say the text as stated here or as in verse 16. The Lord is our peace and he embodies grace. (See on 1 Thess. 5:28 for the significance of *with.*) Again there is no verb. (Cf. 1 Thess. 1:1 and discussion.)

Annotated Bibliography

Lexicons

Arndt, W. F. and Gingrich, F. W. *A Greek-English Lexicon of the New Testament.* Chicago: University of Chicago Press; Cambridge: University Press, 1957. Covers early Christian literature outside the New Testament. Based on Walter Bauer's *Griechish-Deutsches Wörterbuch* and takes account of scholarly work up to 1954. A gold mine for preachers who will take the trouble to dig into it.

Liddell, H. G. and Scott, R. *A Greek-English Lexicon.* 2 vols. 9th ed. revised by Sir Henry Stuart Jones and Roderick McKenzie. Oxford: Clarendon Press, 1940. Liddell and Scott has long been the standard dictionary for ancient Greek.

Moulton, James H. and Milligan, George. *The Vocabulary of the Greek Testament.* London: Hodder and Stoughton, 1929. Grand Rapids, Mich.: Wm. B. Eerdmans. Light is shed on Greek usage by extensive quotations from the papyri and other non-literary sources.

Souter, Alexander. *A Pocket Lexicon to the Greek New Testament.* Oxford and New York: Oxford University Press, 1916. Makes unobtrusive use of new knowledge derived from the papyri. Invaluable for the traveling preacher's briefcase.

Grammars

Blass, F.; Debrunner, A.; and Funk, R. W. *A Greek Grammar of the New Testament.* Chicago: University of Chicago Press, 1961. Highly technical but rewarding.

Goodwin, W. W. *A Greek Grammar.* 2nd ed. London: Macmillan; New York: St. Martin's Press, 1894.

————. *Syntax of the Moods and Tenses of the Greek Verb.* London: Macmillan; New York: St. Martin's Press, 1875. Both books are on the advanced level. The beginner should try something much simpler.

Moulton, James H., Howard, Wilbert F.; and Turner, N. *A Grammar of New Testament Greek.* 3 vols. Edinburgh: T. & T. Clark; Naperville, Ill.: Allenson, 1908, 1929, 1963. Full and even minute attention to detail by a succession of masters in the field.

Robertson, A. T. *A Grammar of the Greek New Testament in the Light of Historical Research.* New York: Hodder & Stoughton and George H. Doran, 1923. Reprint. Nashville: Broadman Press, 1947. Over fourteen hundred pages of fascinating reading written by an eminent grammarian and devout believer. Full enjoyment depends on the degree of competence in Greek.

Turner, Nigel. *Grammatical Insights into the New Testament*. Edinburgh: T. & T. Clark; Naperville, Ill.: Allenson, 1965. Exciting discussions for the general reader as well as for the scholar.

Word Studies

Hatch, E. and Redpath, H. A. *A Concordance to the Septuagint*. 2 vols. Graz, Austria: Akademische Druck-u. Verlagsanstalt, 1954. Hatch and Redpath is indispensable for the discovery of the Old Testament (Greek) background of a New Testament text.

Moule, C. F. D. *An Idiom Book of New Testament Greek*. 2nd ed. Cambridge and New York: Cambridge University Press, 1959. A careful discussion of many passages helps the reader to come to his own conclusions when right interpretation depends on syntax.

Moulton, W. F. and Geden, A. S. *A Concordance to the Greek Testament*. Edinburgh: T. & T. Clark; Grand Rapids, Mich.: Kregel Publications, 1957. A standard work.

Ward, R. A. *Hidden Meaning in the New Testament*. Old Tappan, N.J.: Fleming H. Revell; London: Marshall, Morgan & Scott, 1969. Pictures and movements suggested by the language stimulate ideas and illustrations for preachers and teachers.

New Testament Introductions

Guthrie, Donald. *New Testament Introduction. The Pauline Epistles*. London: Tyndale Press; Chicago: Inter-Varsity Press, 1961. Exhaustive treatment by a well-known conservative scholar. Two other volumes (*The Gospels and Acts*, and *Hebrews to Revelation*) complete the series.

Harrison, Everett F. *Introduction to the New Testament*. Grand Rapids, Mich.: Wm. B. Eerdmans, 1964. A sound work prepared primarily for students, after teaching the subject in the classroom for a quarter of a century.

Kümmel, W. G. *Introduction to the New Testament*. London: SCM Press, 1966. Not so conservative. Very full discussion, including such matters as text and canon.

Theology

Bultmann, Rudolf. *Theology of the New Testament*. 2 vols. London: SCM Press, 1965. New York: Chas. Scribner's Sons, 1970. Radical and to be used with care. More for those who want to know what is going on in New Testament studies and what is being criticized than for the pure expositor.

Cullmann, Oscar. *The Christology of the New Testament*. London: SCM

Press, 1959. Rev. ed. Philadelphia: Westminster Press, 1964. An antidote to Bultmann. A significant examination of the titles of Christ.

Ellis, E. Earle. *Paul's Use of the Old Testament.* Edinburgh and London: Oliver and Boyd, 1957. The value of this profound study is increased by the lists of Old Testament quotations and allusions.

Kittel, Gerhard and Friedrich, Gerhard. *Theological Dictionary of the New Testament.* 8 vols. Translated by Geoffrey W. Bromiley. Grand Rapids, Mich. and London: Wm. B. Eerdmans, 1964–1972. This monumental work is a translation of Kittel's famous *Theologisches Wörterbuch* and is indispensable for the advanced student. Patience and application will yield rich rewards even to those who have only a working knowledge of Greek.

Langevin, P.-E. *Jésus Seigneur et l'eschatologie: exégèse de textes prépauliniens.* Brussels and Paris: Desclée de Brouwer, 1967. Detailed exegesis of texts: over a hundred pages devoted to 1 Thess. 1:10; 5:2.

Richardson, Alan. *An Introduction to the Theology of the New Testament.* London: SCM Press, 1958; New York: Harper & Row, 1959. This study combines the wide sweep of a comprehensive view with consideration of many individual texts.

Stauffer, Ethelbert. *New Testament Theology.* London: SCM Press, 1955. New York: Harper & Row. Profound scholarship and stimulating language. There are extensive bibliographies.

Tasker, R. V. G. *The Old Testament in the New Testament.* Grand Rapids, Mich.: Wm. B. Eerdmans, 1963. A survey of New Testament usage.

Commentaries

Findlay, G. G. *The Epistles of Paul the Apostle to the Thessalonians.* Cambridge Greek Testament. Cambridge: University Press, 1904. Acute discussion of the implications of the Greek.

Frame, James E. *A Critical and Exegetical Commentary on the Epistles of St. Paul to the Thessalonians.* Reprint. Edinburgh: T. & T. Clark, 1966. A worthy member of a distinguished series, The International Critical Commentary, often referred to as ICC. Full introduction is followed by minute examination of the Greek text. This kind of commentary is a must for every serious student of the New Testament.

Hendriksen, William. *Thessalonians First and Second.* Grand Rapids, Mich.: Baker Book House, 1953. Commentary based on a fresh translation from the Greek.

Lightfoot, J. B. *Notes on Epistles of St. Paul from Unpublished Commentaries.* London: Macmillan, 1904. The ripe fruit of the renowned scholar's vast learning.

Milligan, George. *St. Paul's Epistles to the Thessalonians: The Greek Text with Introduction and Notes.* London: Macmillan, 1908. Still a standard work; still valuable; still used.

Moffatt, James. *The First and Second Epistles to the Thessalonians.* Vol. 4 of The Expositor's Greek Testament. 5 vols. London: Hodder & Stoughton, 1897–1910. Grand Rapids, Mich.: Wm. B. Eerdmans. Takes its place as part of a "basic set" of commentaries for the exposition of the New Testament.

Moore, A. L. *1 and 2 Thessalonians.* The Century Bible: New Series. London: Nelson, 1969. Based on the Revised Standard Version. Competent and up to date.

Morris, Leon. *The Epistles of Paul to the Thessalonians.* Tyndale Bible Commentaries. London: Tyndale Press; Grand Rapids, Mich.: Wm. B. Eerdmans, 1956.

————. *The First and Second Epistles to the Thessalonians: The English Text with Introduction, Exposition and Notes.* New International Commentary. Grand Rapids, Mich.: Wm. B. Eerdmans, 1959. The Tyndale commentary is admirable in style and contents. The New International is not just a longer edition but is a completely new and full-scale study with a different approach.

Neil, William. *Thessalonians.* The Moffatt New Testament Commentary. London: Hodder and Stoughton; Naperville, Ill.: Allenson, 1950. Based on James Moffatt's vigorous "New Translation," though the commentator has been left free to take his own line. It seeks to make plain the meaning of the Greek for those who know no Greek.

Oepke, Albrecht. *Die Briefe an die Thessalonicher.* In *Die kleineren Briefe des Apostels Paulus.* Das Neue Testament Deutsch, vol. 8. Göttingen: Vandenhoeck & Ruprecht, 1965. Valuable comments and references.